Contentment is Great Gain

A Missionary Midwife in Sierra Leone

Lois Olsen

First Edition

ISBN:0-9654488-00

Library of Congress Catalog Card Number: 96-095021

Published by
Leone Press
PO Box 93395
Milwaukee, WI 53203-0395

Printed by
Palmer Publications, Inc.
PO Box 296
Amherst, WI 54406

Table of Contents

Part III: Wheels Make a Difference: June 1960 to June 1963

Preface

For 12 years, I was a nurse-midwife in charge of a dispensary and 12-bed maternity unit in a rural African village. This was not what I had intended to do with my life. Although I had planned to be a missionary from the time I was 13 years old, I had always envisioned that I would go to China as a public health nurse and had directed my professional education to that end. In September of 1949 I enrolled at the Yale University Institute of Far Eastern Languages in an intensive study of Chinese, excited by the prospect that I would soon be realizing my dream.

In January 1950 the Communists conquered all of China and that country was closed to Americans.

For several months I was in great despair and was without concrete plans for the future. In September the mission board, to which I had applied, sent me first to London to study midwifery. My assignment was to then proceed to Sierra Leone where I spent the next 12 years; most of that time was spent in a single village, Tiama.

This is the story of those 12 years.

PART I:

The First Step

JANUARY 1952 TO OCTOBER 1954

CHAPTER 1

The Sierra Leone Railway — The Backbone of the Country

It was almost midnight. I was standing on the platform of a small railway station in rural Sierra Leone waiting for the " down" train, which should have arrived at 4:00 p.m., but obviously had been delayed.

It was January of 1952. I had been in Sierra Leone less than a week and I was terrified. I had come to Sierra Leone to work as a nurse-midwife. I had never intended to be a nurse-midwife, nor had I intended to come to Africa. For 14 years I had made preparations to go to China as a public health nurse, but China had been closed to Americans in 1950. I had earned an undergraduate degree in public health. When I was assigned to go to Sierra Leone I was sent to midwifery school in England. The senior medical officer in charge of the medical work in Sierra Leone had insisted that all American nurses were to be trained as midwives in addition to their nursing education.

My vision of working in Africa had not included standing on an isolated train station platform at midnight. How had I gotten into this situation? Any doubts I had about the wisdom of living in a remote village had turned into certainties. I recalled all the tales I had heard about cannibals and witch doctors. I had already seen the graves of the five missionaries that had been massacred in the Hut Tax War of 1898. Sierra Leone was the place where fierce Mende warriors lived, noted for their savagery in battle.

My doubts had been intensified by the conversation I had on Sunday evening in Freetown. I had arrived by boat from England on Saturday. That evening we sat on the veranda of the old mission house, where we had a lovely view of the Sierra Leone River which flows into the Atlantic. The evening breeze was a cooling relief to the heat that had been overpowering all day. The wife of the American missionary superintendent saw fit to prepare me for the existence I was to have, living alone in a small Mende village.

"The Mende men have a reputation for being fierce warriors," she said. "They were some of the strongest fighters during the uprising in 1898."

I had read of this uprising called the Hut Tax War when British, American, and African people had been slaughtered by the local people. The war was a response to a tax imposed by the British colonial government and was so unpopular with the local people that they resolved to drive out all the foreigners. That was more than 50 years ago and there had not been a similar incident. The country seemed pretty peaceful.

She went on, "It is also the center of the Wunde Society, the male secret society; part of their initiation includes cannibalism."

I thought about that. Who did they eat? Was I an intended victim?

She added the climax. "The man that you will be working with at the dispensary in Tiama is one of the chief officers of the Wunde Society."

I thought I didn't want to meet the Wunde Society or any of their members. I would have to watch and listen to see if they were still active. I was too stunned to respond to her. After all, she had lived in Sierra Leone for several years and I had just arrived. I really didn't know much about life here.

Early the next morning, I traveled with a friend to Rotifunk, the site of the major mission hospital of the Evangelical United Brethren Church. I was to stay there for several days before I traveled to Tiama, my new home. The four women missionaries who lived there were very friendly and made me feel welcome. One of them had been my roommate at Yale and it was good to renew acquaintance.

On Thursday during the preparation for the Sunday service, someone realized there was no *Vimto* in Rotifunk. *Vimto* was the grape juice concentrate used by the church for communion. Dr. Mabel Silver, the missionary doctor at the hospital, decided that since I didn't have anything to do, I should go by train to Moyamba, about 20 miles beyond Rotifunk, to buy *Vimto*. A mission school for girls, the Harford School was situated at Moyamba and there were a number of missionaries who taught at the school.

The "up" train was scheduled to leave Rotifunk at 10:00 a.m. I would arrive in Moyamba in time to get the *Vimto* and catch the 4:00 p.m. "down" train. But the "up" train didn't leave until 2:00 p.m. and I had missed the "down" train. Now here I stood at midnight. I debated about what I should do. Perhaps I should go back to the mission school and wait for the next day. Or maybe I should forget the whole thing, go back to Freetown, and take the first boat back to the United States.

As I stood there, a car approached. The driver was a young British District Commissioner. Two of the missionaries from Harford had been having dinner at his house and he was taking them back to school. The car stopped and he got out.

"Are you in some kind of trouble? What are you doing here? Can I be of some help?"

I explained the situation. "I'm a bit concerned, standing here alone." I failed to add that I was terrified and enormously grateful to see a white man.

He laughed and gave me a piece of advice that was a watchword for the rest of my years in Sierra Leone.

"You are probably safer on this train than you would be anywhere in the world. No one will lay a hand on you to hurt you. In fact, everyone will be glad to help you," he said.

He was right. There were many times when I traveled alone in West Africa and was stranded. I was never harmed and there was always someone, American, African, Lebanese, who came to my aid and helped me out of the difficulty.

The three of them waited with me, and in a few minutes, I boarded the train and went back to Rotifunk.

This was my first adventure but not the last, on that unique method of transportation, the Sierra Leone Railway. It provided my basic means of travel when going and coming to Tiama. Construction of the railway began in 1896 and was the first railway built in West Africa. The railroad transformed trade and government. For many years, it was the principle means by which goods and passengers were able to cross the country. By 1952, roads had been built and some goods were transported by lorries; still the railway remained the major means of commerce.

The train started in Freetown and ended at Pendembu on the eastern border where Sierra Leone met Liberia. About 100 miles from Freetown, a spur branched off to the north going to Magburaka and Makeni.

The train left Freetown from the Water Street Station every morning at 7:00. The equipment and schedule had not changed much in the 50 years of its existence. The diminutive size of the coaches and engine, as well as the narrow gauge track reminded one of an adult toy, the sort of thing you see for children in zoos.

There were three classes of coaches. The first class coaches offered a bit more room and comfort than the other two. First class was divided into small compartments, each having four small seats facing each other and a narrow aisle running the length of the car; between facing seats was a small table.

Everything was covered with a thin film of black dust and cinders as the smoke from the engine blew through the open windows. The windows could be closed by pulling up the besmudged glass, but the resulting heat made the journey unbearable. Or, the wooden shutters outside the windows could be closed. This decreased the grime but also made the interior too dark to do anything. The open windows afforded the passengers a pleasant exchange of fresh air and a panoramic view of the green hills, swiftly flowing streams, and mud houses along the track. The open windows also provided an opportunity for the passengers and produce sellers to barter and exchange local products. As I later learned, the open windows also provided an opportunity for alert thieves to snatch whatever the unwise traveler had left on the table top.

Water Street Station bustled with the noise of passengers boarding the train, handing assorted loads through the open windows: footlockers, wooden boxes, colorful Temne blighs (baskets), chickens, bundles of clothes, and assorted produce tied in colorful cloths. Babies were handed through the windows and children clambered through. Family and friends clustered around the cars shouting advice and offering farewells.

Finally, there was an aggressive snort from the engine accompanied by a belch of steam. The train began to inch itself along the tracks. At best, the average speed was 13 miles an hour so that travel through the city was measured in feet rather than miles. A favorite comment from one of our early missionaries was that the Sierra Leone train was mentioned in *Genesis*: "Behold, the Lord God made everything that creepth upon the earth."

The first stop was Dove Cot, only a few blocks beyond the Water Street Station. Additional passengers piled in accompanied by noise, shouts, and movement of freight.

Freetown is situated on a peninsula that juts out into the Atlantic Ocean. In the center of the peninsula are large hills, many of which are not populated, and the city itself nestles on the base of the hills like a necklace. The train progresses through the city until it reaches the open countryside, which is the dividing line between Freetown the colony, and the provinces that make up the rest of Sierra Leone.

At one point after leaving Freetown, the train crossed a remarkable bridge that spanned a deep gorge, at the bottom of which ran a narrow sparkling stream. The bridge was built on a sharp curve so that those of us in the rear coaches could see the engine and coal cars at the front of the train as it rounded the curve.

The next big stop was Waterloo. The use of English names: Newton, Waterloo, Wellington, Hastings has persisted to the end of the

Railway bridge over the Orugu gorge (N.B.).

twentieth century and reflects the lingering aura of colonialism that clings to much of the peninsula. After independence the streets of Freetown were renamed to reflect the glory of the new African heroes such as Stevens, Margai, and Nkrumah, but the villages of the peninsula retain the old names.

Street vendors sold local delicacies at many of the stations. At Waterloo, travelers could buy *Congorings*, crisp dough, deep-fried and laced with hot peppers. In the proper season you could buy local fruits and staples: oranges, bananas, pawpaw, pineapples, guavas, yams, roasted corn, and groundnuts. However, after years of eating bananas during my stay in Sierra Leone, I lost my taste for them. In fact, I have to be extremely hungry before resorting to peeling that yellow fruit, but I have not lost my enjoyment for fresh pineapples, pawpaw, oranges, and groundnuts.

The women sitting near the station had a delightful way of managing oranges. Very often the ripe fruit was not orange but bright green, yet still juicy and ready to eat. The women deftly removed the outside thick rind, leaving the orange covered with the thick white inner portion. Using a sharp knife and with quick strokes pointing away from the body, they changed the green globe into a white one. Then they cut a small piece off the top of the orange. We would take the juicy orange and rotating and squeezing it, suck the refreshing juice until the rind was empty and flat. In a part of the world where water is often scarce or unsafe to drink, people could quench their thirst in minutes with several of these lovely fruit.

The next big stop was Rotifunk, headquarters of the Bumpe chiefdom. It was also the site of the major hospital of the Evangelical United Brethren Church where American missionaries had worked since the 1880's. By 1950 the hospital had 60 beds and a large outpatient clinic. Since it was situated on the rail line, it offered easy access for patients from all over the country.

When we were traveling up country there was often a special treat for us at Rotifunk. Dr. Mabel Silver, the doctor in charge of the hospital, frequently met the train with hot fudge sundaes. This was before the days of electricity when refrigerators ran on kerosene. Of course, all the ice cream was made by her cook. Ice cream in itself was a treat, but hot fudge? Marvelous! Since the trains rarely ran on schedule, it must have taken some intricate planning for her to accomplish this.

After Rotifunk came Bauya. Since this was the junction where part of the train went north to Makeni, while the rest of the train went east to Bo and eventually to Pendembu on the Guinea border, there was always a long stop here. Most of the lines were a single track with double tracks only at the stations. Thus, the "up" train and the "down" train could only pass each other at these stations and this frequently occurred at Bauya. There was usually time to get out of the train, walk around and perhaps restock your lunch basket. It was also an opportunity to visit with friends and acquaintances who were traveling on the opposite train.

At all stations food was usually sold by women and young girls. Dressed in blouses and *lappas* (colorful wrap-around skirts), their heads covered in bright cloth squares, they brought trays of food to the open windows. "Groundnuts dey, groundnuts dey!" they cried. Groundnuts and chili peppers were sold in quantity, measured in small tomato paste tins or in larger amounts in cigarette tins, always piled heaping with an extra measure poured on top so that the excess groundnuts ran back into the tray. Boys in tattered trousers, usually barefoot, were equally energetic in peddling their products: cigarettes sold individually, matches, and hard candy.

There were several more stops until I reached Mano, a small town and the headquarters of the Dasse chiefdom. This was often the starting or ending point of my journey. If the train was on time when I was going back to Tiama, I would arrive there about 4:00 p.m. From there I would get a lorry to Tiama where I lived, a distance of 12 miles.

Lorries were large commercial trucks used to carry goods and passengers. The Tiama lorries met the trains morning and evening so that there was usually no problem in getting back and forth. One night, however, I arrived in Mano about 10:00. I was reluctant to take any available transport (or perhaps there wasn't any) so I knocked on the door of a Lebanese trader with whom I had made friends and who owned a car.

"Mrs. Hamud, there is no lorry to take me back to Tiama. Could your driver take me back?" I asked.

She was gracious in her reply, "He is not very reliable. He is probably drunk at this time of night. I would not ask him to drive to Tiama, but you can stay here and get a ride in the morning."

I was too tired to protest and the offer of the bed was very tempting.

"Boys, get out of bed," she commanded two of her youngsters. "Let Sister Olsen use it."

I lay down on the bed. A few minutes later, the family's large dog climbed up beside me and snuggled in. Neither of us disturbed the other and we both slept soundly until morning and I was able to take a lorry back to Tiama.

The final stop of the day's run of the train was Bo. This was the provincial capitol, a major city where the protectorate government was located. There was also a large government hospital and a boarding school for boys that had been established originally for the education of the sons of chiefs.

The train was scheduled to reach Bo by 6:00 p.m. The "down" train from Pendembu was also scheduled to arrive about this time. Passengers going to a further destination would find lodging for the night before continuing on their journey.

During my first years in Tiama, my only exit from the town was by lorry to Mano and then by train either east or west. It was possible to travel from Mano to Bo by road but that involved riding one of the local lorries. The distance from Tiama to Freetown was 120 miles by train, but the journey took about 12 hours "if" everything went well. Over the years, I became very familiar with the route and the stops of the train.

Preparations for a journey took several days before I was to start out. First, there was food to consider. Traveling whets my appetite and I am apt to start eating only a few feet from my door. The cook would pack sandwiches, leftover cookies, groundnuts and fruit, including bananas. All of this was supplemented by what could be purchased at the stations along the way as well as donations from missionary friends, who had been forewarned that one was traveling, and had come to meet the train.

Next, there were the diversions. Reading matter came first on the list. Books and magazines are usually chosen with greater care than that given to my choice of wardrobe. My own limited supply of books was augmented by borrowing from every possible source. The return journey presented fewer problems since I would have replenished my stock from the excellent Church Missionary Society bookshop in Freetown or by raiding the shelves of my friends.

Occasionally, there were interesting fellow passengers of whom several come to mind. One day a British mining engineer, from the diamond mines in the far eastern corner of the country, occupied an adjoining seat. After an hour or so of rather aimless conversation, he finally remarked that the worst thing that ever happened to West Africa was the arrival of the missionaries. I refrained from responding that an equal disaster was the arrival of the mining companies and the conversation died a natural death.

On another occasion my fellow traveler was a well known Sierra Leone physician. We were having an animated conversation when he suddenly said, "Will you marry me?"

I was dumbfounded. "I'll have to think that over," I stammered.

"I'll contact you in a week or so and see if you are interested," he responded.

He never did follow through and to this day I don't know if he was serious, but for months afterward I was puzzled and always had a bit of regret that I hadn't given him a little encouragement.

One day in 1953, when I was spending several months in Rotifunk, a telephone call came from Moyamba. Neither town had telephone service, but in an emergency, the railway telephone system could be used. The station master at Moyamba reported that there had been a serious car accident beyond Bauya on the road to Makeni. Two tires had blown out and a car had crashed into the ditch. No one was killed, but the English couple in the car had been seriously injured and were now on the train going to Freetown. He asked if one of the medical people at Rotifunk could join the train and go with the couple to Freetown.

Although there was no doctor at Rotifunk, there were two other nurses besides me. We discussed it and decided that I should be the one to accompany the couple. Somewhere along the line, a doctor had seen them and made the decision to send them to better medical facilities. The woman was less seriously injured than her husband. I think she may have had a broken arm. The man was semi-conscious and in much pain. I thought he might have broken ribs and perhaps some internal bleeding. He moaned as the train jerked to stop and start. I was carrying morphine.

"Can I give you something to ease your pain?" I offered.

"I would rather not take anything," he whispered.

It was December and it was hot. The rains had ended in October and the air and ground were dry and dusty. The bright sun produces a heat that encourages you to reduce all activity to a minimum.

The woman and I soaked small towels in water which we placed on his forehead as a comfort measure. We kept the shutters closed to reduce the shock of light and to make the compartment a bit cooler—that also kept out the stares of the curious onlookers at each station. Worry and fear made the heat seem more oppressive. It was a long journey and the slow progress of the train seemed more annoying than usual. Somewhere outside of Freetown an ambulance met the train and carried the couple to Hill Station Hospital. I later learned, to my great relief, that they had both recovered.

At the time, I would often be upset by the slow speed and the frequent delays on the train. As a friend said in 1969, "The Thursday train doesn't arrive until Monday." But I came to realize that the prolonged journeys gave time for relaxation, for reflection, and for meeting interesting people.

In the 1970's the Sierra Leone government was persuaded to dismantle the tracks and discontinue the railroad. It was difficult and expensive to obtain parts for repairs because of the narrow gauge and non-standard size of the equipment. Every year that figure increased and so it was decided to tear up the tracks. In his autobiography, President Siaka Stevens says that he realized later that discontinuing the train was a grave mistake. Even though it was slow and frequently late, it served a purpose.

Today, as you pass the deserted little stations, they are often in the process of collapse. Road traffic has brought other problems. Roads are expensive to build and maintain. Gasoline has risen in price and is often in short supply or there is none at all. Cars and buses also need repairs. With the shortage of foreign exchange, the spare parts for cars and gasoline have become scarce commodities. Each time I have gone back to Sierra Leone, I mourn the loss of that unique means of transportation, the Sierra Leone Railway.

CHAPTER 2

Changed Plans

Setting foot in Sierra Leone was the fulfillment of a dream that had lasted me for 15 years. When I was 12 years old I had made a commitment to lead a Christ-centered life and a year later began the process toward a missionary career.

I was motivated by several generations that had been involved in the church. My maternal great-grandfather and his brother were both pastors in the Evangelical Church in Wisconsin. Both grandfathers were committed laymen and for 39 years, my maternal grandfather had been a voting delegate to the annual conference of the church. In the Methodist tradition, this annual meeting is the legislative body. Every four years the church holds a General Conference, again a national legislative meeting, attended by clergy and laity from all the annual conferences. Grandfather Hess had been elected to two General Conferences.

My father, Clifford Olsen, began his working life as a farmer and school teacher. When I was three he left the farm and attended the Evangelical Theological School in Illinois. When he came back to Wisconsin, he served as a minister for almost 50 years. Although he worked in small towns and rural areas, all of his churches grew under his leadership. He had a deep concern for people and was willing to spend his energy in meeting their spiritual and emotional needs, usually with modest monetary rewards.

My parents always had a strong interest in missions. For five years my mother was the treasurer of the state missionary society of the church. Missionary speakers were welcome guests and usually were invited to stay at the parsonage. Dr. Paul Mayer and his wife, who spent many years in Japan, made a great impression on me. My father's roommate in seminary was a young German student who, with his wife, served in China. Their letters stimulated the family interest in missions. When I was 16, I listened to Miss Nora Vesper, a veteran missionary in Sierra Leone, who was a true inspiration.

Several other interests in the family furthered my decision. My father loved to travel. The unknown road held excitement for him and so the three of us traveled as extensively as our limited resources would allow: the Chicago World's Fair in 1933, several drives to North Dakota to visit relatives, and an exciting tour of Washington, D.C. and Philadelphia. Both parents read extensively and encouraged me to read anything I could get. My mother had attended the University of Wisconsin at a time when few women went on to higher education. My father always regretted that he had not had an opportunity for a college education. They assumed that I would go to college and I made the same assumption.

As a teenager, my dreams became more specific. I would be a nurse and I was going to China. The mission board of the church required that an academic degree in nursing was minimal preparation. I attended the University of Wisconsin in Madison, one of the two schools in the state, at that time, that offered an academic degree in nursing. I pursued my interest in China by taking courses in Chinese history.

At the beginning of my senior year in college, my mother died. My father was alone and many friends suggested that it was my responsibility to stay at home and manage his household. But, by mutual consent, he and I decided this was not a wise decision. I had already made a commitment to the mission board and agreed that to stop my education at this point would only lead to disappointment in an aborted education and career.

In the fall of 1949 I went to start a concentrated course in the Chinese language at the Institute of Far Eastern Languages at Yale University. There were about 65 students studying Chinese, the majority of whom were preparing for the mission field. It was an exciting time. I was awed at being able to attend Yale, although at that time, the Institute was one of the few places on campus that admitted women students. New Haven and New England were fascinating and several times we explored the surrounding countryside as well as visiting Boston and New York.

The atmosphere provided an almost ideal learning situation. We were not awarded academic credit for the courses we were taking, but we were motivated by the knowledge that proficiency in the language would be invaluable when we got to China. There were stimulating instructors; some of them Chinese, others were Americans who had been born and reared in China.

Although we were highly motivated, we were also aware of the events going on in China. Mao Tse-tung and the Communist army were gradually conquering the country and the Nationalist army was being defeated. In January of 1950 the Communists completed their occupation of the Chinese mainland. Missionaries were no longer welcome, particularly American missionaries.

For all of us, it was a period of great despair. I was not the only one who had planned for years to go to China. Many people had strong feelings that it was God's will that they should serve in China. Now this was not possible. When classes resumed in January, the entire group was upset. The faculty noted that there was low morale and no motivation to learn the language. For many of us, the future held only a question mark.

Some of the students left Yale in January and went to other assignments. Some could be reassigned to areas where Chinese was a common language, but the Evangelical United Brethren Church offered no such opportunity. Six of us stayed in New Haven and continued our study while the mission board decided what they would do with us. Eventually, one person went to Japan, and one to Puerto Rico; three of us would be sent to Sierra Leone. Those decisions, however, were not made until much later. For me, the months from January to May were filled with discouragement. Normally, I don't spend much time and energy worrying but, at this point, I could see no future. I had wasted nine months in intensive study of a language that I was never to use. I had no job prospects. My father was planning to remarry, so he didn't need me as a housekeeper. After all those years of expectation about China, I couldn't think of any place that would be as exciting or appealing, certainly not the alternative of a county health service in rural Wisconsin.

To complicate matters, I had fallen deeply in love with a man much older than myself who was also a student at the Institute. He was kind and gentle and we shared a love of music. But, he was also a confirmed bachelor. It was obvious that he had no intention of returning my interest and we parted as friends.

In May I returned to Wisconsin. I was ill-tempered, full of anger, and unsettled. I don't know how my father was able to live with me during those months. Finally, I decided to get a job and also to attend the seminary. Up to this time, all my formal education had been in my profession since the University at Madison had been noted for its anti-religion bias.

The day before I was to go for my job interview, I received a letter from the mission board saying I was assigned to Sierra Leone. First, however, I needed to have midwifery training in London. I was thrilled at the prospect of living in London. I wasn't so sure about midwifery. Where was Sierra Leone? I had read little about Africa and even less about that tiny country (about the size and population of South

Carolina). I didn't know if I would work in a hospital or a maternity unit. My limited ability in Chinese language wasn't going to be of much help, no matter what language they talked in Sierra Leone.

I spent a harried six weeks making preparations for the year in England and three years in Sierra Leone. The future held a lot of question marks, but at least I was going somewhere and I was going to do something.

In November of 1950 I sailed to England where I spent 14 months qualifying for a certificate in midwifery. In the middle of December 1951 I sailed from Liverpool to go to Freetown.

CHAPTER 3

Sierra Leone: A Brief History of the Country and the Church

Sierra Leone is a small country on the west coast of Africa. During the fifteenth century, the Portuguese, encouraged by Prince Henry the Navigator, sailed along the west coast of Africa; the first Europeans to make this adventuresome journey.

The first Portuguese ship anchored in the estuary of the Rokel River in 1447. This river forms the northern boundary of the peninsula on which the current city of Freetown is located. In 1462, Pedro da Centra named the peninsula Serra Lyoa, from which the current name of the country is derived, probably because the hills in the center of the peninsula resembled lions.

Although the early Portuguese carried slaves and gold to Europe, Sir John Hawkins was the first Englishman to conduct a slaving voyage to Sierra Leone in 1562. The English continued to dominate the slave trade, although other Europeans were also involved in the transportation of slaves from the area until the British outlawed the slave trade in 1807.

In a 1772 landmark decision, the English chief justice ruled that a slave could not be forcibly removed from England. This resulted in a measure of freedom for slaves in England. In 1787, the first group of about 400 "Black Poor" was sent to Sierra Leone. The group also included about 60 white women and a few white men. In 1792, the new settlement was named Free Town. This changed to Freetown in 1792 by the settlers from Nova Scotia. In 1791, a private company, the Sierra Leone Company with headquarters in London, took over the administration of the area and it became a British colony.

The next black settlers arrived from Nova Scotia in 1792. They had been slaves in the United States and had been set free at the time of the American War of Independence. Some of them had fought as members of the British Army and were no longer welcome in the United States and so settled in Nova Scotia. They had appealed to the Sierra Leone Company which offered them land in Free Town. They were Christians and brought their churches with them: Methodist and

Baptist. Some of them also brought with them an obscure sect of Christianity called the Countess of Huntingdon Connection. The Countess of Huntingdon had been the leader of a group of Anglicans in England who had separated from the Church of England, much as had the Methodists. Her movement had quickly spread to the American colonies and was found among the Nova Scotia settlers.

A third group of settlers was the Maroons. Originally, they had been slaves in Jamaica. After a slave revolt, they were captured and shipped to Nova Scotia. They suffered from the bitter cold weather and asked to be sent to Africa. They arrived in Freetown in 1800.

In 1807 the British government passed the Abolition Act which made slave trading illegal for British citizens. In 1808 the British upgraded Freetown to a British Crown Colony. The British Navy began to capture ships carrying slaves. Instead of returning the captives to the country of their origin, they brought the slaves to Freetown. By 1815 over 6,000 were settled there.

In 1804 the Church Missionary Society, (CMS) a Church of England institution, sent out two missionaries. The strong Christian influence of the early settlers encouraged the captives to adopt Christianity. Although the captives came from numerous language backgrounds, English soon became the common language. Many people also adopted English names. The settlers blended into a single group called Creoles. Today, the term Krio is the commonly accepted spelling.

The Krios were, and still are, separate and distinct from the indigenous people of Sierra Leone. Although much of the Krio culture was European-based: clothing, houses, and religion, there were certain distinguishing characteristics that separated them from their western origins. The Krios, from the beginning, wore European-style clothing: coats, trousers, and top hats for the men; dresses and feathered hats for the women. Although rice was the staple food for both Krios and indigenous people, certain dishes were a feature of Krio menus: Jollof rice (rice cooked in a tomato sauce); foofoo (boiled and fermented cassava root); and palaver sauce (a peppery stew of greens served over rice).

But the outstanding feature was their language. Although English provided the base, words and phrases from many languages were grafted in. For example, the verb "sabby", to know, is from the Portuguese "sabeir" while "borku", meaning much, is from the French "beaucoup". Some phrases were direct translations from indigenous languages. For example, an angry person is told "Cool your heart" which is a translation from a Mende phrase. A distinctive grammar and vocabulary evolved. For instance, the English sentence "This is the man" in Krio becomes "Nar de man dat". Krio is a common language in Sierra Leone and its use has spread along the coast and is used in Ghana and Nigeria.

In 1896 the British Governor, Frederic Cardew, declared the rest of the country to be a British Protectorate while the peninsula remained a British colony. The Protectorate was organized into five districts, each governed by a British District Commissioner. Districts were divided into chiefdoms, administered by elected indigenous chiefs.

The use of imported administrative officials meant that expenses increased. To meet the cost of the new administration, Governor Cardew imposed a hut tax in 1898. Each house owner was to pay a tax to the government. The tax was exceedingly unpopular. The resentment of the tax, plus the animosity against the government, when they lost their independence to the authority of British administrative officers, was a major impetus that led the people of the Protectorate to declare war on the British government.

During the first months of 1898, sporadic fighting broke out over the whole of the Protectorate. On April 27, a mass rebellion erupted. The uprising was carefully planned by the chiefs and covered the entire Protectorate. The plan was to destroy all Europeans, all Krios, and all government servants. This was extended to anyone who had learned to speak English or who had adopted a European life-style. One historian states that the common statement was "Every man in trousers, every woman in a dress."

The rebellion was soon overturned. The British army, along with a contingent of local troops, advanced through the country. The army soon captured those towns that were of strategic importance, where a powerful chief held authority. This included Rotifunk. In Tiama, a tall, thick wall with a moat in front of it, surrounded the town on three sides. Unable to scale the wall, the army attacked the town from the unprotected bank of the river and Tiama was captured.

The British government enacted swift retribution for the rebellion. Chiefs, in particular, were singled out for arrest and punishment. The historian Fyfe, reports that 96 people were hanged. After the rebellion, the British government consolidated its hold over the country and the number of Europeans in administrative authority was increased.

Following the rebellion, there was consistent development. From 1800 to 1961, the government and the Krios made education a high priority. Christian missionary organizations established a number of schools. The CMS started the Grammar School and the Annie Walsh Memorial School; the Wesleyan Methodist Society established the Methodist Boys High School in 1874 and a girls school in 1880. In 1827 the CMS founded the Christian Institute of Fourah Bay which in 1848 became Fourah Bay College.

A number of Krios went to study in Britain. The first barrister, John Thorpe, a Maroon, qualified in 1850, and James Africanus Horton became the first western-trained doctor in 1859. Samuel Adjai Crowther, the first registered student at Fourah Bay, qualified as the first Anglican Bishop in 1864. Samuel Lewis became the first Sierra Leone Knight in 1896 and was the first to be granted Cambridge and Oxford degrees.

Krio influence extended throughout all of West Africa. Krios were ubiquitous traders, but they were also missionaries, educators, and engineers and were involved in the legislatures of the British West African colonies. Fourah Bay College became the center of learning for the West Coast.

Although control of the country was firmly in the hands of the British authorities, there were some small efforts to involve local people in the governing process. In 1924 a new constitution provided for a Legislative and Executive Council. The Legislative Council of 22 members had eight Africans, three of them elected and five members appointed by the governor.

The Protectorate Assembly was organized in 1946. This was a central representative body which allowed the people a voice in Protectorate matters. It was still under the authority of the Legislative Council. Eventually, some of these elected members were given responsibilities for government ministries. In 1954, one of these men, Dr. M.A.S. Margai, became the Chief Minister and later Prime Minister.

After World War II, the British colonies throughout the world intensified their demands for independence. In most British colonies, Britain granted these demands with few objections. In West Africa, there was no armed struggle such as occurred in Kenya with the Mau Mau opposition. In Africa, the Gold Coast was the first and became the country of Ghana in 1957. Sierra Leone celebrated its independence on April 27, 1961.

The United Brethren Church

The first missionaries of the United Brethren Church (UBC) came to Sierra Leone in 1855. Instead of settling in Freetown, they moved south along the Atlantic Coast and settled in Shenge. Prior to their arrival, work had been established by the American Missionary Association. Eventually, this association transferred all of its property to the UBC. The UBC extended their field of work beyond Shenge to

Rotifunk in 1875 and later to Moyamba and Tiama. Although the UBC missionaries concentrated much of their work among the two largest ethnic groups in the Protectorate, the Mende and Temne people, they also established the King Memorial Church in Freetown. In 1904, they also opened a Boys' High School, the Albert Academy in Freetown. King Memorial had a Krio membership, but the Albert Academy was called the "Mende" school. The majority of the students came from outside the colony.

During the Hut Tax War, the UBC suffered much in the loss of missionary personnel, church members, hired workers, and property. The five missionaries living at Rotifunk were killed. Rev. L. A. McGrew and his wife, Clara, who had been living in Tiama since January of 1898, were taken to a rock in the middle of the Teye River, were killed there and their bodies washed downstream.

After the rebellion was over, the UBC expanded all aspects of their work. New missionaries arrived and some who had been on furlough to the United States returned to continue their tasks. The UBC people, who placed a strong emphasis on education, developed numerous primary schools, usually staffed by local people. In addition to the Albert Academy, the Harford School for Girls was opened in Moyamba in 1898 and in 1937, became the first secondary school for girls in the Protectorate.

In 1904, evangelistic work was started in Jaiama in the Kono district near the border with French Guinea. In addition to the hospital at Rotifunk, the church started small clinics and maternity units at Jaiama, Tiama, and Manjama. Increasingly, local staff were in charge of all institutions. After independence, the Sierra Leone government ruled that all heads of schools had to be non-Europeans.

In 1946 the UBC and the Evangelical Church in the United States merged into one organization called the Evangelical United Brethren Church. This organization united with the Methodist Episcopal Church in 1968 and became the United Methodist Church (UMC). These changes, both in name and structure, were adopted by the church in Sierra Leone.

As the church expanded, the number and authority of the expatriot missionaries decreased and the church and its associated institutions were delegated to Sierra Leoneans. Much of this delegation was necessitated by the rapid growth of the church. Some of the delegation of authority came as both missionaries and Africans were aware of the need of the church to become autonomous and independent. The first African bishop was the Rev. B. A. Carew. Temne by birth, he lived in Mende country for many years and spoke a classical Mende. After

Carew's retirement, the Rev. Thomas Bangura was elected bishop. In 1993, he was succeeded by the Rev. Joseph Humper.

Expatriots continued to perform the medical work. For short periods, Sierra Leone doctors worked at Rotifunk: Dr. John Karefa-Smart and Dr. Moses Mahoi. All of the medical institutions had Sierra Leone staff who worked under the supervision of the missionaries. For a short period of time, a school for midwives was established at Rotifunk. After graduation, these midwives were able to carry some of the responsibilities at the other clinics.

CHAPTER 4

Climbing the Portuguese Steps

January is probably the most pleasant month of the year on the African west coast. The rains finish in October and each day there is brilliant sunshine until the rains resume in April. In December, the weather is often cool and hazy from the Harmattan, a trade wind that develops over the Sahara and blows southwest over West Africa. One anticipates the fierce, hot sun during February and March, but January is still fairly cool and the heat is not as oppressive as it will be in a few weeks time.

It was under this bright tropical sun that the SS Aureol docked in the Freetown harbor and I caught my first glimpse of the city. I had spent the last ten days on board ship in passage from Liverpool. The weather there had been cold and dreary, only gradually did we sail into the warmth of that sunlight.

Freetown has one of the world's best natural harbors. The Rokel River, later called the Sierra Leone River, which flows into the Atlantic, forms a deep bay that allows large vessels to approach the land easily. Today, ships dock at the Queen Elizabeth II Quay. But in 1952 the quay was just under construction. The Aureol anchored a few hundred feet offshore. A number of small boats clustered in the clear water around the ship. In each were several young boys, smiling and dancing and calling out to us, asking us to toss coins into the water. We obliged with shillings and half-crowns, and the boys quickly dove into the water to retrieve them; emerging with shouts of victory, excitedly waving the coins in the air.

A narrow plank was lowered alongside the ship to the small launch which awaited us. It was a bit tricky getting down the gangplank, which was unsteady and tended to list.

As a young missionary, I was very conscious of my appearance. I had waited for this day for 14 years and I was not about to disgrace myself or those folks waiting on the quay. I was wearing one of my better dresses, and perched on my head was a demure blue and white hat that stayed with me for several months. At least in Freetown, my head was covered when I attended church. But I really dislike having anything on my head, and over the years, I abandoned any head covering including a nurse's cap. Eventually, I gave my arrival hat to an African friend who wore it to church each Sunday.

I also had put on nylon stockings. Within a few hours, I found they were very hot and uncomfortable. It may have been the last time I wore them in all my years in West Africa.

The little boat reached the landing. We climbed the so-called "Portuguese Steps" to the top of the quay. These steps had been constructed about 1818, long after the Portuguese sailors had first landed in Freetown. Later I realized that these were the steps used by the slaves captured by the British Navy when they were brought back to Africa and given their freedom.

At the top of the steps, I was welcomed by fellow missionaries. I was particularly pleased that Gertrude Bloede had come down from Rotifunk to greet me. Our friendship dated back to our childhood in Wisconsin. Our fathers had been pastors in the same conference and some of her family had been members of my father's congregation. She and I had been in England at the same time during part of our midwifery training. She was one of the few people I knew in Sierra Leone and hers was the only familiar face I saw on that day.

Many of the passengers on the Aureol were African students returning to the countries along the west coast. Obviously, during the ten days we had been traveling together, we had developed friendships. While we were standing on the quay, one of the students came up to me, holding a coconut.

"Would you like to taste fresh coconut milk?" he asked. "It is really very tasty."

I was eager to start with any new experience I could find.

"I would enjoy it," I replied.

He cut off the top of the coconut with a sharp pocket knife and showed me how to drink from the shell. I was about to try it for myself when the mission superintendent spoke to me very sharply.

"Miss Olsen, I don't think you should do that."

Reluctantly, I handed the coconut back to my Nigerian friend. I didn't know if the superintendent objected to my drinking from the open coconut or because I had accepted the gift from one of the African students, but it was clear that he thought my actions were inappropriate.

We left the bright sunshine of the quay and passed through the cool, dark customs shed. I don't remember much about what I had carried with me on that first trip. I had only six weeks notice before leaving the United States in October of 1950. Things were still heavily rationed in Britain so that it was difficult to obtain much in the way of supplies. As I recall, I had packed a four-piece place setting of plastic dishes. My clothes and linens were packed in an upright steamer trunk that had drawers on one side. The left side was equipped with hangers so that the trunk could function as a closet both on board ship as well as in one's home. I had three prized possessions. One was a small and very old pump organ. It lasted through the three years of my first term in Sierra Leone. The second and third were a hand-wound phonograph and a 20-record set of the "Messiah." Sadly, one record of the set got broken on the journey out. To this day, I know where some of the records had to be turned over in order to pick up the rest of the melody.

The buildings of Freetown showed a great variation in style and construction. There were large houses of stone and concrete blocks, as well as small structures made out of flattened kerosene tins and indigenous buildings made of sticks and mudaub with thatch roofs. Roy Lewis describes Freetown as having "the serene unhurried pace of a small English port, further slowed by tropical languor." The streets of the central part of the city were set in an orderly grid, but began to curve and twist as the city had grown around the hills. The streets also rose steeply as they reached the center of the hills.

The Evangelical United Brethren mission house was just up a small hill from the Portuguese Steps at No.5 Gloucester Street. It was a large three-story building made of cement blocks and was sandwiched between the General Post Office and the City Hotel. The ground floor included a large dining room, a kitchen, and a business office. There was a large parlor and several bedrooms on the second floor. Both floors opened out onto verandas that ran the length of the north side of the building. Beyond the ground floor veranda was a lawn enclosed by a high wall. Blooming hibiscus, poinsettias, and towering palm trees enhanced the beauty. From the second floor balcony you could see, off in the distance, the harbor and the north bank of the Rokel River.

The guests at the mission house used it as a hotel when coming to and leaving Freetown. Many other travelers besides the missionaries were welcomed as guests. During World War II, when shipping was often disrupted, people sometimes found themselves stranded in Freetown for weeks and were able to use the spacious rooms in the house.

The immediate view from the second floor veranda was of the City Hotel. Readers of Graham Greene's *Heart of the Matter* will recognize the Freetown landmark. The squat two-story building was, for many years, the only hotel accommodation in Freetown. Its bar was the center of much of the social activity in the city.

Two activities caught our attention as we sat on the mission house veranda in the cool of the evening. One was that numerous men used the outside wall of the hotel as a latrine. It surprised me that men had no hesitation about relieving themselves in any public spot. Usually, however, they stood with their backs to those passing by, although this did not prevent them from turning their heads to observe the local traffic, including anyone walking on the road. The second thing was the numerous liaisons that developed around the building. I suppose that Freetown had an organized system of prostitution, but the City Hotel was a gathering place for a large segment of the male population, offering a choice venue for trade.

Someone has said that Freetown was as British as boiled cabbage. In 1952 independence was still nine years away. Colonial trappings were much in evidence. Government offices were housed in buildings with Victorian architecture, their counterparts to be seen in the outposts of the Empire such as Accra, Lagos, and Nairobi. The police wore navy blue woolen uniforms despite the heat. School children marched to classes and sports activities in bright uniforms. British literature dominated the curriculum of the schools and proficiency in written and spoken English was the norm. Even the sports were British, with football being the most popular.

The Krios had retained some of the flavor of their British and West Indian origins, but a unique Krio culture had evolved. The women wore a distinctive dress; floor-length, voluminous, and decorated with intricate stitchery. On their heads, they wore complicated folded material, often of a material matching the dress. Men usually dressed in trousers, shirts, and colorful neckties. Alridge, writing in 1900, remarked that "Men preferred woolen suits to cotton, and top hats and spats were a common feature on the Freetown streets." By 1952 the top hat and spats had disappeared and it was common to see African men wearing Khaki shorts and shirts in Freetown. However, as late as 1980, an African male friend of mine delayed going to lunch until he had changed his shorts for long trousers.

The most persuasive influence in the colony was the British Colonial Administration which influenced not only the official life, but also the political and social life. Although the senior British officers were in charge of the administration, the movement towards African participation had begun.

The Americans living in the country adapted to the local culture, both British and Krio in a variety of ways. Some attempted to accept British customs such as serving tea at four o'clock in the afternoon and using British terminology and spelling. Some people became fluent in the Krio language and learned to cook and enjoy the local dishes. I was aware of some of these adaptations during my first Sunday in Freetown.

We walked to service at King Memorial Church, the largest EUB church in Freetown, and except for the church in Tiama, probably the largest in the country. The church building was near the center of the city, on the corner of two very busy streets. Like many African church buildings, it was a rather graceless structure, rectangular in shape. In the sanctuary, a small platform in the front held a plain table that served as an altar as well as several chairs for the officiating clergy. On the right was an organ and several benches for the choir. Fitting the Wesleyan tradition, an elevated pulpit stood to the left of the platform.

My missionary friends advised me how to dress. In addition to the hose and hat, I wore, as did all the women, a dress with long sleeves and a pair of white gloves.

Although I had been raised in the Evangelical Church, I was not prepared for the formal liturgy that greeted me that morning; written prayers, chanted responses, and a rigid order of service.

I have never adapted to this formal structure. I was fortunate that the two churches in Sierra Leone, where I most frequently worshiped, used a more spontaneous worship experience. However, the singing was lusty and enthusiastic and most of the hymns were familiar, such as "What a Friend We Have in Jesus," "The Old Rugged Cross" and "Sweet Hour of Prayer."

Except for the six or eight of us white Americans, the congregation was all African. It was to become a familiar experience, being in the minority and a foreigner. Only occasionally was I conscious of how conspicuous my white face and blond hair was in that sea of blackness.

Most of the congregation were Krios, with everyone well dressed. Men wore suits and ties. Some of the women wore Krio dresses and headties while others were dressed in the latest European fashions as well as smart looking hats. Like me, most of them wore white gloves.

When the service was over, we marched back to the mission house for dinner. No haphazard meal, this! The large table in the dining room was covered with a white linen tablecloth. There were linen napkins and an array of silverware at each place setting, arranged in an orderly fashion on both sides of the plate, with dessert utensils on the top. Courses were served by the white-coated servants. The first course of a cream soup was followed by rice and stew. It was the custom on Sunday to serve Jollof rice (the rice cooked in a tomato sauce with several kinds of meat, often chicken, beef, and fish) as well as some vegetables cooked with rice. It is often cooked with a strong lacing of chili peppers. It was, and is, my favorite West African dish. In addition, local vegetables were served as side dishes. Tomatoes and cabbage were plentiful, while carrots were more difficult to obtain. Fried plantain, a form of banana, provided a tasty addition to any meal.

Finger bowls were passed before we were served dessert. They were really unnecessary, for when we were served bananas, we were expected to eat them with a knife and fork. The custom was to cut the banana down the center lengthwise, cut the flesh in portions and extract each section with a fork.

We spent the afternoon inside the house to avoid the hot sun. Most people took a nap or caught up on their reading. In the evening, we gathered on the northern veranda for a time of conversation. The cool evening breeze was a welcome relief from the afternoon heat. However, while the veranda offered a charming view and pleasant breeze, it also made us prime targets for local mosquitoes. It would be some time before I realized that such exposure was hazardous. Historically, all of the west coast was known for the virulence of its mosquitoes. Sierra Leone has been called the "Whiteman's Grave". The very earliest visitors and settlers had been victims of malaria and this visitor was no exception. I had more than my share of malaria attacks and through the years, I have learned to be wary of charming, open verandas in the early evening.

On Monday, Gertrude and I boarded the train to go to Rotifunk. At that time, and still after 40 years, I questioned why we were in such a hurry. Freetown was, and is, a fascinating city. I wanted to explore its streets, look at its Victorian architecture, visit the markets and shops, but the mission policy was that one did not "waste time" in Freetown. As a missionary, you came to work, and that meant going directly to your posted station. Even though I wasn't to be posted at Rotifunk but to Tiama, I, too, left the city.

Before I left, the superintendent gave me a few words of advice.

"I know," he said, "you will run into some difficulties. It will not be easy to be alone in Tiama."

This was not news to me. I expected I would have some difficulties. I didn't know the language. I was going to have to adjust to a completely different diet. I didn't even know what foods were available in Tiama; was there bread, or milk or fresh meat? I knew I would be confronted with medical emergencies with which I had not the knowledge, the skill or the equipment to manage.

He continued, "No matter what troubles you have, you are not to discuss these with any of the local people. You must not admit to any of the people in Tiama that you are having problems."

I nodded in agreement. I didn't know what to say. If I couldn't discuss it with the Africans, and they were the only people there, what was I to do? He didn't give me any suggestions.

"And further, if you know of any problems and difficulties between other missionaries, you are not to talk about that either."

"I understand," I agreed. But I didn't understand. It was probably the worst advice that anyone ever gave me.

His advice reflected on the concept of the superiority of white people over black folk. But the idea of the invincibility of white people was patently ridiculous. I knew that and the Africans knew it. Not only that, they quickly estimated the character of each newcomer and gave an appropriate name to describe the person's character. They were aware of the animosities and personality clashes, as well as individual affinities and were often able to use them to their own advantage. If one missionary refused to share money or food, they would turn to the person who gave things generously. They frequently visited the persons who kept their door open and shunned the closed and uninviting door.

For about nine months, I followed his advice. Then I realized that I needed the help of someone older and wiser than I and turned to the African pastor and his wife for help. I soon found that they had understanding, listening ears and sound advice.

CHAPTER 5

"And Are We Yet Alive?"

Rotifunk was located about 40 miles from Freetown on the railroad line. At that time, there was no motorable road into the town. The town was the site of one of the oldest United Brethren mission stations in Sierra Leone and the site of the mission hospital, a primary school and, of course, a church. The earliest missionaries had come to Rotifunk in 1875. As in much of West Africa, many of the missionaries survived only a few months before succumbing to malaria. The cause of malaria was not determined until the end of the nineteenth century. Although quinine had been in somewhat limited use since the 1650's, widespread use was not initiated until the early 1900's.

As discussed in Chapter 3, during the Hut Tax War in 1898, the five missionaries at Rotifunk had been killed. In commemoration of this, numerous reminders were scattered over the grounds of the hospital compound. The recovered bodies were cremated and the ashes buried in the local cemetery, next to the compound, and were marked by an appropriate headstone. In addition, prominent markers noted where a particular person had been killed. The hospital was called the Archer-Hatfield Dispensary, named after the two single women doctors who had died in the raid.

The church contained even more commemorative plaques, mentioning those who had died of fever and other causes, including one person who had been killed by lightning. The plaques were placed along the walls at eye level of those sitting in the pews. It was sobering to be confronted with the past devastations during every worship service. In addition, the services were conducted with the same dull formality of the Freetown church. I often felt that when the Lord wanted to punish me, he sent me to attend the services at Rotifunk.

The compound was about 500 yards from the railroad station and consisted of four buildings. The church was a single-roomed square building made of cement blocks, painted red, on the outside. In the interior, there was a simple platform that contained the pulpit, lectern, and a communion table. A reed parlor organ was the source of musical accompaniment and on several occasions, I was allowed to play it.

The single missionary residence was a wooden building with a large veranda on the east and north sides of the house. The house was built on a slope and was partly supported by concrete pillars. A large sheltered area was underneath much of the house. Later, when an influx of leprosy patients came for treatment, many of them found shelter in this area.

The inside of the house had a long, central living room flanked by two bedrooms and a bathroom on the south side, with another bedroom, storeroom and a rather spacious dining room on the north side. A door from the dining room led to the kitchen which was separate from the house. The house was constructed so that there was no cross ventilation, which made all the rooms, including the living room, uncomfortably hot. One of our builders once said the mission residences were designed for Indiana and not for the tropics.

When I arrived in January of 1952, four single women lived in the house: Gertrude Bloede, a nurse-midwife; Esther Megill, the laboratory technician; Winnie Smith, a young doctor and Dr. Mabel Silver. The younger women had been there for about a year, but Dr. Silver had been there since the early 1930's. (See colorplate 1).

A second house was being built which eventually provided housing for Gertrude and Esther and later for other missionaries. But for one year, all the American personnel shared one house, and I am sure, that at times, the tensions must have been unbearable. Sometimes, the group included families with small children. There were few opportunities for outside social activities and travel was hindered by many difficulties. Single women were forbidden by mission rules to own a car. Even if they had one, there were few roads on which to travel. In 1957, more roads had been built, and one single woman broke the rule, bought a car, and by 1958 several of us were able to own and drive a car.

The other two buildings on the compound made up the hospital. They were made of cement blocks and painted white. The clinic building had a large covered veranda where the patients gathered early in the morning to wait for treatment. Dr. Silver saw patients in a large sunny room. To save time and energy, it was the practice to bring 10 to 20 patients into the room at the same time. She would question them, examine them, and prescribe treatment. She often distributed medicine from her desk, although there was also a pharmacy where medicine was distributed. She was fluent in several local languages and had little need for an interpreter. Ernest Koroma, a dispenser, who had been there almost as long as she had, gave injections at a table situated at the side of the room. The laboratory was in a side room.

Originally, another building had housed in-patients. Later, two more wards were built to house male and female patients, then an operating room and a maternity wing.

After I had been at Rotifunk for several days, all the missionaries traveled back to Freetown for the annual missionary council and church conference, which were two separate meetings. The first included only the missionaries. The second was the annual meeting of pastors and lay members of the church. This Methodist tradition had its origin when, in the eighteenth century, John Wesley met annually with the pastors in a meeting that combined procedural concerns and matters of doctrine. The EUB church had its roots in historic Methodism and continued to meet in an annual conference. While Africans were not a part of the missionary council, missionaries were expected to attend the annual conference.

The system was beginning to change in the 1950's. Many of the major decisions about the work of the church were still made by the missionary council. Missionaries were the heads of institutions such as secondary schools and the hospital. It was at this council in 1952 that plans for restructuring the administrative system were being discussed. Advisory committees were to be formed to deal with such matters as education, medical services, and evangelism. These committees were to be comprised of Africans and missionaries. The evolution from missionary control, to joint management, to African control took a long time. Gradually, the committees were asked to make decisions about institutional policies. How many children should be admitted to a primary or secondary school? Where would a new secondary school be located? The medical committee made the decision to establish a school of midwifery at Rotifunk. The evangelism committee encouraged the establishment of new congregations in the Temne and Kono areas.

I have always been rather proud that the EUB church, and after union with the Methodists, the United Methodist Church, saw the necessity for this shift in leadership and responsibility. Some denominations have dropped the word missionary, and have designated their expatriot workers as fraternal workers.

Much of the discussion in January of 1952 included the practical measures necessary to organize the committees and to finance such things as transportation, accommodations, and methods of procedure. How were the members of the committees to be chosen? The missionaries assumed they would elect their own representatives, but who would choose the African members? Some people felt they should be elected by the conference, with the missionaries having no vote. Others felt that at least some of the members should be appointed by

King Memorial EUB Church, Freetown.

the missionary council to assure that the "right" people would be on the committee. I remember a saying that Dr. Silver often used, "Every missionary has a blind spot in his eye for one African!"

Finally, came the most important questions of all, "Who will be in charge of the money? Who will collect it? Who will spend it? Who will decide the budget?" We couldn't agree on that among ourselves, how much harder it would be in a larger group.

Suddenly, the quiet voice of one of the senior missionaries said, "If you are going to share responsibilities with Africans on these committees, it means you are going to have to eat with them."

Had I heard right? Of course, we would eat together. I soon found out that he was not objecting to the practice. Indeed, his home, his table, and his heart were always open to people of all races and backgrounds, but he knew that was not true of everyone in the group; his openness was a part of his success as a missionary. Again, I had to realize that not everyone who came to Africa to serve the Lord felt an equality with all God's children.

The annual conference meeting followed. In many ways, Methodist conferences are the same the world over. There is a joy of reunion with friends and colleagues, often after a year's separation. It is a tradition that the conference is opened with Charles Wesley's hymn "And Are We Yet Alive and See Each Other's Face." The third stanza has always seemed so relevant to me. "What trouble, fightings without and fears within, since we assembled last." But the hymn ends triumphantly, "Let us take up the cross till we the cross obtain and gladly reckon all things lost, that we may Jesus gain."

The Methodists, by tradition, have expressed their devotion by lively, enthusiastic singing, this conference was no exception. To quote John Wesley, "Sing lustily and with a good courage."

Finally, the conference was over and I was ready to go to Tiama. I was grateful for this opportunity to meet the other missionaries as well as to meet African pastors and lay members. I had some understanding of the extent of the growth and work of the church. I also realized that tensions existed between missionaries and between Africans on matters of money and authority. None of this was important at the time because I was going to an adventure in my new home.

CHAPTER 6

To Tiama

Dr. Silver and I traveled from Freetown to Rotifunk and then to Mano. I have described the train journey in Chapter 1. At Mano, we were met by Pa and Ma Leader, the senior EUB missionaries. They had worked in Tiama for over 20 years and were largely responsible for the growth of the church in Tiama, as well as in surrounding villages, and for the development of the school and the agricultural program. They now lived in Bo, about 60 miles away, where they were responsible for starting a Bible school for pastors and evangelists. They were knowledgeable about the local people and customs and had close personal relationships with many of the people who lived in Tiama. They had come from Bo to escort me to my new home and to introduce me to the local people.

The work of the church in Tiama had three parts: the medical work, a primary school, and the church. The latter two were managed by local people, only the medical work still used a missionary. The primary school had about 800 students and was about two blocks away from the dispensary.

The church building, my house, and the dispensary were situated on a triangle of land in the center of town. (See colorplate 1). The church was a red cement block building which faced the main street of the town. Farther along on that street was the chiefdom court building, called a barri, and a distance to the north, the Teye River. To the south of the church, separated by a fence, was my house, also made of cement blocks and painted white; next to the house was the dispensary. (See colorplate 2). The two buildings were connected by a short wall with a gate.

Inside the wall was a pleasant patio. A long veranda fronted the south side of the house. A rope hammock was a part of the patio furniture. Numerous flowering plants ornamented the patio and the veranda: brilliant red hibiscus, towering poinsettia and pink bougainvillea. The bougainvillea climbed the side of the house and inched along the roof.

East of the house, but in a separate building, were an outhouse, kitchen and two storerooms. An ample lawn, which stretched on the east side of the house, included a number of fruit trees: limes, avocados, and papayas which the local people called pawpaws. Imagine being able to go out in the early morning and pick a bright green pawpaw from the tree to be enjoyed at breakfast. The entire compound was surrounded by a wire fence. I'm not sure of the purpose; to keep me in or to keep intruders out? When we built the new compound, there was no such protection or hindrance.

At first appearance, the house seemed spacious and comfortable. I'm not sure what I expected. Like many Americans, did I think everybody lived in mud houses with thatch roofs and mud floors? I came to appreciate the low-hanging eaves which kept out the rain and the hot sun, but allowed for a free circulation of air. The inside whitewashed walls allowed for reflection of available light and were a welcome contrast to the continuous green of the African landscape. Since the windows on the south side opened onto the covered veranda, there was never any reason to close the shutters, even in heavy rain.

I was grateful for these comfortable surroundings. I loved being in the center of the town with the bustle of the village easily heard; the children playing, ceremonial dancers passing on the street, an occasional car coming down the hill, the chatter of the people passing, going to market or to the court.

Kori Chiefdom Court barri, Tiama.

The maternity building was about two blocks away, up a small hill. It had two wards with six beds each and a delivery room. It was a real sprint from the house to the delivery room for an emergency delivery and I didn't always make it on time.

The house had four rooms, an attic, and a closed-in veranda on the east side. Very few buildings in rural Africa had two stories. In fact, only one other house that I lived in had a second story. The floors were cement, the ceiling was wood, and the roof was of corrugated iron. One of the most comforting sounds I know is the sound of rain on a metal roof. Since Sierra Leone has a six-month rainy season, there was plenty of time to enjoy that sound.

Light was provided by kerosene lamps, of the type called Aladdin lamps, which had a small cotton mantle and a tall glass chimney. The lamp was silent, relatively easy to care for, and gave good light. It is no longer available, but has been replaced either with pressure lamps that are noisy and much more complex to operate or by hurricane lamps that give only a dim light.

Our water supply was stored in a cistern attached to the dispensary. All the EUB mission compounds were built with cisterns. During the long rainy seasons, the cistern filled with water which usually lasted through the dry season. Our cistern was equipped with a hand-operated pump similar to the one that supplied water in my childhood home in Wisconsin. The water was carried in a bucket to wherever it was needed. The maternity unit had its own cistern.

Years later, when I lived in Liberia, the water system was operated by electricity which only ran for eight hours a day. It meant that for much of the day there was no water. I wondered why no one had built cisterns for the hospital and houses on the mission compound such as we had in Sierra Leone.

The front section of the screened veranda contained the kerosene-burning refrigerator which was a bit tricky to operate. A long container at the base held the kerosene which fed the round wick at the rear. If the wick became uneven, the unit smoked, staining the wall behind it, and decreasing the efficiency of the cooling system. Otherwise, it worked fairly well. One could even freeze things in the freezing compartment, including ice cream. The back section of the veranda was closed off to form the bathroom. Because these early houses did not contain a bathtub, it had a small galvanized washtub that was the bathtub, and a hole in the floor leading to the backyard served as a drain. A small wash basin was used for washing. The toilet was a wooden box with a bucket underneath the seat. Daily, the watchman opened the door on the outside wall, removed the bucket, and emptied it in the

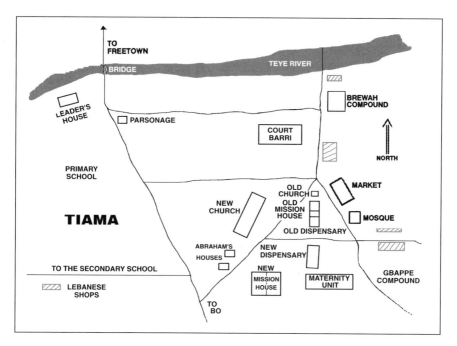

nearby pit latrine. Why didn't I use the pit latrine in the yard? Looking back, I must say, it would have been easier for everybody. But it seemed the custom that all the houses in which Europeans lived used the same system and I just followed the custom of the country.

In 1954 a new house was built and equipped with a proper bathroom, including a flush toilet. I have always enjoyed tub baths, plenty of water and some bubble bath. I have a special fondness for perfumed soap, so I insisted that the new house have a bathtub. If one couldn't be made or purchased in Sierra Leone, I threatened to tow one behind the ship on my way back from America. That wasn't necessary, a bathtub was included in the house.

But after the new house was under construction, I began to worry that it was too ornate. I feared my living style would alienate me from my neighbors who didn't have flush toilets and bathtubs. The latter was not too important, since most of my neighbors preferred to either bathe in the river or bathe by pouring water over themselves, but nobody in Tiama had a flush toilet. I had just moved into the house when the chief Muslim in town, Alhadji Samba Fofana, came to inspect the building. He carefully looked into each room, including the bathroom. Then he said, "You should have had a bathroom like this long ago."

To the east of the house were two important community institutions; the first was the village market. Although it was only a small, open-air building, it seemed adequate for the town. African markets continue to fascinate me. Among others, I have wandered through the enormous markets in cities like Treichville outside of Abidjan, the huge city market in Nairobi, the ancient market in Mombasa, and the colorful markets in the center of Monrovia, Liberia.

The Tiama market was very small compared to these others. A short, small wall surrounded much of the building which was covered with a metal roof. The open walls allowed for circulation of air, provision for light, and opportunities for the shopper to see what was being offered for sale. Inside, rickety tables were arranged in rows. The market was limited to fresh foods: rice, cassava, greens, chili peppers, mangoes, oranges, and bananas. Markets were usually organized by produce so that all the rice was sold in one area, the bananas in another. Some things, such as rice and chili peppers were sold by cigarette tin. The buyers brought their own containers in which to take home their supplies. In 1952 a locally woven basket was usually used which was big enough to carry rice, vegetables, and fruit.

One corner of the market was screened off for the butcher shop. For many years, a cow was killed once a week on Friday. Abraham Lavaly had been taught how to cut up a carcass so that there were recognizable cuts of meat. I think beef was about two shillings a pound, 45 cents in American money. You took what you could get, but I was fussy. I didn't want the tail or the head, but boneless chuck. So I was charged 2/6 or 60 cents a pound and got a piece that could be used for stew, ground for hamburger or even roasted.

Pork was unavailable. Chickens were scarce and were both expensive and tough to eat. Sometimes fish was available, but whenever someone came to sell fish, the cook always told me "E no fit for white person to eat." I marveled that it always seemed to be fit for black people. However, I've never been that fond of fish, so it wasn't too important.

Next to the market was the mosque. The early morning call to prayer was often the first sound I heard on waking. The evening call to prayer came at sunset. It was rather a modest mosque, built of mud with a roof of sheet metal and without minarets, it had no sound system. There was a broad covered veranda all around the building where the women prayed, while the men prayed inside.

In 1989 I revisited Tiama. Little had changed. The mosque, the court barri, the market, the old church, and the whitewashed house were still standing. The main street had been covered with tar. The town had extended to the south. At one point, a water system had been installed in the town but was no longer functioning. A few private homes and businesses had generators, but as a whole, the people were still using kerosene for lights and three-stone fires for cooking.

CHAPTER 7

Abraham Lavaly

Abraham Lavaly stood with a grave manner and great dignity. Holding out his hand he said, "Welcome to Tiama." In the bustle of our arrival there had been general greetings and welcome. Now the two of us stood alone, the beginning of what was to be eight years of a close-working relationship and lifelong friendship. In those eight years, I learned to respect and appreciate his intelligence, common sense, and skills. (See colorplate 2).

During those years, I also learned about his background. The Lavaly family held a position of honor and power in the Kori chief-dom. In the earlier days of British rule, the chiefdom had been one of the most powerful on the West African coast. As the British extended their control over the Protectorate, this chiefdom was one of the last holdouts during the rebellion of 1898.

One of the warriors involved in that conflict was Abraham's father. He was still living during my stay in Tiama, a tall, dignified man whose placid appearance gave little hint of his militant past. It was my understanding, although it was never clearly stated, that he was the leader of the male secret society, the all-powerful Wunde Society. This group held the economic, religious, social, and political authority with-in the community. The Wunde Society controlled behavior of the inhabitants, including sexual behavior. It was rumored that the politi-cal power extended beyond the chiefdom to provincial and national politics. The society organized military training which had allowed the Mende to be such a powerful fighting force.

After the war in 1898 the British resumed their control over the country. Those mission stations that had been closed or destroyed were reopened and rebuilt. In 1902 Miss Minnie Eaton, one of the early UBC missionaries, came to Tiama and was responsible for building the school and church building. She also started the first primary school. In time, the government insisted that every family had to send at least one boy to school. It should have been the firstborn son. Since the first wife was the "big wife," the one who exerted authority over all the other

39

wives, her first son was held in greater esteem than the other boys. But people remembered that those who had been killed in the Hut Tax War had been those who were educated or who adopted foreign ways so many families were reluctant to send the oldest son. Instead, they sent a younger son, or in some cases, the son of a slave. The story was that Pa Lavaly refused to send his oldest son. He looked out into the rice field, saw one of his sons, and sent him to school. As a result, Abraham was one of the few in the family to be educated.

Miss Eaton, and later Charles Leader, had the philosophy of education promoted by the United Brethren missions, that said academic learning, such as reading, writing, and arithmetic should be accompanied by education in manual skills. The school at Tiama had an active carpentry and tailoring department as well as a large agricultural project. Abraham acquired the necessary academic skills, but also learned such practical skills as carpentry and equipment repair.

After finishing primary school, he came to work as cleaner and yardboy at the dispensary. He was soon promoted to dispenser. He was quick to learn and had acquired many technical skills. He took advantage of the knowledge of the medical staff that ran the dispensary. He could pull teeth, suture wounds, give drop ether, and acted as the pharmacist in preparing many of the medications that were dispensed. He also ran the temperamental steam autoclave by which we sterilized some of our supplies. We made an effort to meet the expenses of the clinic by charging fees for treatment and by selling medication. One of the most popular was a combination of petroleum jelly, mentholatum, and chili peppers called capsicum. It was a "rub medicine" which created a feeling of heat when applied to the skin. It sold extremely well and was one of the things that Abraham mixed for us.

As befitting a man of much community stature, Abraham's father, Pa Lavaly, had a large number of wives. His first wife, the "big wife," was a soft-spoken, mild-mannered woman. It seemed unlikely that her gentle nature would allow her to exhibit the kind of control needed to run the large compound. Abraham's mother, on the other hand, was a strong, forceful woman who exerted influence not only over the compound, but over her family including the grown children.

Abraham's wife was another extremely quiet and unassuming woman called Mabel. He had previously been married to a very bright and charming girl. Many people told me of this woman's engaging personality, her beauty, her friendliness, her intelligence, and her qualities as a good wife. She had borne him a son who was named Amos Kakpindi. Traditionally, in many African societies the woman breastfeeds for at least two years after birth, during which time the couple does not have intercourse. In some instances, the wife goes back to her family until the child is ready to be weaned, then the intercourse resumes and the woman starts her next pregnancy. This is so traditional that even in the 1990's, if one knows the age of the oldest child, one can assume the ages of succeeding children, and indeed, the age of the woman herself.

In the Mende tradition, men had no participation in anything to do with childbirth. In fact, a man was not allowed to touch a pregnant woman. Abraham's first wife was only a few weeks pregnant with the second pregnancy when she had a miscarriage and then had a severe hemorrhage. No one called her husband until she was close to death. It was too late to do anything to save her. He was grief stricken, his sorrow overwhelming. His consolation seemed to be in his young son. Amos was to be given the best care available.

It was unthinkable that Abraham should be without a wife. His mother particularly, threatened, cajoled, and pressured. One day, so I heard, he was walking through a village, saw a young girl, and said, "I'll take that one." It was Mabel.

Although lacking some of the graces of the first wife, she was a good wife. She kept his house and his clothes clean. She cooked good meals and agreed to his careful handling of money. She gave him five children, the first a boy. When he agreed to take an orphan girl into the family, she also raised Naomi. Behind her shy smile lurked a bubbling sense of humor. Like many Africans, Mabel was a great imitator and reduced me to laughter when she imitated me. One day when I was walking past her, in exact imitation of me, she repeated my favorite exclamation, "My gosh!" We both burst into laughter.

One evening she came to me in tears. Abraham had accumulated a nice supply of household equipment including in this case, a pretty china teapot. Mabel had broken the handle. "He will be furious," she said. "He will scold me terribly."

I had a teapot that was similar to the one that was broken and gave it to her. Abraham did not recognize the substitution. At Christmas, I gave him a new teapot, told him the story and claimed my own. He laughed when he realized that he had not noticed the substitution.

Our relationship was not always calm. He was sometimes annoyed by my various American habits. It bothered him that the missionary children called me by my first name. Occasionally, we would argue about British colonial rule, American politics, church organization.

One morning he was very angry when he came to work.

"Now what's the problem?" I inquired.

"That Mabel," he answered. "She never answers back. When I get angry and scold her, she just stands there. Why doesn't she argue with me?"

I was quick to respond. "Well, you won't have to worry about that when you come to work. I'll always give you a good debate."

In the early months of 1952 Kori chiefdom was without a chief and the election was to be held in June. The chieftaincy was held by hereditary right so that only certain families could hold the post. Voting was by representation, each village having a headman who could cast one vote. I soon found out that Abraham was one of the candidates. He wanted the post very badly. The position provided certain financial rewards and carried some power, but by tradition it was a position of prestige. The chief was recognized as a person of authority by the provincial administration and by the colonial government. Even if the chief was old and incompetent, he was regarded with honor by the local people. Great chiefs were historical legends, remembered in story and song and some even found their way into the history books.

It seemed as though attainment of this position was Abraham's ultimate goal, overshadowing every other aspect of his life, except his love and pride in his son, Amos. He campaigned with great vigor. He tirelessly visited village headmen, using every minute of his time away from the dispensary to solicit votes. For several days before the election, he took a leave and spent all of his time on campaigning.

Finally, the day came for the election. It was held in the court barri, a spacious building covered with the usual corrugated iron roof but open on three sides. On the platform sat the officials; the court president who was an official from the chiefdom and the British commissioner. The main floor of the barri was emptied of spectators and the candidates stood in front of the officials. All of us watching the event stood outside the building looking over the low walls. I think there were about seven candidates of whom I remember only three: Abraham, Alfred Brewah, and James Gbappe. The crowd of spectators was very quiet, but as they pressed forward toward the barri one was aware of the tension. One by one the village headmen were called and came to stand in front of their choice. When the last man had been called, Gbappe had one more vote than Abraham.

I had mixed feelings. I was disappointed for him, but if he had won I would have been without my main support and my most experienced employee.

Abraham was obviously terribly disappointed. His first words to me were, "Well, I guess I'll be back working with you."

The next few weeks were very difficult. Abraham was physically ill and stayed in bed for about a week. When he came back to work he continued to express both his anger and disappointment.

The new chief was elderly, uneducated, and infirm. Although he had chronic elephantiasis, he was a cheerful man, and one who seemingly exerted little authority. The assistant to the chief was called the speaker and often deputized for him. Abraham was appointed to the speaker's post and probably did much of the administrative work of the chiefdom.

I am grateful to Abraham for all he taught me. He was very patient to explain local customs and to tell me when I offended someone. He helped me learn the proper Mende grammar and vocabulary. He knew far more about local disease and the medicines used for treatment, of which I had very little knowledge, and he curbed my curiosity when I got too nosy.

After several months, I noted that a number of Chief Gbappe's wives were coming in for delivery so I brought the subject to Abraham.

"I don't understand how all these wives are pregnant," I complained, "when Chief Gbappe has elephantiasis."

The reply came quickly, "That's none of your business."

He was right, it wasn't any of my business and the subject was closed.

He also taught me some philosophical precepts. One of his favorite sayings was "contentment is great gain." And so it is. One needs to learn to be content within themselves whether you are living in the center of an American city or in the African bush.

Thank you, Abraham Lavaly.

CHAPTER 8

The Team

Clinic Staff

Her name was Jeanette, and she was the first of a series of young women who came to "help." With respect for the African regard for titles, they were called nurses and wore uniforms, but their training was strictly on-the-job.

Jeanette previously worked as household help for the other single woman missionary who lived in the village. In this job she had demonstrated neither enthusiasm nor intelligence. I am not sure if I was aware of this before I hired her, but it was quickly evident when she started to work at the clinic. One of her tasks was to translate the local language, Mende, into English for me since preparation for my position had not included any language training in Mende. She also assisted me in the outpatient clinic, prenatal, and baby clinics.

The small maternity unit was the only inpatient unit of the clinic. During the first year about 50 babies were born there. Management of labor and delivery were my responsibility, and Jeanette was there to help me. After babies were born she bathed them every morning, helped to keep the building clean, and was responsible for making sure there was an adequate supply of kerosene for the lantern we used at night. It was not a very taxing job.

My outstanding recollection of dealing with Jeanette was trying to teach her how to read the thermometer. The effort lasted a month before I gave up. I held the thermometer in my hand, pointed out the lines that indicated degrees and tenths of degrees. This alien concept took a long time for her to understand. I drew graphs and made models until I thought that Jeanette knew how to read degrees, but finding the mercury on the thermometer was a mystery never to be fathomed. The little red line did not exist for her. Eventually, I admitted defeat, deciding that my teaching ability was not equal to the task.

Sometime later I made the same effort with Amos, the school boy who did the sweeping and dusting at my house. In less than a half hour, he was accurately reading the thermometer. My ego was restored.

Soon my tolerance for Jeanette was reaching its end, and I sought a way to terminate the relationship with her. Fortunately, she solved the problem by becoming pregnant. The rule of the mission was that unmarried pregnant women could not be employed. It was a relief to wish her well and send her on her way.

It was necessary to find another girl to assist me. By local custom, a man was not allowed to be present during labor and delivery. Even after the baby was born, the father could not visit his wife for three or four days so it was essential that I have a female helper.

Abraham suggested that I hire Musu Morsay, a girl from his household. When his first wife died, her family had given him a small child as a replacement and Abraham's mother-in-law had raised her. Musu had attended school through the eighth grade, but there was no money or opportunity for further education so Musu became part of the staff.

Musu was a short, plump, jolly girl, reasonably intelligent, and willing to learn. She applied herself well in the new position and was a part of the staff for the next eight years. She was industrious and came to the maternity ward early each morning. All the babies were bathed and dressed before she came to the clinic at 8:30 a.m. to start the day's work there. She oversaw the sweeping and cleaning. It was also her responsibility to clean the delivery equipment and boil the instruments to prepare for the next delivery.

Just as men were not allowed to observe a delivery, neither were unmarried women who had not had a baby themselves. For the next two years Musu never saw a delivery. One day I missed a delivery. The woman had been in labor all night, a labor complicated by malaria. I examined her early in the morning and decided it would take some time before the baby would be born. I went home, bathed, had breakfast, and started to see the patients that had come for treatment. Suddenly, someone ran from the maternity unit saying the baby had been born. I sprinted the two blocks up the hill to the maternity unit and found the woman in bed, the crying baby lying on the bed in front of her. Where was Musu? From the adjoining room, she emerged from under the bed where she had been hiding.

There was a fourth member of the clinic staff, Francis Ngegba; patient, quiet, hardworking, and gentle. He was like a quiet shadow of those two exuberant personalities, Abraham and Musu. I appreciated his consistent service, reliability, and his talent for working harmoniously with the rest of us. One of his best assets was his kind manner towards the patients, always responding to their queries in a gentle voice.

There was also usually a yardman. The one I remember best was Dulu, which means duck in Mende. His walk did resemble a duck. At one time he had leprosy but was now cured. Lepers and ex-lepers are not always accepted by the community, but the clinic staff took in Dulu as a part of the group.

A more flamboyant member was Pa Gbondo the night watchman. As it was with John, the cook, there was a constant skirmish between him and me to see who was in charge. I lost more battles than I won.

First, Pa Gbondo had no ability to manage money. Each payday, he would spend all of his money by going to the Lebanese shops and making a down payment on something. Of course, he never had enough money to make the rest of the payments. In a day or so he would come and ask for an advance on the next week's pay. If I refused, a few days later a note would come from one of the shopowners asking for the payment. This went on for a year. As I remember, he was paid three shillings six pence, about 60 cents a week for both his watchman duties and the daily task of emptying the latrine bucket. At this time, a loaf of bread or a cupful of groundnuts cost three pence.

At one point, Abraham and I tried to solve the problem by offering to pay him six pence every day instead of giving him his pay once a week. But that backfired when he asked if he could be paid both the daily coin, and the three and six at the end of the week, too.

When I first arrived, Pa Gbondo was the watchman for the other woman missionary living in Tiama. Because she worked with the women through the whole church in Sierra Leone, she was frequently gone for several days at a time. During that time, Pa Gbondo guarded her house. He was supposed to stay awake all night. Instead he usually slept through the night. His tools consisted of a small hurricane lamp, a large stick, and a machete. The job was a lonely one. Apparently, the man was considered quite attractive, as he had at least one female companion. The rumor was that he had several "friends." At any rate, he was often missing from his duty post. When questioned his excuse was that he had just gone to the latrine. I began to suspect prostate trouble.

One night before I had gone to sleep, he came pounding at the outside gate.

"Please, Ma," he begged. "Have you been up to the house?"

"No, I haven't been out all evening. Is there some kind of trouble?"

"Someone has stolen my lantern and my machete."

I didn't understand how that could happen. "Weren't you there?"

"Please, Ma, I just go latrine."

I had no answers, but I had a few suspicions. On the next morning, I confronted the staff.

"Who stole Pa Gbondo's lamp last night?"

Abraham confessed immediately. "He always says he goes to the latrine so I put the lantern and the machete in the latrine."

After the other woman missionary left in August of 1952, I inherited Pa Gbondo. He was to stay on my veranda and guard my house at night. However, frequently after I had turned out my light, I could hear the front gate, which squeaked badly, open and close. Usually I ignored the problem. One night in irritation, I went out, brought the lantern inside the house, and placed it just inside the door so that when Gbondo returned he would see the lantern. But to wake me and ask for it, would mean admitting that he had gone out. He couldn't use the latrine as an excuse since there was one available near the house. In the morning I put the lantern outside the door so that we both knew that I was aware of his absence.

Eventually, his fiscal problems caught up with him. I had refused to give him more advances, his debts overwhelmed him. One of the merchants had him arrested and put in the local jail. Alarmed, I went to Pastor Carew.

"Do you think I should bail Pa Gbondo out of jail?"

"No," replied Pastor. "I think a few days in jail will do wonders for him. It might help him to learn how to manage his money better."

That sounded good to me. His work would not be done, but we could manage for a few days. Then I found out that as his employer I had to pay one shilling a day for his keep in the jail and provide his food as well. I immediately went down and bailed him out.

Household Help

One of the criticisms of missionaries has been their practice of hiring household servants. After all, we don't usually have servants when we live in the United States. We do most of our own household tasks, with the aid, of course, of refrigerators, electric stoves, washers and dryers, fast food restaurants, and numerous other conveniences.

During my stay in Africa, I always had some household help; from school boys who worked for me while I was in Liberia, to Ibrahim Mujuri in Kenya, who cooked, cleaned, shopped, and did the laundry. The help allowed me to put my energy into my job and other projects where I could use my skills. Since food sources were limited and diets tended to be monotonous, it was often too much effort to prepare meals. But if food was on the table at noon, I would eat. Since I always lost weight when I lived in Africa, I could afford to eat one balanced meal a day without worrying about weight gain.

One of the first things Dr. Silver and I needed to do in Tiama was to find someone to help. For several years there had been no medical missionary there and the house had been empty. The man who had cooked for an earlier missionary appeared and we hired him. He was a disaster. He was a poor cook, had a violent temper, and argued loudly with Dr. Silver. Staples and equipment disappeared with amazing rapidity. He was sent away with almost as much rapidity.

Shortly after that, teacher Francis Brewah, nephew of the acting chief, came to the door with his brother, John, who had spent many years cooking for bachelor Englishmen, who held administrative posts in the county. Now John had a wife and child and wanted to come back and live in Tiama. He had good letters of reference. He turned out to be a good cook, although the shift from bachelor Englishmen to an American spinster took some major adjustments. For instance, I drank coffee in the morning and not tea. I like my tea with sugar and not milk. I have never learned to like Yorkshire pudding and think macaroni and cheese is an adequate entree for dinner. I refuse to eat baked beans on toast at any time. I wanted my main meal at noon and not at eight o'clock in the evening.

During the interview, I should have wondered why John never uttered a word. He was hired and the next day I found out why he had been so silent. He stammered very badly. He seemed not to stammer in Mende, only in English. Two circumstances increased the stammer: guests in the house and his consuming a little too much liquor. I also discovered that he suffered from epilepsy. The attacks occurred infrequently and apparently he had a strong warning aura, which is a warning that an epileptic attack is about to begin. When word came from the Brewah compound that John was ill, I assumed that he was having a seizure and that he would be back to work in a day or two.

John ran the household. In addition, there were always "small boys" in the house; school boys who came before and after school and usually on Saturdays. It was their responsibility to carry wood and water. Help with cleaning and laundry, and carry messages and do other small tasks. Most of the boys were in some need of help with school expenses, and the money they earned went toward school fees, books, and uniforms. (See colorplate 3).

A few days after our arrival, Dr. Silver asked Abraham if he knew of some school boy who needed to earn some money.

He quickly volunteered, "I will send my oldest son, Amos, to help you."

Dr. Silver protested, "That will not be necessary, surely you need him at home."

"He was born in your hand," Abraham responded. "He needs to say thank you to you." Indeed, twelve years earlier, she had delivered Amos. He came to work and after Dr. Silver left in March, he stayed for the next year until he went to Bo to secondary school. Our friendship has been sustained through the years. There have been numerous get-togethers in Sierra Leone, Britain, and one memorable three weeks when he and his family came to stay with me in the United States.

Amos was the sole surviving child to Abraham's first wife. Not only was he the delight of his father, but he had been raised and cared for by his doting grandmother, Mama Simitie. As a child, his health had been precarious. Abraham blamed it on the fact they had tried to raise him on "American food." His father usually called him Amos, rather than by his Mende name, Kakpindi. As other children were born, Abraham resorted to his African heritage; the children were raised by Mende custom, their Mende names were used, and they spoke only Mende until they started to learn English in school. As a result, they were comfortable in both languages.

John Brewah, his wife Ami and two daughters.

Amos was, and is, organized. He was conscientious about cleaning and straightening things, neither of which are assets of mine. On Saturdays, for example, there was a flurry of sweeping, mopping, and dusting. Books were put back on the shelves, papers were straightened, items picked off the floor. Unfortunately, by Wednesday I was still trying to sort out the straightening process. After a few months we compromised, the desk and the papers were off limits, to be touched only by me no matter how untidy they looked.

Because of his less-than-robust health and his father's ambition for his future, Amos was encouraged to excel in his school work. He had a great interest in reading. Of course, there was no library in Tiama and even the school had a very limited supply of reading materials. But for me, books were as essential as food or sleep. I had brought some with me and I borrowed others. Amos began to borrow them and was soon reading as avidly as I.

At the end of the year, Amos went to attend the prestigious Bo Government School. One British author has called it the "Mende Eton." The school had been developed for the sons of chiefs after the 1898 raid, and it was now open to all segments of society. It maintained its reputation for excellence and was the outstanding school for boys outside of Freetown.

One of my concerns for the staff was the lack of materials to encourage Christian growth. Most of what I used were devotional materials provided by the Scripture Union Organization for various reading levels. I had obtained several of these which I distributed to the staff. I also sent a copy to Amos in Bo. One morning as he was reading his Bible and the commentary, he felt the need to make a firm commitment to Christ. He knelt by his bed and made that commitment. It was the end of the month and the end of the quarter. The Bible commentary was ended and he didn't have one for the next month. In much simplicity, he asked the Lord to provide some scriptural guidance. When he went to his mail box, there was a commentary for the next quarter, sent by a student at Harford School for Girls. Amos' commitment has continued and his witness as a Christian has been a part of his life at Bo School, Fourah Bay College, in advanced schools in Britain and Canada, and at his present position at the School of Education at Njala University College in Sierra Leone. He is a credit to his father's care and concern. I am grateful that some of my interest helped to influence his contribution to his country.

CHAPTER 9

Delivering Health Care

As the weeks progressed, I had a growing realization that although I had nearly eight years of professional preparation and 14 years of expectation, I was not well equipped for the responsibilities I was expected to assume. I had no knowledge of local customs and had a minimal knowledge of tropical diseases and treatment.

This quickly became apparent to me when a few days after our arrival, Dr. Silver and I had a startling experience. One evening several people came to the door. One of the women was carrying a very sick child about a year old. The child had an elevated temperature and was on the point of convulsions. Dr. Silver gave the child two injections: an anti-malarial and a sedative to reduce the convulsions. I administered a cold enema in an effort to bring down the temperature. Just as I finished the enema, the child gasped and died.

I felt terrible, but Dr. Silver didn't seem too upset. "I think this child has probably been ill for several days," she said. "I don't think it just started this evening. The family probably tried 'country medicine' first and when that didn't work, they came to us."

Country medicine was that used by the local herbalists and medicine women. Some of it was herbal remedies, but it often included magic spells and talismans.

In Mende custom, an adult death was greeted with loud wailing, crying, and violent body movements. The grieving family would sometimes roll on the floor. However, such signs of grief were not usually demonstrated when a child died, but this woman defied custom. She flung herself on the floor, screamed, and tore at her clothes. She refused to take the dead child.

Dr. Silver stood quietly, holding the baby in her arms. A crowd soon gathered. Someone sent for Abraham. He and a few others in the crowd finally got the woman to quiet down. Someone took the baby and the family moved off. Abraham told us that the woman was cursing Dr. Silver, saying she had killed the baby. Abraham was "vexed" and told us the next morning that he had not slept all night.

The next day, one by one, people came by to sympathize with us. It seems that the woman had a reputation of being a troublemaker. One old woman came in and said, "Since my hair turned white, I have never known such nonsense that Dr. Silver would kill a baby." I was grateful that this had not happened to me while I was alone.

Dr. Silver was loved and respected all over the country and such was her reputation, that the community relied on her good judgement and her concern for her patients. The death of the infant did not deter people from coming to the clinic for treatment.

The days soon settled into a routine. The mornings were occupied with the daily clinic which we started with a short devotional session with patients and staff. We sang a hymn, and had a short prayer and a message, often a simple retelling of a Bible story. All the staff members, including me, were expected to participate in leading this exercise, a different person giving the message each day. The rest of the staff, of course, did theirs in Mende, while someone interpreted my talk into the local language.

After the service, we started seeing those patients who had come for treatment. Mostly we treated malaria, diarrhea, skin problems, colds, and coughs. A small number of people came for leprosy treatment. Abraham pulled teeth and sutured wounds.

I had little knowledge of the treatment for malaria or diarrhea. I had to learn the difference between bacillary diarrhea, amebic dysentery, and typhoid. My knowledge of the course and progress of leprosy was very limited. The new medications for treatment and cure of leprosy were just being introduced. I certainly had no skill in tooth extraction or in suturing wounds.

Some diseases occurred seasonally. Measles, diarrhea, and typhoid were more common in the dry season usually starting in January. These diseases often resulted because as the water supply decreased, the villagers turned to water from contaminated sources.

Intestinal parasites were a perpetual problem. Babies were free of them until they were old enough to sit by themselves, but then began to pick them up from the mud floors they were sitting on. The parasites plus the malaria were the cause of much of the anemia we saw. Dr. Silver felt that severe anemia was a primary cause of infertility and started treatment in these cases by eliminating the worms, treating the malaria, and providing iron therapy.

School children were treated free of charge. Because the children rarely wore shoes, they developed sores on their feet and ankles. Initially, we dressed these in the morning before school started, but since the children frequently appeared just before the morning bell was rung, this made them late for class. After awhile, we changed the dressing time to after school. Although these simple dressings were something I could do, I didn't enjoy it, but felt I couldn't ask the staff to do something that I didn't do. Everyone pitched in and got the job done. Dressings were usually done with lengths of torn sheets sent to us by the church women in the United States.

Burns were another common problem. Everybody cooked on a stove that consisted of three stones with the cooking pot set on the stones. Firewood was inserted between the stones and the heat was regulated by the number and size of the sticks. Sometimes these fires were kept outside the house, but in the rainy season, the cooking was done inside. It was very common for children and toddlers to fall on the stones or the fire. At that time, we dressed burns with ointment and cloth dressings instead of painting them with an antiseptic solution and exposing them to the air.

Another cause of burns were explosions of the stills used to distill the local liquor. The brew was called *omole* and could be distilled from either sugar cane or palm wine. The liquor fermented in copper stills and it was common for them to explode. The scalding malt and liquor caused severe burns, but since distilling liquor was illegal, no one wanted to admit they had been burned in this manner.

One evening very late, a group of men appeared at my door with a boy about ten years old who had been severely burned. The entire front of his body from his head to his feet was raw flesh. He bore his pain with stoic silence. I was appalled. I tried to find out what had happened, but my Mende was too limited. I sent for Abraham.

"How did this happen?" I asked. They had told me the boy had fallen into the fire, but I couldn't understand how he could have developed such extensive burns.

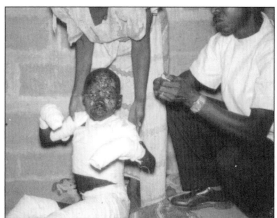

Child burned from an exploding still.

53

Abraham started in Mende. "Tell her the truth," he said to the men. They did not lie to him. "The still blew up and caused the burns."

"How long ago did this happen?" I inquired.

"A week ago."

Abraham filled in the details. One of the other treatments for burns was to paint them with a solution of methyl violet. This has some antiseptic qualities and was frequently painted on burns to help the healing process. "Some men came a week ago and asked for methyl violet. I would only sell them a very small bottle. Several men came and each bought another small bottle. I refused to sell them anything in a larger container."

By this time, of course, the burns were infected and the people had come for help.

"Is he the only one who was hurt?" I asked.

"No," the answers came reluctantly.

"How many are there?"

"Eight."

It was a depressing situation. If we tried to dress nine people with severe burns, it would take the staff all day. I turned to Abraham.

"Now what do we do?"

"You know the district commissioner is in town. He is camping up on the hill. I think we should go to him," Abraham said. "This is not only a medical matter, it is a legal matter. We would have to report the incident anyway."

So at midnight, the two of us climbed the hill and woke the District Commissioner and told him the tale. He was gracious and sympathetic. Early in the morning, the government lorry carried the nine men to the hospital in Bo.

That was not the only time we saw burns from an exploding still, but we never again saw such extensive burns or so many people involved.

Gradually, the community began to accept me. Sometimes this took a funny turn. One day an old man came for treatment and after I had seen him and prescribed some treatment, he went to talk to Abraham.

"Is the pumoi (white woman) married?" he asked.

Abraham assured him that I was single.

"I would like to have her for a wife," he offered.

"How many wives do you have?" Abraham asked.

"Thirty-nine," was his response.

Abraham told him he didn't think I was interested in being the fortieth wife in his compound.

When I wrote this home, my grandfather's response was, "You should have taken his offer. That was the best you have ever had."

With some people I had to make a harder effort to win approval. One of the older women in the community, Mrs. Sillah, was known to have an intense dislike of all missionaries. She had previously had some disagreement with several of my predecessors and made every effort to avoid me.

I was determined to win her approval, my ultimate goal was to have her speak at my farewell service when I went home on furlough.

One evening Mrs. Sillah rushed to the dispensary with her two-year-old granddaughter who was convulsing with malaria. The child was her favorite and the woman was very distressed.

By this time Dr. Silver and Abraham had taught me how to treat malaria. We gave the child an anti-malarial injection, a sedative, and immersed the child in a cool bath to reduce the temperature.

After several hours the temperature came down and the child responded, but the next night the child had a repeat seizure. Again, we gave treatment. It was repeated twice more until the malaria responded to treatment and the child recovered. Two years later when I was ready to go home, Mrs. Sillah came to the service and gave me her blessings.

A big part of our service was offering prenatal and well-baby care. One of my missionary co-workers once accused me of being interested only in mothers and babies. He wasn't far from wrong. Although we treated many problems, our major emphasis was on preventive care for mothers and infants.

We followed the established principles of a well-baby clinic. We weighed the young babies every week. After a child was older, the mothers came less frequently. Although we kept a record for each child, the mother also carried a card on which we recorded both the infant's progress and any medication. Each child was given malaria prophylaxis. There was no charge for any care given in the baby clinic.

For several years, we received non-fat dried milk from the United States government which was distributed to the mothers. All babies were breastfed and the milk was supposed to supplement the infant's nutrition. The local diet was particularly deficient in protein which meant that kwashiorkor was fairly common. Kwashiorkor is the condition found in infants who are fed a protein-deficient diet. A child with this condition has thin, spindly legs and a protruding abdomen. The child is listless and whiney. In the final stage, the black curly hair becomes straight and reddish in color.

One of the best treatments is to give the child protein, and the best of these is non-fat dried milk. One of the first signs that the child is improving is when he begins to smile.

As the word spread, attendance at the baby clinic mushroomed. It became almost unmanageable. So we divided the mothers into two groups: the women from the surrounding villages came on Wednesday and the Tiama women came on Thursday. From 1960 to 1963, we operated a clinic in a village about ten miles from Tiama which we staffed on Fridays. We attempted to start another clinic in a town about five miles to the south of Tiama, but somehow we were never able to establish a routine and eventually dropped the idea.

I thoroughly enjoyed the clinics. I enjoyed meeting those young, cheerful mothers and as my Mende improved, was able to engage in limited conversation. It was fun seeing those fat, happy babies. Often the women brought their two- or three-year-olds along and I was able to develop a happy rapport with these uninhibited toddlers.

We spent a great deal of time teaching preventive health measures. Abraham accused me of preaching the gospel of orange juice and dug latrines.

One of my regrets was that we never did immunizations. More recently, vaccines have been provided free of charge in all developing countries by the World Health Organization (WHO) and by its associated organization UNICEF, but this was not true in the 1950's. It was the policy of the mission board that vaccines were too costly and an unjustifiable expense. In terms of child mortality and morbidity, I now feel it was a short-sighted view.

The knowledge that immunizing women against tetanus would provide protection for their newborn infants was not available until the 1960's. The unprotected infant can become infected at the time the umbilical cord is cut. It was one of our promotion points for a hospital delivery that we had never had a case of neonatal tetanus develop in a baby born at the maternity center. When babies infected with tetanus were brought to us, it was very difficult to save them. It was a long, expensive, and tedious process, and in my experience, rarely effective. The infant had to be sedated to stop the muscle spasms. The tetanus itself was treated with medication. Another name for tetanus is lockjaw, and the child could not suck since the facial muscles are paralyzed. The infant had to be tube fed for nutrition and hydration. Most of these babies died from an overwhelming infection.

The prenatal clinic was held on Tuesday. The local people wanted to be "sounded" when they came to the clinic. This principle of hands-on-care, during which the practitioner touches and examines the patient with his hands, has proven to be valuable even in these days of highly technical medical care. A stethoscope and thermometer proved to be valuable adjuncts for making a diagnosis. This was particularly true in the prenatal clinic. Our facilities were very limited. We listened to fetal heartbeats with a pinard stethoscope, an instrument about six inches long, bell-shaped on one end, which is placed on the abdomen. A flat piece on the other end is where the listener puts her ear. We were able to use the three most important methods of prenatal care: weight, blood pressure and urine testing; much later I learned to do simple hemoglobin measurements. Still later, we sent blood samples to the hospital lab at Rotifunk to be tested for syphilis.

During my midwifery training in Britain, I had conducted 60 deliveries and felt I had an adequate background of practice and knowledge of midwifery. But nothing could have prepared me for practicing in an isolated area without electricity, 60 miles from any consultation or help and with limited access to equipment and medications.

Local maternity care was given by traditional birth attendants. These women, and they were always women, served a long apprenticeship with another traditional birth attendant. Deliveries were done in the woman's home or sometimes in the confines of the women's secret society, the Bundu Bush. The laboring woman sat in a semi-reclining position, her arms supported by another woman who sat opposite her and encouraged her to push the baby out. The birth attendant had only crude ways of handling obstructed labor, such as pushing on the top of the abdomen to assist the birth. They had no medications for controlling hemorrhage.

When the first trained practitioners arrived, the community was slow to accept their help. The turning point in acceptance had come when my predecessor, Dr. Everett Lefforge, had heroically saved the life of a woman in labor on Christmas Day in 1949. After that, women had come willingly and in increasing numbers.

The first woman in labor came during my second week in Tiama. I felt totally unprepared and was about to send her away. Dr. Silver remonstrated, "If you send her away, no one else will come." So I admitted her into the maternity unit.

Her name was Boi Brewah, one of the wives of the acting chief. Fortunately, it was an easy delivery. She was a cooperative patient and it was her third child. Delivery was a bit delayed as she tried to push the baby out against an anterior lip of cervix, a frequent occurrence in deliveries other than the first baby. Part of the uterus hasn't quite opened up and the baby cannot be born. As the woman pushes, the cervix becomes more edematous, which is an obstruction to the descent of the baby's head down the birth canal. I may have been warned about this in my student days, but I hadn't been told how to handle it. Eventually, I used my common sense, pushed the cervix past the baby's head and the baby was born.

With that delivery, I started a practice that I maintained all during my years in Sierra Leone. I allowed, even encouraged, the presence in the delivery room of the women who had accompanied the patient to the hospital so that I could encourage by example. I washed my hands before examining the woman before delivery, the woman lay on a clean sheet. The instruments used to cut the cord were sterile. I am not sure if the women knew the significance of the latter, but at least they knew that special care had been given to those instruments.

The delivery equipment was reduced to the utmost simplicity. It consisted of two clamps and a scissors to cut the cord. After each delivery, these were boiled along with two small basins. After boiling, the tools were immersed in a diluted Dettol solution, a compound similar to Lysol, with which I hoped to maintain their sterility. After the cord was cut, it was tied with a short string. I made the cord ties out of heavy crochet thread or fishing twine. These were also boiled and placed in the Dettol. A sterile towel was placed on the tray. This would be used to wrap the baby after delivery. The entire tray was covered with another sterile towel.

Immediately after delivery, the baby was placed on a nearby cot. It was left there until I had finished the rest of the delivery. I would not let anyone handle the baby until I had retied the cord, dressed with a sterile dressing, and covered it with a belly binder. This prevented anyone from handling the cord and contaminating it with tetanus. In retrospect, it also delayed the normal process of separation of the cord. The current theory is that allowing the cord to be exposed to the air and being kept dry will hasten normal separation.

I never wore rubber gloves in all those 12 years; they were too expensive and difficult to obtain. There was no oxygen, nothing to warm the baby, no intravenous equipment. The oxytocic drug used after delivery to control hemorrhage was a liquid form of ergotrate, and was used only when I saw signs of excessive bleeding.

The problem of hospital laundry was solved by sending the soiled linen home with the women who had accompanied the patient. There was a taboo against men handling such linen. Linen was never stolen and it was carefully returned and was spotlessly white. It had been taken to the riverside, beaten on the rocks, and dried on the bushes.

As an aside, my personal laundry was washed in a similar fashion. On my first furlough home, my stepmother offered to wash my clothes in the washing machine saying, "I'll get them really clean for a change." As I handed them to her, she said, "But they are clean!" Of course!

The next four deliveries were not so fortunate. Again I realized that my knowledge was inadequate and my prior experience was not enough to enable me to handle the complications I saw in labor and delivery. Three of the next four babies either died or were stillborn. It should have been a warning to me of what the future would hold. I delivered one woman in her home, with the only light a tiny kerosene lamp. The patient lay on the mud floor and I knelt beside her. The woman had a spinal deformity and the baby was born dead. That was the only home delivery I did in 12 years. In that delivery not only was the equipment and the light inadequate, but the position was most uncomfortable for me. I found the kneeling position for a long time was painful and exhausting. It also limited my ability to assist the mother as she pushed and made delivery of the baby's head more difficult. In a home delivery if the labor was delayed, I would spend a lot of time away from the clinic and my other responsibilities so I resisted all lures to do home deliveries. Even if Musu wasn't present for the birth, I could leave her with a laboring patient, trusting that she would call me at the crucial moment.

Dr. Silver left Tiama in the middle of March and went home to Rotifunk. My apprenticeship was over and I was on my own. A few hours after she left, a woman was brought in bleeding about two months before her expected date of delivery. She probably had a placenta that had improperly implanted and as the uterus began to contract in pre-term labor, the placenta started to separate and the hemorrhage resulted. I got out my midwifery text. I was so ignorant that I didn't realize the possible causes. The textbook suggested that the woman be given a warm douche to stop the bleeding. I heated the water and gave her a quart or so of fluid, but that didn't stop the bleeding or the labor. Eventually, the baby was born. She weighted two and a half pounds and had one tooth protruding from her lower jaw. The tooth dropped out a few days later.

As I think about it, I am horrified at my management of the case. I am equally amazed at the advice from the textbook. Again, it is only God's grace that the woman and the baby didn't die.

If I didn't know how to manage an antepartum hemorrhage, at least I did know how to handle a premature baby. I made an incubator out of a cardboard box lined with a heavy blanket. In the folds I placed three hot water bottles which I changed at least every three hours. I used an eye dropper and fed the baby every three hours with diluted cow's milk.

The baby survived and thrived despite my bumbling treatment, but I succumbed. At the end of a week, after nights of exposure to mosquitoes and interrupted sleep, I had my first attack of malaria. I was prostrate. My head ached, my face ached, every muscle that I had ached. I vomited and had diarrhea. I was too sick to move beyond my bed and the bathroom.

I was also concerned about the baby, but the mother, more sensible than I, simply picked up the baby and put it to her breast where the baby sucked vigorously. She kept it warm with her body and the baby lived.

The family called the baby Mami Casey since I had kept it in a cardboard case. It is the custom in many African families that when a child is two years old and has been weaned, it is given to someone else to raise. The mother is now busy with a new baby that takes all her energy, plus the new family is not as apt to spoil the child as the mother will. Sometimes the baby is given to the grandmother, aunt or prominent family who can give the child material and social advantage. When Mami Casey was two years old the family appeared on my doorstep. Because I had shown so much attention to this child, they would now give the baby to me and let me raise it, but I had learned a few things in the intervening years. I knew now that I couldn't carry on my responsibilities in the clinic and take care of an active, growing child. My main responsibility was to the medical work. I turned down their generous offer.

The experience of caring for a pre-term baby taught me an even more valuable lesson, never again did I try such heroics. Small babies were given to their mothers who gave appropriate care. I never again was successful in raising such a small baby. Even babies who were much larger, at times, failed to survive. Even if they lived for several months, they seemed to have less resistance to infection and were frequently the victims of malaria or diarrhea when they were a few months old.

Several other deliveries stand out in my mind in those early days. Gertrude Bloede came to spend a few days with me. Gertrude was a friend from my childhood in Wisconsin and was working as a nurse-midwife in Rotifunk.

While she was visiting me, a woman was brought in from quite a distance. She had been in labor several days and had not delivered. By local custom, a dead woman with a fetus inside would not be buried undelivered. The local midwives would cut the dead woman open and bring out the body of the fetus. These women charged a great deal of money. When it looked like the woman would not survive, she was often brought to the maternity center. Perhaps there was some hope that we could save the life of the mother and child. If not, perhaps we could get the infant delivered. We didn't charge anything extra to deliver the baby. Even though the fetus was dead, we were often able to get the body out although we didn't always save the mother.

The woman was brought at night and was semi-conscious. Her pulse was rapid and her breathing shallow. The fetal head was in the pelvis, but the shoulders would not pass through the pelvic inlet. The baby had been dead for sometime and the skull was collapsed. Obviously, numerous attempts had been made to get the baby out because the vagina contained leaves, sticks and other materials.

Gertrude and I conferred and together we were able to push the head back into the uterus, turn the baby around, bring the feet down, and deliver the baby by breech extraction.

When the process was over we carried the woman to a bed. Within a few minutes, Gertrude observed the patient gasping for breath and she soon died. It was my first, but not my last maternal death.

Twins were a fairly common occurrence. Twice during my stay in Tiama, I delivered triplets; both times the babies were very premature. In one instance, all three babies together weighed less than two pounds, and of course, did not survive.

Early in 1952 the wife of one of the local evangelists appeared with what I had diagnosed as twins. I safely delivered the first child, but what I had supposed was the head of the second twin was a large uterine tumor. These tumors usually present serious problems during the delivery and afterward, predisposing the woman to postpartum hemorrhage. Fortunately, I was able to control the bleeding in this case and the woman went on to have future pregnancies.

I was severely handicapped by my inability to speak the language. I quickly learned to say "push" and "don't push" in Mende, but I needed more than that. One night four women brought a woman in labor. With the women was a school girl that was attending Harford School. Obviously, she was unmarried and didn't have a child, as the other women would not allow her to come into the delivery room. She stood outside the window as I called out my questions to her in English and she repeated them in Mende to the women inside the room. The response then went in the other direction. Fortunately, the case was uncomplicated and we were able to manage with this second-hand conversation. I soon picked up enough Mende so I could manage the antenatal clinic and deliveries without too much help.

During that first year, I delivered 48 babies; six were still-born, three died within 24 hours, and one mother died. The next year there were another 49 deliveries; ten of these were at Rotifunk during the time I was staying there. There were two maternal deaths, six still-births and three early deaths. In the ten months of 1954, I did 40 deliveries; five still-births, no maternal deaths, and three neonatal deaths. Three sets of twins were born. My notes from that time are very sketchy but complications included amebic dysentery, tuberculosis, typhoid and sickle cell anemia as well as the usual obstetric problems: obstructed labor, antepartum, and postpartum hemorrhage. I notice that at one time I applied forceps to assist a delivery and removed one placenta manually, although without anesthetic.

Finally, the community taught me valuable lessons. One day a man brought his wife who had been bitten on the foot by a snake. I admitted her to the maternity ward. Her baby was only a month old and of course, was still breast-feeding.

I took the baby off the breast and started him on formula. Neither the mother or the baby were doing well. About the third evening, I walked to the maternity unit to check on their progress.

The young husband was standing outside the building, throwing stones at the big mango tree.

"What are you doing?" I inquired.

"There's a boa in the tree and I am driving it away," he replied. The boa, in this case, was a symbol of impending death and needed to be driven away by whatever means.

I tried to reassure him that no one was going to die, but when I walked into the ward the baby was dead. I wasn't sure why it died but thought it might be related to the formula. If I had only let the mother continue with breast-feeding. The mother was recovering nicely.

I sat on the delivery table and cried and cried. The young father came in, patted me on the shoulder and said, "Please Ma, don't cry. Now God."

I was grateful that he didn't blame me even though I was sure that I was at fault.

But I realized I had to place more faith in God than in my own abilities. God had led me to this place, he would also see me through my trials.

"Now God," was a good word for the future.

CHAPTER 10

If Possible, Live in Peace

Innumerable books have been written about and by missionaries. Many times these individuals are pictured as plaster saints without a spot of blemish. In reality, missionaries are human beings who are motivated to leave home for a variety of reasons, often reasons they deny to themselves and others. Since it takes some determination to leave home, family, and friends, most missionaries are fairly resolute and usually have strong opinions, voiced or unvoiced, that determine their mode of action. Often the very leadership qualities that sent them away from home bring dissension when they are working with others. The examples are unending.

Albert Schweitzer's drive to be independent severed him from established mission organizations and led him to develop a medical facility that had no strings attached to an existing organization. Caroline Alexander in *One Dry Season* says:

> *"If one delves into the annals and letters of the men who preceded Schweitzer, one soon comes to realize that one of the greatest difficulties about being a missionary was working with one's fellow missionaries, and that the craving for an independence was not unusual... Schweitzer's independence, therefore, would perhaps not be seen as an additional burden, it was something many missionaries desired."*

In another example, Winifred Harley wrote a brief account of the life of her husband, Dr. George Way Harley. The Harleys established the Methodist Hospital in Ganta, Liberia where George Harley supervised the construction of the buildings on the hospital compound as well as conducting the medical work. In addition, he investigated the healing arts of the local traditional healers in eastern Liberia. His book *Native African Medicine* is a well documented discussion of both the local herbs and medical practices. Winifred Harley was an authority on local fauna, particularly ferns.

However, Dr. Harley consistently had difficulty in working harmoniously with his missionary co-workers. This became such a problem that at one point, the bishop remonstrated with him and suggested that he needed a conversion. Several times the other missionary family moved to another station to avoid the conflicts.

Over the years, I heard stories of personality clashes among missionaries. I have mentioned the confined living quarters at Rotifunk and a similar situation existed at the Harford School for Girls at Moyamba. The habits of untidy persons grated on the people who were tidy. Some people adhered to a strict time schedule while others ate or slept on a more relaxed routine. Even more difficult to cope with were widely separated theological beliefs. Those people who felt that evangelism could only be demonstrated with enthusiastic preaching clashed with others who felt personal example and individual contacts was the best way to witness.

Perhaps it was to my advantage that I spent so much of my stay in Africa living and working with minimal contact with missionary co-workers. Since habitually I am rather untidy, my careless ways didn't irritate another person. I learned to adjust my schedule to the local disregard for time. Babies don't arrive on order and I had to adjust my habits to sleepless nights and missed appointments.

On the other hand, one of the happiest times in my life was when Gladys Fahner Galow and I shared living quarters and working assignments. She was relaxed about time. I confined my untidiness to my bedroom. In addition to the pleasure we shared in midwifery, we both loved to read. We enjoyed singing together and were able to adjust our food tastes to accept the local diet. The friendship has lasted through the years. I look forward to our reunions even though they occur infrequently.

During my first two months in Tiama in 1952, Dr. Silver and I lived together. Wise in the ways of Africa, she was an invaluable help to me. She organized the household, introduced me to the local shop owners, and advised me about what I could expect to buy locally and what I would have to purchase in Bo or Freetown. She supervised the work in the clinic, told me how to order medical supplies, and gave me advice on local diseases and medications. She was a dedicated Christian and applied her theology in a most practical way in her loving care of patients who came for help.

There was at that time another missionary woman in Tiama, Jane, who directed the work among the women in the conference. This was a combined educational and evangelistic project. Classes were conducted for the local women in nutrition, child rearing, and household practices, always accompanied by stories and lessons from scripture.

Jane's assignment involved much traveling. Sometimes she conducted long institutes when women from a wide area would gather for educational sessions. Jane had no vehicle, but had to travel on public transportation, carrying not only her teaching materials but often food and some bedding.

It was decided that while Dr. Silver was still in Tiama, I should accompany Jane on one of her teaching treks. We went to Dodo and Blama about 60 miles east of Tiama. To get there we had to take a lorry to Bo, then to Kenema, then north to Dodo and Blama. I don't remember much about Jane's teaching sessions, but other impressions about the trip remain very clear.

Scattered throughout the country were government rest houses, permanent houses built for the accommodation of traveling government officials. The houses were prepared for temporary accommodation and were usually sparsely furnished if they were furnished at all. One could rent these for several nights' stay.

The first night out we stayed at the government rest house at Dodo. To say it was sparsely furnished was an overstatement. There were four walls and a roof. The windows were without glass, screens or shutters. We set up small cots equipped with mosquito nets. It was February, when the days were excessively hot, but the nights were always comfortably cool. The sky during the African night presents a canopy of brilliant stars because the absence of artificial light allows the splendor of the stars to dominate the sight. During the full moon the light is enough to illuminate the path while walking.

I lay staring at that magnificent sight. Birds flew in and out of the open windows. Beyond the walls I could hear the comforting sound of frogs and chirping crickets.

Early the next morning we were up and on our way. We hiked five miles into a village where there was an active church and women's group. We were warmly greeted and treated to the generous African hospitality which is usually accorded to guests. We were given separate bedrooms equipped with beds and mosquito nets and presented with gifts of a live chicken and rice. Because we had walked so far in the dust and heat, warm water was brought to us and we were allowed to bathe and change clothes. In the meantime, the chicken was killed and cooked. When the food was ready, we were invited to eat. As often happened, we were served and ate by ourselves. Later on I would protest and insist that my hosts join me as we ate together, but that was after I had become more familiar with the local customs.

We may have been served separately, but we were not alone. At each window and door was a group of curious and interested observers. We were the first white women to have visited the village and as such were the objects of much comment.

After the meal I was asked to see several people who were in need of medical care. I can't have carried much medicine, probably some aspirin and anti-malarials, but I dispensed what I had along with some advice, probably not very helpful.

It was now 11:00 p.m. and we had not yet had the teaching session. We may have been tired, but the villagers wanted to hear what we had to say so we proceeded to give our health message, probably about the value of giving orange juice to small children and the advantages of dug latrines. Jane gave a short sermon. At midnight we gratefully fell into our beds, but we were up at 4:00 a.m. hiking back to the main road in time to catch a lorry that would take us towards home.

Jane was not an easy person to live with. Life had been "difficult" for her. She was born and raised in Pennsylvania and came from a relatively poor family. She felt that she had been denied many advantages. Even in her own family she had not been given as many opportunities as had other members. A brother had died tragically at age 13 and even this was taken as a personal affront. Because the local community had failed to appreciate her gifts and talents, she had come to Africa. She started out by teaching at the Harford School for Girls, even there she felt that no one appreciated her efforts. She had been assigned to women's work where she might function as independently and creatively as she desired.

This job, too, had its drawbacks. She had no transportation of her own. Communication by mail was slow and uncertain, and of course, there were no telephones. It was difficult to plan trips and institutes. Sometimes she would arrive at a church only to find that the letter, mailed weeks before, had not arrived and nothing was ready for her classes. Her living accommodations were far from adequate in her estimation. She was living in a house that Abraham Lavaly had recently built for his family, but which he now rented to her. Three small bedrooms and a large living-dining room made up the house. The living room was enclosed on two sides by a low wall with the top section covered by screening. This design made the room light and airy with the opportunity to catch the available breezes to keep the room cool. Low, overhanging eaves kept out the tropical sun and also gave protection from the rain. The house was well built with cement blocks and the usual metal roof. The exposed living room resulted in a lack of privacy since anyone could walk up to the room and peer in.

According to Jane, there were other problems. The house was only a few feet from the main street so that dust from the passing trucks billowed into the house. The numerous neighborhood children were noisy and disturbing. She had no electricity and food was limited in both choice and supply. Because she was gone much of the time, she didn't have full-time household help, but hired a girl who helped Jane when she was home.

It was true that food was limited in its variety. We usually ate rice every day. A cow was butchered once a week, and with a refrigerator, you could usually keep a supply of meat for a week. But if you weren't in town on the day the cow was killed, you didn't get meat. Other meat was unobtainable, but we were rich in sweet fruits and vegetables: bananas, oranges, guavas, mangoes, and tangerines. My mouth waters just thinking about them.

I was fortunate. Patients frequently brought me gifts in appreciation for the treatment they received at the clinic: two or three eggs, some bananas, several mangoes. A particularly sweet type of mango was found near the village of Pelawahu, and occasionally, when the women came to baby clinic, I would have some to eat. Feeling sorry for Jane, I would share my bounty; one egg for her from my two, two bananas from my four, a share of the oranges, but this brought complaints. Why didn't anyone give *her* oranges? After awhile I stopped sharing and kept quiet about the small "dashes"(gifts) I had received.

When Jane was at home in Tiama, we shared our evening meal, alternating houses. Although I welcomed the company and the conversation, I often found it difficult to listen to the constant complaints about people, incidents, and food.

The situation came to a head in June. Jane had been gone for several weeks. During this time she had spent a few days at Rotifunk. When she returned to Tiama her discontent was even more bitter. For several days I listened to the unhappy conversation. Everyone at Rotifunk had been too busy to spend any time with her. The trains were late and dirty; she got to Mano very late and had trouble getting a lorry back to Tiama. She had arrived in Tiama on Tuesday and no meat was available. Her complaints ran on and on.

In my weekly letter to Dr. Silver, I asked what had happened at Rotifunk. Had there been some particularly difficult episode?

The mail came in the evening. On that night I had opened my letters before supper, including one from Dr. Silver. She had said there had been no unhappy experience while Jane was in Rotifunk. In fact, they had thought Jane was unusually happy and cheerful during her stay.

We ate supper. I usually walked Jane to her house after we had eaten, but I remembered that I had promised to see a patient in town before I went to bed. I suggested that Jane wait at my house and when

I came back I would walk her home. I took the medicine to the patient, returned home, and we walked together to her house.

When we reached the house, the storm broke. She had read my letter from Dr. Silver. In strident tones she told me her opinion of me as a missionary.

"You really are a most unacceptable missionary," she said. "You are unkind and unthinking."

"What do you mean?" I stammered.

"I read the letter from Dr. Silver," she responded. "You had no reason to complain about my behavior. And furthermore, you are incompetent. You really are not suited for this job."

I was too stunned to complain that she had read Dr. Silver's letter.

"I don't know why you thought you could be a missionary," she continued. "You have none of the qualities it takes to do your job. I can't imagine how the mission board ever sent you here. I think you should go back to the United States."

I was devastated. She was right. What business did I have to come to Africa? Why had I come? And she was also right, I should leave and go home. I had prepared for this experience for 15 years and all my efforts in that time had been in preparation for life service on the mission field, but now I was told that those dreams were in vain. Her criticism only reinforced the feelings of inadequacy I had felt since my arrival.

As I walked away from her house, I began to cry and then I resorted to something that has long been a release for frustration: I walked; I walked all around the village.

One of my first impulses was to confide my problems to one of the Africans. I walked past Abraham Lavaly's house and hesitated, but the superintendent had said I was never to confide in any African. I walked past his house, up the hill, circled around the village, past the school. I don't remember meeting anyone, but perhaps I was too blinded by my tears. I walked to the river, back through the village. At the parsonage I hesitated again. Perhaps if I went to talk to Pastor Carew and Betty they might give me solace, but the superintendent's advice lingered in my ears. I finally found my way back home to a sleepless night.

I resolved a few personal issues in that long walk. Living and working here was the fulfillment of a lifelong dream. I was resolved that six months would not finish my work experience. If I didn't know enough, I would learn. The condemnation of one person would not deter me, I would stay.

In the morning, I sent a note to Jane saying "All is forgiven, please come to supper tonight."

The matter was never mentioned by either of us again. In August she left Tiama to go back home. As she was leaving, she thanked me for being such a true friend. I only saw her once after that, but we corresponded at intervals through the years.

Sometime after she went home I discussed the matter with Pastor Carew. By that time I realized the folly of the superintendent's advice. I had learned that keeping one's problems pent up inside was not good medicine. I needed the advice and help of this wise man. After I had told him of that stormy night, he gently scolded me for not coming to him. He was aware, he said, of the problems I was having with Jane's personality. It was one of my learning experiences.

CHAPTER 11

The Cathedral in the Bush

The church in Tiama was well-known throughout Sierra Leone. It was a growing, lively, enthusiastic body of Christians. The church had been nursed through its birth pangs by the early missionaries: the Magrews, Miss Minnie Eaton, and Charles and Bertha Leader to mention a few. When Pastor B. A. Carew came, the church was given safely into the hands of a dedicated, competent African pastor.

The original church building was in the center of town near the native court barri. On ordinary Sundays, it was filled with worshippers. The building could seat about 150 people, including those who sat on benches in the aisles. On special Sundays like Easter, there were as many people outside the building looking in through the windows as there were inside the building.

A new building had been started about two blocks away up the hill. This building was made of cement blocks and could seat about 900 people. During the early months of 1952 the construction was in progress. It is unheard of for most African churches to have a mortgage or to borrow money to finance the construction. When all the current funds are spent, construction stops until additional funds are found. Some of the money and the labor are provided by the local people, but frequently appeals are made to organizations and individuals overseas for money. This is the way it was for the Tiama church.

On my first Easter in Tiama, Jane warned me that the church would be filled, so we went to the little building very early in the morning and found a place to sit.

As always in Tiama, Easter was a very special celebration. There were extra hymns sung with great vigor. Pastor Carew loved "Thine Be the Glory, Risen Conqu'ring Son," sung to the rousing tune composed by George Handel. It was taught to the congregation and was sung not only at Easter, but on many occasions. Another favorite was Charles Wesley's triumphant "Christ the Lord is Risen Today." Services in Tiama were never limited to an hour, but often went on for two to three hours.

The Tiama church was the only established one in the chiefdom of some 70 villages, but in many villages, small chapels made of mud and thatch were constructed. Services were held in these buildings several times a week, led either by one of the local evangelists or by a lay person in the community. Frequently, it was a teacher in the village who conducted the service. Members were all considered to be a part of the Tiama church where baptisms were administered and the Lord's Supper celebrated. Members were expected, if they were able, to attend the services in Tiama at least three times a year. Some people attended every Sunday, often walking an hour or more to get to the service. Early responses to the gospel were often among children and old women, but the strength of the church in Tiama was evidenced by the participation of a group of dedicated and interested young men.

After services many of the villagers met at the parsonage where food was prepared, mostly donations brought by the villagers. However, Betty Carew supervised the preparation of the food. Perhaps this is what it was like in the early church described in the Book of *Acts*, when members had all things in common, and work and food were shared. It was not just a time of physical refreshment, but also a sharing of joys and fellowship, including news of births and deaths in each community. Prayers of joy were offered for blessing of growing crops as well as prayers of concern for illness or other troubles.

Before the next Easter the new building was completed. The building was in the shape of a cross with an elevated platform on the south end which contained the altar, pulpit, and lectern. Pastor Carew was a skilled carpenter and had made the pulpit furniture himself using the plentiful supply of mahogany logs found in the area; a generous supply of windows brought in both light and air. The congregation segregated itself by age and gender. The men sat in the eastern wing of the cross, just behind the organ. The women occupied the northeastern section of the long nave while the school children sat, and sometimes slept, on the opposite side of the long aisle. The western arm of the cross was designated for guests, and sometimes important people in the town like the assistant chief or the court president. (See colorplate 3).

The day of dedication was a day of great rejoicing with about 2,000 people gathered for the celebration. Many of the Christians in Kori chiefdom came joined by Christians from many remote towns as well as the missionary staff in Sierra Leone. We gathered at the old building and marched to the new one. Since 2,000 people couldn't be seated inside the building, many people stood outside and joined in the service, singing their praise through the windows.

I have some vivid memories of the worship services. Much of the service was in the Mende language. Gradually, as I became familiar with the language, I was able to understand and participate in the worship. Parts of the service, including the hymns, were in English when school was in session, particularly after the secondary school was opened, as many of the students did not "hear," that is understand, Mende. The Bible was sometimes read in Mende, sometimes in English, and then translated into Mende.

Over time I learned to appreciate Pastor Carew's sermons. People listened eagerly and sometimes responded with comments. When the sermon was long and he noticed some people nodding (not surprising after an hour's walk in the hot sun), he would interrupt the sermon and ask someone to start a song. The most inspiring part of the service were Pastor's prayers. Always spontaneous, his heartfelt thoughts and concerns were expressed with sincerity and depth of feeling. (See colorplate 4).

Despite the emphasis on education (there were some 600 students in the primary school), many of the adults in the village were illiterate. Since it is difficult to build a congregation where people cannot read the Scriptures for themselves, great emphasis was put on efforts to teach adults to read. Eventually, a literacy institute was held every December. The harvest was over and the farms would not be planted until March. The weather was warm and the rains had ended in October and would not resume until April so travel was fairly easy. The adult learners would come to stay for several weeks, and instruction was by the Laubach method which uses pictures to each reading. This was helpful because Mende had been a written language for less than 100 years and the spelling was phonetic. It is possible, at least in the early lessons, to teach someone to read without the teacher knowing the language.

A few people returned year after year for the literacy institute until they became proficient in their reading ability. Unfortunately, other than the Bible, there was little literature available printed in any of the local languages of Sierra Leone. It was gratifying, when in the service, the Bible was read in Mende rather than translated spontaneously from English. I always had a question about the accuracy of this off-the-cuff translation.

Pastor Carew encouraged the development of local evangelists. These men, and I think they were all men, usually lived in a village outside of Tiama but would travel to other villages to hold services. Two such people stand out in my memory.

Matthew Mwami was blind. He was a man of outstanding intelligence and contributed both his ability to preach and his talent for composing hymns in Mende using local musical patterns. He traveled many miles through Kori chiefdom, singing and preaching. He was, like many Africans, a superb storyteller. In traditional fashion, he would gather people and tell the ancient stories, ending with the Biblical tales including the "Old, Old Story" of salvation.

A second evangelist was Peter McCauley, who had attended school and was literate. He had worked outside the chiefdom for several years, but had now returned home. He lived about ten miles from Tiama. Peter's most noticeable trait was an overwhelming stammer. Every sentence was uttered with great pain, facial contortions, and agonizing slowness. How could this man be an evangelist?

I wanted to find out and repeatedly pleaded with Pastor to take me to Peter's village. He finally consented and we started off. The village was off the road on bush paths so we went by bicycle. Pastor had long experience with missionaries who easily succumbed to the local illnesses and heat. It was even more risky to pedal the ten miles with this white woman who was likely to fall and break a leg so he coerced Teacher Sesay, a husky male teacher, to go with us to help take care of me.

I had not yet purchased my own bicycle so we borrowed a man's heavy bicycle. There were no women's bicycles in the town since women didn't ride bicycles. It was never acceptable for a woman to wear trousers, but this was one of the few occasions when I wore blue jeans after apologizing to Pastor and Teacher Sesay for my inappropriate attire.

We crossed the Teye River in the dugout canoe and then cycled the ten miles. The bush paths were usually just wide enough for one cycle.

We reached the village safely and were met with the usual warm hospitality. Peter cooked for us and we enjoyed the traditional rice and stew. To my great surprise, for dessert we had a lovely baked bread pudding complete with raisins. It seems that Peter had once cooked for an Englishman and this was one of his culinary accomplishments.

Then it was time for the service. This village did not have a chapel building. The meeting was held under the shade of two large mango trees. Benches were provided for the guests and elders of the community. The rest of the people seated themselves on the dry ground next to us. We sang several hymns, had Scripture, prayer, and then Peter preached. Gone was the stammer, facial contortions, and the belabored sentences. His effectiveness as a preacher was witnessed by the response of the people of the village.

I was humbled as I realized that God's message is often preached effectively by the most unlikely people: a blind musician, a healed leper, an illiterate peasant, and a man whose stammer disappeared when he was led by the Spirit. It is a lesson that every missionary needs to learn. The Gospel is not only spread by educated people, particularly foreigners. God sends his word forth in many forms and shapes, relying on the Holy Spirit to bring His Kingdom.

There is a brief postscript to this story. After the service, about 3:00 p.m. in the heat of the day, Pastor decided to take an alternate route back to Tiama. We pedaled along until we came to a small pond across the road. It was not possible to go around the pond due to the thick undergrowth. It wasn't very wide and didn't look very deep. Pastor thought he and Teacher Sesay could wade through and I saw no reason why I couldn't do the same thing. By this time, a group of villagers had gathered.

"I think I can wade through the water," I suggested.

The village headman objected. "Please, Ma. You should not do that. We have a canoe and we can take you across."

I didn't see the canoe. "Where do you keep it?"

"It is in the water, but we will bring it out and take you across in the boat."

The men pulled out the canoe with much difficulty. The canoe was about eight feet long; crescent shaped. The two ends rose in the air and sloped to the center.

Hesitantly, I stepped into the boat. The accumulated mud was very slippery and with my first step, I slid lengthwise to the center, thoroughly coating myself with mud to the uproarious laughter of the group. It was funny and I laughed, too. I was quickly ferried to the other side of the pond. Some of the village women brought dried grass and some old clothes and helped me clean off the mud before we continued on our way home.

CHAPTER 12

Lebanese Families in Tiama

Among the many non-African settlers in West Africa, then and now, are many Syrians and Lebanese; even very small villages had a few resident Lebanese. In Sierra Leone they are usually called Syrians even though most of them came from Lebanon originally. They are traders and transporters; they buy local produce such as ginger and palm kernels, then carry them to the major markets. They also operate retail shops; selling such essentials as soap, kerosene, canned margarine, and sugar as well as cloth and agricultural tools.

When I lived there the Lebanese tended to live apart from the Africans who often said, "there are three groups in Sierra Leone: whites, Africans, and Lebanese." Some of the Lebanese were married couples with small children who were sent back to Beirut for their education while others attended the local schools.

There were large numbers of single men, and different types of arrangements were made for them to marry. In some cases, the brides were ordered from Lebanon; in others, men went back to Lebanon to claim a bride; still other men took African wives. Some of these unions were legalized and some were not.

Among the Lebanese there was a wide range of financial stability. In large cities, including Freetown, they owned large commercial firms. Some of them were involved in construction; others in remote rural villages, lived on the brink of poverty.

In Tiama there were three Lebanese couples and three men with African wives, two of which were permanent, stable relationships. Two of the families had children. The Habibs had only one son, terribly spoiled and naughty. He was indulged with anything he wanted, and at age five, he was still occasionally solacing himself at his mother's breast. The parents were a rather carefree couple, friendly and hospitable. Like many Lebanese, they lived in a few rooms behind their crowded shop.

The second couple was fairly young and had four or five children. Both of them were good-looking. The husband was a devil-may-care type, dashing and not very interested in shopkeeping. The wife, Serena, was a business woman. She was literate in French and Arabic, but her English both spoken and written, was limited. On a few occasions, she asked me to write a business letter for her.

As our friendship grew, she told me about herself. When she was 13 her husband returned to Beirut and they were married. They immediately started back to Sierra Leone by ship. Because she was so young, an older woman accompanied her. Very quickly she learned that her husband enjoyed the good life, pretty women, and liquor. He left her and her companion to their own amusements while he enjoyed his. She must have been terrified. As was to be expected, she immediately became pregnant. They came back to Tiama where she delivered a baby that weighed nine pounds. She told me of the excruciating labor and the severe lacerations. Three other children were born in quick succession.

Her husband maintained his regular habits. The end came one night when he brought in a woman and used Serena's bed. After the ensuing quarrel he left Tiama. Since she had conducted the business when he was there, she continued and made a profit.

Now that she was alone, we became friends. Several afternoons a week I went to her shop and shared Syrian coffee, a thick, black mixture, heavily laden with sugar and served in minute demitasse cups. I soon acquired a liking for the new taste.

Our means of communication was in Krio since her English was limited. I have very little talent to learn another language, although I have been exposed to 20 during my lifetime. In most of them, I have a smattering of words and little grammar. I have always maintained that I can say "push" and "don't push" in six languages, but I quickly acquired ability in Krio and shared long conversations. She had a lively curiosity beyond the local gossip and I learned about Lebanon. She was also an excellent cook, and I added a relish for Lebanese food to my diet.

The third couple had no children. The wife was considerably older than her husband, squat and dumpy, decidedly not pretty, and not terribly bright. She owned the shop. In their case, the husband had been sent for from Lebanon to marry her. He was tall, well-built, and probably ten years younger than his wife. He was soft-spoken and always very pleasant. They had a very large shop, the biggest in town and the best stocked. In fact, it was the only two-story building in town. Their living quarters, on the second floor had four or five spacious rooms and a shady veranda around the whole of the second story. Not only did they stock their shop with a greater supply of cloth and tools,

Lebanese shop and house.

but they also owned two large lorries which were used to transport the ginger and palm kernels raised by the local farmers.

After her husband left her, Serena soon took to sharing her meals with her neighbors. The outcome was inevitable. She was lively and pretty, he was young and handsome, his wife was old and dull.

One day Serena asked me to visit her and told me she was pregnant. She was very unhappy. Would I give her an abortion? Even if I had known how to do it, it was against my professional and religious beliefs. Wouldn't I at least give her some medicine to induce the abortion. No, that wasn't possible either. Somehow she obtained a supply of ergotrate, a medication classified as an oxytocic which causes the uterus to contract. It is not usually used to induce labor since it causes sustained contractions which can be fatal to the baby, and in large enough doses, fatal to the mother. It takes large amounts of ergotrate to induce abortion, and even then it may not be successful. It also causes vasoconstriction, a tightening of the blood vessels. Cases of ergot poisoning have occurred in various parts of Europe. Some of the physical results of overdoses of ergot are insanity and loss of limbs from gangrene. This is because the blood vessels become so constricted that there is no blood supply to the extremities and they must be amputated.

Several days after our conversation about the abortion, Serena sent for me again. She had managed to abort the pregnancy, but now was in the agonies of vasospasm with an excruciating headache and severe pains in her hands, feet, and abdomen. There is no antidote for ergotrate poisoning. Eventually, she recovered.

In 1955 when I was home on furlough, she again became pregnant, but this time she carried the pregnancy through to term. She was determined to deliver in Tiama but there was no midwife there. She asked Abraham if he would deliver her. She had a long history of massive postpartum hemorrhage, probably related to that first enormous baby. He refused and told her she would have to go to a properly staffed hospital. She didn't go, but waited until she was in labor and sent for him. He quickly got a lorry to try to transport her the 60 miles to Bo, but the labor was too far along and she delivered a few miles out of town on the way to Mano, accompanied by the expected hemorrhage. He was able to control it and she and the baby were well.

Eventually, the older woman died and Serena married the man. She left her little shop and moved into his spacious quarters. They had several more children, some of whom were sent back to Beirut to school. The oldest son eventually went to Paris and graduated from the university. Serena proudly went to France for the graduation ceremonies.

Contacts with the Lebanese in my early years were not always pleasant. My days were well occupied with the clinic, midwifery cases, and the dispensary was open every morning. Even on Sunday we treated emergency cases and children who were acutely ill. Services at church occurred on Thursday and twice on Sunday. I saved my Sunday afternoon as my only totally free time. For weeks that time was violated by the arrival of Lebanese families seeking medical care because it was their time away from the shop and their free time, too. I was annoyed and cross and gave treatment reluctantly. Dr. Silver remonstrated with me, saying that they, too, were people in need, but I continued to protest about the intrusion on my time. Eventually, we talked it over and came to a compromise which included a duty-free Sunday afternoon. They agreed to come when I was working at the clinic.

The couple that came most often were from Mano about 12 miles away. They had a number of children, five or six. The oldest were a pair of twins, one of whom had a form of Thallassemia called Cooley's anemia, an inherited condition found among eastern Mediterranean people; one of its features is an abnormal blood clotting factor. Like Sickle Cell Anemia, the affected person is often stunted in growth and has periodic painful crisis during which the joints become swollen, and are so extremely painful the person does not want to move. Usually these people have a shortened life expectancy.

The contrast between the twins was striking. The healthy boy was tall, vigorous, and well-built. The affected twin was spindly with thin arms and legs, a prominent forehead, and little energy. Mrs. Hamud's visits were in search of treatment and a cure for this sick son. The Hamud's had a car as well as several lorries. It was not unusual for them to arrive in the middle of the night seeking help. Some nights they came and got me and took me to Mano. On another night I accompanied them on a frantic dash to take the boy to Bo to the hospital.

There was no cure for this condition, only supportive and palliative care, but Mrs. Hamud explored every possibility. At one point, she carried her son to Beirut where he had an extensive course of treatment.

In the 1960's a Roman Catholic nun and physician, Sister Hilary, came to Sierra Leone. She originally practiced in Bo then later moved to Serabu south of Bo. There she developed an extraordinarily effective community health program. Mrs. Hamud was quick to avail herself of Sister Hilary's expert care. One of my missionary compatriots complained about this change of allegiance, but I made no protestation. The child would eventually die, and I didn't want it to happen when he was under my care.

In 1980 I visited the shop in Mano. The affected boy was dead. His stalwart twin, amazingly resembling his father, was in charge of the store and was running a successful business.

After the atmosphere between the Lebanese community and myself became more hospitable, Mrs. Hamud would invite me for meals, sending her car to take me to Mano. I especially remember with delight her chicken soup.

CHAPTER 13

The British

Sierra Leone became independent in 1961. Until then Freetown was a British Crown Colony and the rest of Sierra Leone was a British Protectorate. The Queen's chief representative was the Governor General. The country was divided into administrative areas each administered by a British official, the three provinces by a provincial commissioner, and the districts by district commissioners. Each district was divided into chiefdoms administered by a locally elected chief who was the only African in the list of officials.

In addition, British people were in charge of many government institutions such as secondary schools and hospitals. Njala, the site of an agricultural station and a teacher's training college, was about six miles away from Tiama. Most of the senior staff was British and on the whole, they were kind, friendly, and hospitable.

I soon found myself invited to Njala for social occasions, in particular afternoon tea and dinner. There were wonderful amenities at Njala: electricity, telephones, running water, and above all else, bathtubs. My enjoyment of hot tub baths quickly became known and I was usually invited to indulge myself. I remember one hostess, with much embarrassment, offering me a bath. I told her not to be embarrassed; it was not a statement about my state of cleanliness, but rather a source of real pleasure.

Going to Njala was like entering a different world. There was little, if any, social mixing of Africans and Europeans, and life was centered around social events. The women, particularly, led an inactive, and to me, boring life. Servants were plentiful, cheap, and usually well-trained. What was there for a woman to do? None of them had jobs outside the home. One woman spent her time in endless knitting of cardigans and pullover sweaters. I always wondered who wore them. Another woman admitted to me that she spent her time reading books. The club had an extensive library, and I was invited to borrow as many books as I could read. During the heavy rainy season, outdoor activity was limited if not impossible. I enjoyed my visits to Njala, but I didn't want to live there.

A typical visit started with tea. To Americans, tea is a hot or iced beverage. To the British, it is often a meal. Sometimes it is limited to just a drink, but it will surely include something sweet to eat, and many teas include sandwiches and salads as well as cakes, cookies, and pastries. Tea was followed by my bath. Then there was a visit to the club where the entire group gathered for drink and talk. (What was there to talk about? Surely the conversation must have been repetitious.) My teetotalling habits always caused consternation. I usually accepted a glass of squash, a mixture of water and artificial fruit concentrate, which I sipped very slowly rather than be overwhelmed with floods of fluid. I was teased about being non-alcoholic and was often threatened with secretly spiked drinks.

Eventually, we went back to someone's house for dinner. Everyone dressed for dinner; the men in suits and the women in long gowns. They all wore knee-high mosquito boots for protection against malaria, but the women often had low-cut dresses and bare shoulders. Njala was situated on the Teye River and the windows had no screens. Those bare arms were perfect targets for the ubiquitous mosquitoes and their malarial aftereffects.

I had no mosquito boots and had only one long gown which was inappropriate for such occasions so I usually wore the better dresses that ordinarily I wore to church on Sunday.

Dinner was a protracted affair. The meals typically had four or five courses which were served formally. There were linens, candles, china, and good silver. Abraham once asked me how I could eat so much at one sitting. I assured him that the portions were small, if numerous, and that overeating was not a problem.

Even at Njala there was not much variety to the food, but since it was an agricultural station, there were a few more choices. They usually had fresh meat which included chicken and pork as well as beef. There were also more varieties of vegetables. As a rule, meals were bland, a startling contrast to the spicy rice "chop," the feature of most African meals.

Sometimes someone would offer to let me sleep at their house rather than being sent home to Tiama late at night.

I became most closely associated with the principal of the training college and his wife, Mr. and Mrs. Wright. During World War II she had been evacuated from Britain to the United States and had lived there for four years. She had many fond memories of the time spent there, but particularly remembered pumpkin pie although she had not been successful in making it.

I finally got enough courage to invite them to Tiama for a meal which included pumpkin pie. The house was cleaned, the best dinner-ware was used (I had a set of plastic dishes with four place settings.) The cook had been told what to serve.

John, the cook, had been begging for uniforms, but I refused to grant his request. To me, it was ridiculous that I should sit alone at the table with a single plate of rice and stew being served by a white-uniformed cook, but I should have been prepared.

Mr. and Mrs. Wright arrived for dinner. The food was cooked. We sat down to eat. John brought in the first course wearing his heavy Wellington boots, and his oldest, most disreputable, torn shorts and shirt. There was nothing to be done; he had made his appearance. To remonstrate, at that point, would only have exaggerated the situation so I suffered in silence. Fortunately, there was no problem with the food, and the pumpkin pie lived up to Mrs. Wright's expectation. The showdown with John was left until the next morning.

I suppose my life was as much an enigma to them as theirs was to me. One night when Mr. Wright brought me home, he asked me how I could tolerate life in Tiama. He thought my existence was pretty grim, just as I thought much of theirs was pretty frivolous. I must have given some explanation. After a little thought, he added, "But of course, you like the Africans." I thought it was one of the nicest compliments I had ever had.

CHAPTER 14

How to Entertain Yourself

Dr. Silver left Tiama on March 15, 1952 to go back home to Rotifunk. From then until September, I stayed in Tiama except for brief excursions around the chiefdom or to Njala.

In that part of West Africa the rainy season starts in April. January, February, and March are hot and dry. In March the fields are prepared for planting by using the slash-and-burn method. Some of the larger vegetation is cut down and the rest is burned. In March the sky is illuminated by bright flames, spiraling smoke and the pungent smell of burning wood fills the air.

In April the rains are heralded with thunder, lightning and heavy winds. Occasionally, the lightening will ignite one of the thatched-roof houses and the inhabitants will be killed by the sudden and engulfing fire. Often there were reports of people who were struck and killed by lightning. The local people believed that these victims were the result of someone invoking the thunder medicine.

In this case, medicine is not something bought at the pharmacy or prescribed by a physician. Medicine may be a liquid or salve made from plants or leaves. It may include the use of artifacts such as cowry shell, amulets, or carvings and may involve the invoking of unseen spirits by means of ceremonies or incantations. Medicine can be used for producing good or evil. Kenneth Little, in the definitive work *The Mende of Sierra Leone,* defines medicine as "any physical object or instrument employed to secure certain ends by supernatural means."

The most powerful medicine among the Mende was the thunder medicine. One person in the chiefdom was designated as the custodian of the thunder medicine. The medicine itself contained some stone figures, metal objects, and bones. When retribution for a crime was to be invoked, the thunder medicine man was called. He announced his arrival by beating on a dried turtle shell. His curse promised that the evil doers would die by lightning. The curse covered the entire extended family so if a distant cousin was killed in Freetown or a house burned on the eastern border, the curse had been fulfilled.

Rains in West Africa are an overwhelming downpour, often all day and all night, every day. From April to October, the atmosphere was wet; shoes and books grew mold; boots, umbrellas,and raincoats were mandatory attire. Gradually,the activities of town slowed to a barely perceptible movement. Attendance at church services dropped since only the people from Tiama came. While in March the Teye River was so shallow people could wade across it; in July the river was about 20 feet deep. Crossing the river with a canoe became so treacherous that few people attempted to come to Tiama. Attendance at the clinic decreased and the number of patients who came for treatment dropped.

Just as the local people were confined to their houses, I, too, was confined to the immediate vicinity of the house, clinic, and church. My only means of locomotion was my two feet. I had no radio and had only a limited supply of books. As the years went on I learned to have a supply of diversions on hand: knitting, embroidery, more books. During my second term I had a small short-wave radio. By my third term I had a good radio and phonograph, all battery operated. I acquired a bicycle and later a Volkswagen Kombi which was like a minivan with two rows of seats for passengers and a space in the back where luggage or supplies could be carried. Once the bridge spanned the river, visitors came through Tiama and often stopped. I was able to move with more freedom.

The days were long and the evenings even longer. I studied Mende. My first Mende teacher was Pastor Wolseley, the assistant to Pastor Carew. Later on Teacher S. K. Carew gave me some lessons. There were no dictionaries or printed grammars. Since neither of these men had a background in teaching Mende to non-Mende speakers, we worked together to help me understand the grammar.

I found that following my Bible while the Scriptures were read in the service gave me some help. The limited amount of linguistic training I had received while studying Chinese at Yale gave me some help. At Yale, we had been told "listen and repeat; listen and repeat, the only way to learn a language is to listen and repeat." It was not surprising then that my first words in Mende were the terms used in the clinic and the delivery room. In fact, I never got much beyond that. Eventually, I could understand all of the church service, even the sermon and could follow some conversation, but never got to the point where I could preach or even pray in Mende.

I wrote a lot of letters. I wrote a weekly letter home, but other people also heard from me frequently. In addition, there was an active exchange of letters with other missionaries in Sierra Leone. Dr. Silver was most faithful with a letter every week. I am not sure if I ever expressed to her my gratitude for those frequent communications. I am sure it took considerable effort on her part to find the time to do this for me.

Then we played games. The younger staff and neighborhood youngsters were eager to participate. Amos became an expert at Chinese checkers and eventually was able to beat me. We played endless games of Parcheesi. One evening we had played until midnight. Musu was in tears because she was losing; about an hour later she was jubilant as she had won.

There is a board game played with many variations all over Africa. In West Africa, it is called warri. A series of holes line both sides of the board and at each end is a pocket in which the markers are deposited. Each hole contains markers, beans, stones, or buttons, and each player, in turn, moves the markers around the board. The board used in Sierra Leone contains six holes on each side and there are four markers in each hole. Gradually, I developed some skill at the game and was at least able to beat the school boys.

In my travels I have collected several warri boards. There is a beautifully carved one that was made at the leper colony in Liberia. I bought another small one in Kenya where there are different playing rules. When I tried to buy my first one in Sierra Leone, I ran into difficulties. Abraham warned me that this was a gambling game and wasn't suitable for me to play.

One of my self-imposed rules was that nothing was to be purchased on Sunday, following the Biblical injunction that the Sabbath was to be kept holy. But one Sunday morning, two small boys appeared on the veranda with a locally produced warri board which they were selling for 60 cents. The board was in the shape of a boat with each end curved slightly upward. The exterior was carved with an intricate design and mounted on a pedestal. Although it does not have the finished look that the Liberian board has, it has the beauty of the locally produced carving. I quickly paid for it. It offered years of entertainment and has traveled with me from house to house.

I must admit that there were many hours of loneliness. When I would return to the United States, people often asked if I wasn't afraid living alone in Tiama. I don't remember being afraid but was often terribly lonely. Confined by the rain, stymied by my limited ability to speak the language, and frustrated by the narrow topics of conversation with even those local people who could speak English, there were many periods of unbroken silence.

Through the years I have come to enjoy those quiet times and miss them, particularly in the United States where life becomes hectic with professional activities, church responsibilities, and social contacts. Maybe that is why I have returned to Africa so many times in order to recapture those hours of reading and quiet reflection.

CHAPTER 15

The Bishop Comes to Visit

It had been decided (by whom? not by me!) that a study conference would be held in Tiama during the week prior to Christmas. How I had the temerity to accept this responsibility I'll never know. I don't think I would attempt it now, but this ignorance was a part of my inexperience as was the euphoria that clouded all reason.

The guests of honor were the American bishop, Ira D. Warner, who had responsibility for overseeing the conference in Sierra Leone, and Dr. Samuel Ziegler, the American executive secretary of the board of missions. All of the EUB missionaries were expected to attend all or part of the conference. The conference was to include a series of Bible studies and services attended by Africans and missionaries alike.

Because it took the better part of the day to travel to Tiama, it was necessary for people to stay overnight. Most of the missionaries would come to Mano on the train which arrived from the west about 4:00 p.m.; from Mano to Tiama, they would come by lorry. When they left the journey was reversed and they would have to be in Mano by 10:00 a.m. in order to catch the "down" train.

For me, the problem was where to house these people. Two people could sleep at my house. Jane's house was empty so there was room for six people there, two to a bedroom. The old mission house where the Leader's had lived was still habitable and a number of people could stay there. All the missionaries ate at my house (where did I find enough dishes to serve them?).

When the first guests arrived, we ran into the first housing problem. A number of men were traveling without their wives, including two men from the United States. I had planned to put two of them together in a bedroom which meant they shared a bed. The bishop took one look at the bedroom and said adamantly, "I never sleep with anyone."

I thought he was joking and said, "Well, I guess this is one time when you'll have to break your rule."

He wasn't joking. Now what were we to do?

The superintendent had come prepared with portable cots and mosquito nets. We set up two beds in the big, open living room where he and someone else slept. Dr. Ziegler and the bishop both had a room of their own.

The bishop also asked that each morning at 10:00 a.m. he be provided with a thermos of hot coffee and a container of freshly-squeezed orange juice. We assigned one schoolboy with this specific task. It was not difficult to prepare the coffee and the juice, but we never knew exactly where the bishop was during the morning. Each day, at 10:00 a.m. the boy would set off with his supplies to track down the bishop and bring his refreshments.

Food was not usually a problem. It was expected that local food would be served and anybody who didn't like rice or wouldn't eat it, was out of luck. Endless combinations of stew can be served over rice. Fruit was plentiful in December and there was a responsible bakery in Tiama so bread was available. Coffee is grown in Sierra Leone and could always be purchased in the local shops.

The biggest problem was supplying an adequate amount of safe drinking water, even the water from the cistern was not safe to drink untreated. It all had to be boiled and filtered and no one wanted to drink slightly warm water so it had to be boiled, filtered, and at least allowed to cool and, if possible have some time in the refrigerator. It

Bishop Warner and Pastor Carew conducting baptisms in the Teye River.

took almost one person's time to keep on top of the demand for water. All the water used for hot drinks had to go through this process as well. John outdid himself. He not only supervised the water and prepared the meals, he managed to provide some good desserts, and made sure that the coffee and fruit juice were ready for the bishop each morning.

The seminar was organized to provide time for discussion and reflection, a Bible study was included. The bishop chose the book of *Romans* for the topic of his Bible study. Everything he said had to be translated at least into Mende, and perhaps into Temne, a laborious process. Much of the New Testament is relatively easy to understand. The parables of Jesus, for example, are often simple stories with obvious meanings, but *Romans* is heavy going with deep theological content. Even in English it is often difficult to understand the meaning and implications of the text. This is compounded when the speaker has no knowledge of the local language and little understanding of the local culture.

The bishop got himself into several quagmires. One day he started telling a story about the Pennsylvania Dutch people.

"A farm woman was selling apple butter and smearcase," he began. He stopped. "How many people know what smearcase is?"

One of the missionaries answered, "It is cottage cheese."

He continued, "How many of you know what cottage cheese is?"

Only the missionaries raised their hands.

"Then how many of you know apple butter?" he persisted.

Again only the white hands went up while our African friends only looked puzzled. He admitted defeat and dropped the subject.

At another time Dr. Ziegler was talking about the number of Christians in Africa and quoted an estimate. For many of the local people concepts of numbers were limited to several hundred. I am not aware that there is a word for thousands in Mende. The translator coped by saying there were many Christians in Africa. Dr. Ziegler followed this with the number of people in all of Africa, stating the comparative number of Christians per populations. That illustration was lost, too.

One of the highlights of the week was a visit to a nearby village where the people had constructed a chapel. It was the usual mud-and-stick building, but it had a metal roof and a cement floor. The building was whitewashed both inside and out. The inside walls had been decorated by a local artist who had painted pictures of Biblical characters. The bishop was to dedicate the building.

A group of church women had prepared some music. They sang several hymns in Mende and then did one in English. The bishop was delighted and encouraged them to sing another. The women were reluctant, but he insisted. Finally, they sang a lively version of "My California Sunshine". Since they probably weren't aware of the meaning of the English words, they probably didn't know that the song didn't fit the occasion.

The week finally ended. John, the schoolboys, and I were all relieved. We had managed that everyone had a place to sleep and was fed. I was glad it was over. We were ready for the next flurry of excitement, a wedding.

CHAPTER 16

Winnie's Wedding

On the Saturday after the conference, my friend, Winnie Smith was to be married. Winnie and I had been roommates while studying Chinese at Yale University. She had lived in New Haven from September until December 1949, where she met a young forestry student, Lester Bradford. Their friendship grew into romance. After she left Connecticut to work at a mission hospital in Kentucky, they became engaged. She left Kentucky, went to Britain to study tropical medicine and arrived in Sierra Leone sometime in 1951.

They planned that Les would come to Sierra Leone and they would be married there. This plan engendered much discussion among the mission leadership. The mission urgently needed a doctor, but what would they do with a forester? While Winnie was studying in Britain, Les had obtained a master's degree in agriculture from Cornell University. An agriculturist would be more useful than a forester so it was finally decided that he could come to Sierra Leone.

Les arrived in Freetown on a Monday and the wedding was set for Saturday. The day after the conference ended in Tiama those of us still there started the journey to Rotifunk.

The train was crowded. It was only a few days before Christmas. School children were traveling home for the holidays. Many people were also going away for vacations and annual leave, even the first class carriages were crowded. The train made it to the Bauya junction. Just beyond Bauya was a rather steep hill. The little engine started out bravely and made it part way up the grade but couldn't reach the top. It backed up, made a dash and tried again only to fail. There was a third try, and a fourth but the hill was simply too much for the power of the engine. The train returned to Bauya where the front cars were uncoupled and taken over the hill. The engine then returned to the station and picked up the rest of the cars, carried them over the hill, reunited the train, and continued on its way to Freetown.

The people going to the wedding got off at Rotifunk. Where did we all stay when we got there? I don't remember. There must have been some crowded sleeping quarters.

A wedding between expatriots was an unusual occurrence. While there were several single white women in the mission, single white men were a rarity. At one time, the mission board had a rule that a single man could not be sent to the field. I have never understood the reasoning behind this ridiculous rule. It seems that single men were not capable of managing for themselves and needed women to run their households. During the years that I was in the field, only once was a single man assigned to work there. Government officials and single men in other mission stations seemed to be able to manage.

On Friday night we had a big pre-wedding dinner. The living room of Dr. Silver's house was occupied by a long table set with linen and Dr. Silver's best flatware. I had taken John along as a reward for his yeoman's service during the week in Tiama, and he helped to serve the dinner. All the waiters were dressed in white jackets, a legacy of Winnie's intern days. It was a festive occasion.

The wedding on Saturday was held in the Rotifunk Church. Bishop Warner conducted the service, and I supplied the music, pumping with enthusiastic energy on the small reed organ.

The service itself was delayed. This may have been my first wedding in Africa, and since then I have come to anticipate a delay of anywhere up to four hours before the festivities begin. I now go prepared, sometimes armed with a book to read while the lengthy preparations go on.

Part of the delay was due to the awaited arrival of the people from Harford School. A newly-made road covered the 20 miles between Moyamba and Rotifunk. The Harford people had hired a small truck to bring them to Rotifunk. One of the bridesmaids and a trio of singers were arriving by road. Eventually, everyone arrived and the ceremony began. The church ceremony was followed by a huge feast of Jollof rice and a traditional wedding cake.

The local community enhanced the celebration with traditional dancing and drumming. One of the local devils made his appearance and entertained us with dancing and acrobatics.

Les and Winnie went off on their honeymoon to Bonthe Island which is in the Atlantic Ocean off the coast from Shenge. At one time, Bonthe was a prominent port for shipping produce to Europe. The Victorian-style houses and shops were a reminder of the early traders. It was also the site of some of the earliest UBC churches and schools. Once the railroad was built, Bonthe lost its importance as a trading center. It was still a charming island with lovely beaches and beautiful flowering trees.

The Bradford's went first by road to Mattru Jong where they caught the launch that took them across the open sea to the island. They carried provisions and equipment to be used while they were in Bonthe when the launch capsized. The couple reached land safely, but lost all of their belongings: their clothes, a typewriter, and the dishes and flatware that Dr. Silver had lent them. We were grateful for their safety.

Despite a rather disastrous start to the marriage, they have led a safe and satisfactory existence. In addition to their years of service in Sierra Leone, they also worked for several years in Bangladesh, employed by one of the United Nations agencies.

I went back to Tiama on Monday accompanied by one of the Harford teachers. We spent a quiet Christmas. I remember that both of us spent long hours in our own bed, sleeping and reading. At last, I was ready to go back to work on a regular schedule.

CHAPTER 17

Two Sick Missionaries

Ruth Harding came back to Sierra Leone in May 1953. She had previously lived in Tiama and had managed the clinic there. Ruth was effervescent, hard-working, charming, and much-loved by the local people. In fact, I was quite jealous when I arrived because so many people told me what a good job she did and how popular she was in the community.

Ruth and Dr. Silver were particularly good friends. Ruth was now assigned to Rotifunk since Gertrude Bloede had gone back to the United States on furlough. Ruth was there only a few weeks when she became ill. Illness among expatriots, as I have mentioned, was fairly common. Despite the use of modern anti-malarial medications, bouts of fever were common, not to mention the occasional attacks of diarrhea and some skin infections. But Ruth didn't have malaria and the illness persisted. It was characterized by fever, vomiting, and prostration, and no treatment seemed to work. The executive committee of missionaries suggested that she should return to the United States, but she didn't want to go home. Dr. Silver decided that she could stay at Rotifunk, perhaps with the hope that whatever was causing the problems would disappear and she would become healthy. Dr. Silver informed the missionary community about the problem but asked us not to send any information to the United States. She felt that if the board at home knew about the illness, they would insist that Ruth be sent home. She was probably right.

In July, Betty Beveridge came to Rotifunk. Betty had been a senior midwife at the hospital in London where several of us had trained as midwives. As we came to know her better, we encouraged her to apply for a position at the hospital in Rotifunk. Betty was both experienced and knowledgeable, in contrast to those of us who had gone to Sierra Leone immediately after we finished our training and had no experience. She was hard-working, enthusiastic, and had an air of authority that enabled her to make some necessary improvements in the maternity area.

I was pleased and excited about her arrival. Although she had been a senior nursing sister at St. Alfege's, the hospital where I had done my training, she had been kind and friendly to me. I had been the first American student to train at that school and had sometimes found the adjustment to the British nursing system somewhat frustrating, but Betty had been sympathetic and occasionally bailed me out of a difficult situation. She was a committed Christian and welcomed this opportunity for service.

Not long after she arrived, Betty developed the same illness that Ruth had. She, too, didn't want to return home. Now there were two bedridden patients that needed intensive nursing care: care during the periods of vomiting and diarrhea, bed baths, backrubs, administration of pain relief for headaches and muscle pains as well as the preparation of small meals and appetizing snacks to tempt nonexistent appetites and to reverse weight loss. There were no other expatriot nurses on that station. To further complicate matters, Dr. Silver had a mild heart attack in February and was restricted in her activity.

Early in September, the mission superintendent sent word to me in Tiama that I should go to Rotifunk to help. I expected to be gone for a few days, but was there for over four months. I packed a small suitcase. Eventually, I had to send back to Tiama for additional equipment and clothing. I went with reluctance. I would have been even more reluctant if I had known it was going to last for so long. I was happy at Tiama, I was needed there, and I didn't like Rotifunk.

Although I was involved doing some of the nursing care for Betty and Ruth, my major responsibility was to see patients in the office, supervise patient care in the wards, and help with deliveries. Esther Megill, the missionary laboratory technician, was a great help since she was aware of the day-to-day running of the hospital. Abbie Johnson, one of the Sierra Leone senior nurses, was drafted to help with the nursing care of the missionaries. Infinitely patient, she was indispensable in her ability to meet the needs of the two sick women. We were soon joined by Charles and Bertha Leader who were scheduled to leave shortly on furlough. Mrs. Leader assumed some of the nursing care and Dr. Leader made himself generally useful.

The two patients were seriously ill and all efforts to make a diagnosis were futile. Dr. Silver sought advise from the British and African medical experts in Freetown. Blood samples and a description of the disease were sent to the University Hospital in Ibadan, Nigeria. They, too, were baffled. Tulane University in Louisiana was one of the few tropical disease hospitals in the United States at that time. Blood samples were sent to Tulane. They responded that it was either a form of leukemia or infectious mononucleosis, however, neither diagnosis seemed to be correct.

Dr. Silver felt that the disease existed in a mild form in several people including a number of Africans. I think that I had a milder and shorter form later on. I had vomiting, diarrhea, and fever which did not respond to malaria medication. I lost my appetite and a lot of weight. Although it is only speculation, I have wondered if it might have been a milder form of Lassa Fever that appeared later in Nigeria, Liberia, and Sierra Leone. When that disease was initially diagnosed, it was almost always fatal.

We all kept our promise about not sending any news of the illness back home,but my parents were concerned. Since I gave no reason for being at Rotifunk, they assumed that I was ill and was keeping the information from them. They wrote repeatedly that if I were ill, or in any kind of trouble, there was always a place for me at home and someone to take care of me. This was reassuring, but it didn't solve the problem.

It was a difficult time. We all became very much concerned about the two nurses, particularly when the illness persisted for several months. As Esther and I walked to the hospital each morning, our comment was always the same, "This can't go on much longer. Somebody has to do something to stop it." Nursing care was strenuous, both physically and emotionally. I was carrying the bulk of the hospital responsibilities which were beyond my knowledge and expertise. I was dealing with more complicated cases than I usually saw in Tiama, including some that required surgery. I was unfamiliar with some of the medications that Dr. Silver usually prescribed. I was overwhelmed. I was very unhappy.

During this time, there were a series of interesting and challenging cases. One of our patients was the former chief of a neighboring chiefdom, a position in Sierra Leone that carried life tenure. Although it was an elected position, it also had hereditary implications, for only certain families could propose candidates. It was a serious matter for the government to depose a chief and could only be accomplished after proof of complete incompetence or serious malpractice. It usually meant that after death, the chief could not be buried on the ancestral ground. I don't know why Chief Mahoi had been deposed, but he no longer held the position. I had been acquainted with one of his sons who was studying medicine in the United States.

The chief was dying in the terminal stages of liver cancer and was receiving only supportive care: pain relief, skin care and adequate hydration. He had only a few days to live. When an adult dies, the mourners made ritual wailing that often went on for hours, sometimes days or weeks. The chief died one evening. For a brief time there was no wailing, then after about a half hour, a solitary wail started in Chief Caulker's compound on the other side of town. Like a great wave, the sound increased and crossed the town until people gathered outside the hospital and joined their voices in the lament. The wailing continued all night. The next morning the body of Chief Mahoi was buried in Rotifunk, denied the right to be taken back to his chiefdom.

Although some of the deliveries were managed by the hospital staff, I also conducted some and Dr. Silver did a few. Early one morning, she delivered a baby that was an anencephalic. This is a condition where a baby is born without a developed brain and usually without any skull bones. The baby is often still-born, and if it is alive at birth, will die within minutes since there is not enough brain tissue to control breathing or a heart beat.

I was glad that I had not done that delivery, but did go later to look at the baby. It is a sorrowful occasion for the mother and the family and it is also a sad event for the medical personnel involved. Since then I have seen several such babies, both in Africa and the United States, but have never had to deliver one.

One Saturday afternoon I was called to help with a breech delivery. Again, these are often very difficult. Even with the best of care, the baby may have brain damage or may die during delivery. The delivery was complicated by having a very uncooperative patient. I delivered the legs and body of the baby, then had a problem in delivering the arms which extended over the baby's head. When I got the arms out, I couldn't get the head out. The patient turned from side to side, kicked one leg, then the other, then lifted her buttocks off the bed, crying, and yelling. Within a few minutes the baby was dead. I still couldn't finish the delivery.

I finally sent word to the house asking Dr. Silver for help. She was feeling ill and couldn't come. Eventually, Esther Megill came and administered drop ether. The patient relaxed enough so that I was able to get the dead infant out.

During the delivery I had cut an episiotomy, but the patient refused to let me suture the cut. I was too worried, tired, and discouraged to argue for long. If the wound became infected it would just have to happen. When I got back to the house, Dr. Silver scolded me, but I was too tired to care. Eventually, the episiotomy healed without problems.

In the meantime, the crisis with the nurses continued with no improvement in their condition. One day the vomiting would stop and they would be able to eat small amounts, only to have the vomiting resume the next day. Because of their severe headaches, they were frequently sedated with increasing amounts of Demoral.

While they were treated with a variety of pharmaceuticals, we didn't neglect access to spiritual healing. Among ourselves, we prayed frequently and fervently. Dr. Silver was fluent in Krio, but said she never used Krio in her prayers. Now she found herself resorting to talking to God in Krio. We knew that the church in Sierra Leone was joining us in our petitions, and the whole of Harford School took a full day to pray for the recovery of the nurses. We followed the New Testament injunctions. Dr. Leader conducted a service of anointing and healing; but the healing did not come.

One of the most difficult problems was the dreadful hallucinations that accompanied the elevation of the women's temperature. Betty had been a nurse in London's East End during the German bombing. During the days of her illness, she relived those days of terror. She would suddenly dive off the bed and onto the floor to escape the falling bombs.

Then, Mrs. Leader got sick. She had previously had some cardiac problems and now began to develop some symptoms: mild chest pain and shortness of breath. One more bedridden patient needing close nursing care would have made the situation intolerable. The Leader's had extended their stay to help us in the emergency but decided that the sensible thing to do was to leave for the United States.

Without their help, the situation became even more difficult. Esther was also due to leave on furlough. Ruth had now been ill for four months with no improvement. A nurse from the British Methodist Church was scheduled to leave for England, and it was agreed that she would take Ruth with her on the ship. Air travel was still not common and was very expensive. As the ship sailed northward, Ruth made steady recovery and was better by the time she reached Britain. She was hospitalized, but after numerous examinations and tests there was still no diagnosis. She returned to the United States and had no further recurrence.

Next Esther went home. Since Betty had still made no improvement, it was decided that Dr. Silver should take her to Britain. During that time, word had come that Dr. Silver had been awarded the honor of Member of the British Empire (MBE) by the Queen, part of the 1953 Birthday Honors list. It was the first time an American citizen had been so honored in Sierra Leone. In the normal course of events, the medal would have been presented to her by the Governor General in a formal ceremony on New Year's Day. Due to the emergency, the medal was given to her in a private ceremony.

In my collection I have a picture of her holding the medal just as she was about to take the launch to cross the river to the airport. I went to Freetown to see them off. Betty was carried on a stretcher and was heavily sedated.

This was before the days of jet aircraft, and the trip from Lagos, Nigeria to London took three days. The passengers spent the nights in a hotel on the ground, and the plane even landed at noon for lunch.

Betty recovered in Britain. She later returned to Sierra Leone where the same illness recurred. Eventually, she recovered totally.

The two passengers left Freetown on the American Thanksgiving Day. Later that afternoon I joined several other Americans in Freetown for the traditional feast. Then, I traveled back to Rotifunk to stay until someone came to relieve me. There was no time for vacation. The house at Rotifunk was very quiet. The hectic activities of the last six months had disappeared. With Dr. Silver gone, fewer patients came to the hospital. I had a lot of time on my hands.

Among the reading material in the house were copies of the magazine of the women's missionary society dating back to 1898. The earlier copies were destroyed in the Hut Tax War of 1898. In graphic detail, these magazines told of the deaths of the seven missionaries who had been killed. Of all the material I chose to read in those weeks alone, only these accounts made an impression on me. I was not frightened or worried for my own safety, I felt very secure. I was grateful for the lives of those early dedicated people who were willing to sacrifice themselves for what they believed. My own troubles began to shrink in comparison. My sick friends were on their way to recovery. I was not ill or in trouble, things could only get better.

Gertrude Bloede came back from furlough in early December. There was someone to share the work, someone to talk to, someone to eat with. Since she had spent her furlough in Wisconsin, she came with news of friends and family.

A week or so later, Amy Skartved came to join us. Amy was assigned to Nigeria and had lived there for some time. She had just finished her midwifery training in London and was to spend several months in Sierra Leone to help us out in the crisis.

It was during this time that I got a letter from the Freetown office. The new superintendent, a man who had served in Sierra Leone in several capacities, wrote to reprimand me for not sending my monthly reports from Tiama. I was righteously indignant and fired back an angry letter. I had not asked to come to Rotifunk, I didn't want to stay, and any time someone wanted me to go back to Tiama and write reports, I would start immediately.

A new American secretary had recently joined the office staff. Later she told me that she read my angry letter and wondered about the caliber of the missionaries in Sierra Leone. What kind of person would write such a letter? We have laughed about it many times.

But I didn't go back to Tiama immediately and I suppose that eventually, the reports were submitted. Christmas was very quiet. After the holidays, we traveled to Freetown for the annual conference. Finally, in the middle of January, I got to go home to Tiama.

CHAPTER 18

A Bridge Across the Teye

As I have mentioned, the principle means of transportation in Sierra Leone was the railroad, but increasingly the government made efforts to build and improve roads. Freetown and Bo were connected by a road, a very poor one. Logically, the best way to cover the distance would be for a road to go south from Yonibana to Tiama and Mano and then east to Bo. The biggest obstacle to that road was the Teye River at Tiama. For years, people had crossed the river by wading in the dry season or by dugout canoes when the river was flooded during the rainy season.

By 1952 the road from Yonibana to the river was under construction. The engineer in charge was a young Sierra Leonean, Wadi Williams, one of the earliest and perhaps the first Sierra Leonean engineer. He was a self-assured, competent man, who was not particularly friendly to non-Africans. Although we never had a hostile encounter, we didn't have very many friendly ones either even though he and his family lived in Tiama. Since the road was finished to the point where cars could travel on it, a ferry was developed so that cars could cross the river.

So Tiama was changing. Increasing numbers of cars came through the village, and the number of people who stopped to visit or stay for a meal increased. My house became a convenient place to stop for a drink of water or a chance to use the toilet.

Our most memorable visitor was the Prime Minister, Dr. Milton Margai. Later he became Sir Milton, honored by Queen Elizabeth. Dr. Margai, a Mende, had been trained as a physician, the first person from the Protectorate to be so educated. He had graduated from the Albert Academy in Freetown and maintained his membership in the EUB church. A major organizer of the Protectorate politics, he became the Chief Minister in 1953. At independence, in 1961, he became the first Prime Minister.

One day he was traveling from Bo to Freetown and planned to cross the ferry at Tiama, but there was a delay due to some malfunction at the ferry. He drove up to the dispensary and asked to see our building. My remembrances of that occasion are that he was very unassuming and friendly. He was dressed not in a suit or uniform, but in a long, traditional Mende gown. He walked to the compound, and in a quiet voice, introduced himself. He asked about the types of cases we were seeing, what our staffing patterns were, and about our finances. It was as though a favorite, caring uncle had come to see us and was concerned about our welfare. Although the staff was pleased and excited about the visit of such a distinguished person, they were not intimidated, and we all had a pleasant visit. His English was faultless, although he obviously could have carried on the conversation in Mende, and probably in several other local languages.

Finally, construction began on the bridge which had two main pilings and three spans. One of the pilings was anchored on the rock in the river where the McGrews had been massacred in 1898. The simple stone that commemorated their martyrdom was moved to the river bank and placed next to the bridge.

Mr. Williams was severely criticized for his building methods. Some of the other government engineers declared that the design was unsafe and the wrong materials were used in the construction. I always doubted their decision but eventually, the bridge was declared unsafe and a second bridge was constructed a few yards downstream. However, in 1989, both bridges were standing and still being used. The original construction was done with almost no modern machinery. The loads of stone and sand were carried in basins on men's heads. After the concrete was mixed, it, too, was carried in similar basins to the appropriate site.

When at last the bridge was completed, the opening ceremony was spectacular. The local secret societies were represented in full

Bridge over the Teye River during the height of the rainy season.

Several chiefs at the bridge opening.

costume. Those members of the male society, the Wunde Society who dressed in women's clothes, paraded in colorful dresses. The warriors marched with swords and shields. Several clown devils, arrayed in raffia suits with large, carved wooden masks on their heads, provided songs, tricks, and dances.

A police band was imported to play for the occasion. Important officials, both British and African, including a number of paramount chiefs, came for the occasion. Although women chiefs were rare, one of them came dressed in a great flowing gown of pink net with a matching head tie. A few of the male chiefs wore floor-length white gowns, the necklines covered with colorful embroidery. The guest of honor was the Governor. Dressed in a white uniform which included a tall hat with white plumes, he approached the bridge from the north and at the center cut a white ribbon, officially declaring the bridge open.

The building of roads and bridges was one of the most beneficial policies of the colonial government. Later when I traveled and lived in Liberia, the lack of transportation facilities was a serious handicap to development. Only a few towns in the far north and eastern parts of Sierra Leone could not be reached by road. These roads encouraged the transfer of goods, people, and services. Locally grown produce such as palm kernels, ginger, and rice could be sent to markets in Freetown or for export, while necessities such as kerosene, sugar, and medicines could be brought to even the farthest corners of the country.

CHAPTER 19

Educate a Woman

A pervasive theme of Christian missions has been to improve the lives of women. Frequently, the church was the first organization to establish schools for girls. Medical care was provided in pregnancy and childbirth as well as care for children in well-baby clinics.

The EUB church in Sierra Leone was no exception. In addition to institutional efforts, there were many informal efforts. For years, one woman missionary was designated to be the woman's worker who organized workshops, did evangelistic work, and promoted homemaking skills. One of the more successful projects was teaching methods of soap making. Soap was a necessary item in housekeeping. Commercially it was expensive, but it is fairly easy to make and easy to store. It became a popular feature of the women's institutes.

In the local culture, the women's secret society, the Bundu Society, was the time-tested organization for educating girls and preparing them for marriage and motherhood. The girls spent weeks, sometime months, in a secluded area, being taught by the older women in the community. At one point, Dr. Milton Margai, as a medical officer in the Protectorate, initiated a plan whereby educated women were encouraged to go into the Bundu Bush to teach modern hygiene and child care to the girls. He asked some of the missionaries to be involved in this effort and several of our women's workers joined the elders of the town, adding to their teaching.

The Tiama church, under the direction of Pastor Carew, also provided educational programs. Because of the large congregation and school, a core of educated women provided education for other women. The leader of this group was the pastor's wife, Betty Carew. Under her initiative, we started a series of projects beginning with sewing, knitting, and crocheting. Many of the women were very skilled at crocheting. Those houses that had chairs and tables displayed the skilled handiwork of the women which included chair covers, table cloths, and bedspreads.

However, women who had not attended school usually didn't

have such skills. Sweaters for babies were some of the most desired objects. Since I was pretty adept at knitting, teaching it became one of my assignments. I'm afraid I didn't accomplish much. The job was complicated because many of the women were illiterate and couldn't follow a pattern. They also had trouble with the fine motor skills required to accomplish their task. One woman somehow kept accumulating stitches in a manner I couldn't fathom. I started her with 20 stitches on a needle only to find that a few rows later she had accumulated 120 stitches.

Later in Kenya where the temperature was much colder, I saw many women, some of them illiterate, and working without patterns, knit good-fitting sweaters often with intricate designs.

The women also wanted to learn how to sew, usually clothes for their children. I was totally inept at this. I had a sewing machine as did several of the educated women, but even with the machine I didn't turn out things that looked good. However, it was impractical to teach the local women to sew with a machine since no one had access to one. The illiterate women had to be taught to sew by hand.

I watched with amazement as the educated women made paper patterns and accurately cut the material into good-fitting garments. My task involved teaching the women how to thread a needle and tie a knot at the end of the thread. I felt I knew instinctively how to do this since I had done it from my childhood, but it proved to be a complex skill for those unfamiliar with thread and needle. Frequently, after several attempts, a woman would bring the tools to me and ask me to thread the needle.

A second effort was promoting literacy. Again, this was a long term project on the part of the church. In fact, an early EUB missionary, Minnie Eaton, had produced one of the earliest Mende-English dictionaries in the early 1900's.

During his tenure as pastor in Tiama, Pastor Carew had developed a month-long literacy institute in December of each year. It was the dry season so travel was easy, the harvesting was finished, and planting had not yet started. Usually these sessions were attended by village men with very few women participating.

But the women were eager to learn to read. The women of the church started their own literacy sessions with small classes that met at irregular times whenever the women were free to come. We used the Laubach method in which simple pictures represent letters which are then put together as words and sentences.

As was to be expected, there was a wide variation in the ability of women to learn. One woman was exceptionally bright, learned very quickly, and was soon reading with some ability. I was thrilled. Suddenly, she stopped coming. I waited several days, but she didn't come back. Finally, I went to talk it over with Betty Carew.

"I don't know what happened to Adama," I started. "I don't think she is ill. Do you know what is wrong?"

Betty said, "I think she went to her village."

"But why? She was making such good progress and was doing better than any of the other women."

Betty explained. "You know her husband can't read. Do you think he will let her learn how to read when he can't read?"

Of course not. The woman never came back for lessons.

At one point, someone had sent me some children's jigsaw puzzles with large pieces. They became a favorite attraction at my house with both women and children coming to put them together. One of the puzzles had a picture of an American cartoon character, Howdy Dowdy. I never did successfully explain who he was.

One of the women who came frequently to do the puzzles was Kadi Jalloh. Fairly early in my stay in Tiama I had delivered her first baby. It had been a long and tedious labor and when a baby boy was born there was great rejoicing. Kadi was the fourth wife of one of the leading Muslims in town. She was young and pretty with a delightful, cheerful disposition. The completion of the puzzle was accomplished with many pleased giggles from her.

One evening I thought, "This is foolish. She ought to be doing something more profitable."

"Kadi," I said, "why don't I teach you how to read?"

"I have to go home and ask Pa Jalloh," she said.

He was agreeable and we started the Laubach primer. She was making good progress and was learning quickly, but after about a month she came one evening and said, "Pa Jalloh said I should learn to do something useful. I should learn to sew."

We put the primer away and started with needle and thread.

*Dr. Mabel Silver,
senior medical officer
of the EUB mission.
See page 30.*

*First EUB church building in Tiama. The mission residence and dispensary are
visible behind the building, on the right side of the picture. See page 34.*

COLORPLATE 2

Old dispensary in Tiama. See page 34.

*Abraham Lavaly,
senior dispenser.
See page 39.*

COLORPLATE 3

John Brewah,
who ran my household
for twelve years.
See page 48.

Interior of the new church sanctuary. The altar furniture was made by the pastor,
Rev. B. A. Carew. See page 71.

Pastor B. A. Carew and his wife, Betty. See page 72.

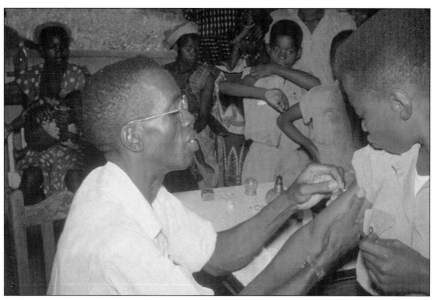

Abraham Lavaly vaccinating a school child against smallpox. See page 128.

Girl initiates in the Bundu Society. Costumes, head adornments, and necklaces are specific to the society. See page 129.

Clyde Galow and Gladys Fahner on their wedding day, standing in front of a poinsettia bush. See page 131.

Mother (on left) with her twins. Her mother is holding one of the babies. See page 136.

EUB church building on Bonthe Island. See page 145.

Acrobatic clown devil at Chief Dudu Bona's compound, Jaiama.
See page 163.

Yumba Pettiquoi, head nurse at the Jaiama Clinic, holding Tamba,
an orphan she was raising. See page 163.

Wunde warriors. See page 192.

Ceremonial dancers at University of Ibadan, Nigeria. See page 235.

CHAPTER 20

Parting is a Sorrow

Sometime during the rainy season of 1954 I became ill. I had rather frequent attacks of malaria, especially after I had been without sleep for several nights when spending the night with patients in labor, but this was different. I was in bed for ten days with malaise, vomiting, and fever. One morning I seriously considered that I should leave and go home before my three-year assignment was over.

The African staff was wonderful to me while I was ill. Often Musu stayed at the house all night so that I wouldn't be alone. Many people came to visit and offer condolences. Krio has a phrase, "Ash" which expresses sympathy for illness, disappointment or loss. Many people came to tell me "Ash."

I lost my appetite and didn't want to eat. John cooked anything that would tempt me. He squeezed endless numbers of oranges to make juice. When I had been in Freetown I had looked at the imported Irish potatoes which were very expensive. I didn't buy any since I thought they cost too much. When I mentioned this to Dr. Silver she said I had been foolish. If potatoes were the only things I wanted to eat, I had better buy potatoes. They were not for sale in Tiama or Mano and my trips to Freetown so infrequent, I wasn't able to obtain any. Eventually, I recovered from that initial attack only to have short, recurrent bouts about once a month.

My furlough was due in October. I had planned to go to Britain by sea, spend two weeks in London, and then sail to New York. The mission executive committee had promised that someone would be available to take my place at Tiama while I was on furlough. But they knew, and I knew, there was no one to take my place.

On the day I was scheduled to leave Tiama, I refused to go. At my last scheduled baby clinic, there was a tearful farewell. Some of the mothers brought farewell gifts: a few pennies, an egg or two, some oranges and bananas. The pennies totaled to a little over three pounds. There were 78 eggs. For three years I had scarcely seen an egg now I was rich! Only about half of the eggs were edible, however. For two weeks I ate eggs cooked in every imaginable way. I resolved to use the money for some token of remembrance.

The executive committee was determined that I had to obey orders. Several of my missionary friends pressured me to change my mind.

The new superintendent came to Tiama to convince me. On his way, he stopped at Harford School.

"I am going to Tiama and insist that she leave," he told one of my friends.

"That will never work," she replied. "But if you reason with her, you can probably persuade her that it is in her best interest to take her leave."

I finally admitted to myself that no one was coming to relieve me and I agreed to go home.

On the day before I was to leave Tiama, Miss Nora Vesper arrived, the oldest missionary in the field. Small, slightly plump, with white hair and a disarming smile, she was energetic, but most of all, governed by common sense. She had retired twice and came back each time to help out in an emergency. I had tremendous respect and admiration for her. I am sure that she was deliberately chosen to make sure that I left since I would hardly refuse her anything.

At the end of the last day I carefully washed my delivery equipment, oiled the instruments, and packed them away. At 8:00 p.m. a woman arrived in labor. I took the equipment out of the containers and delivered the baby. Again I washed and oiled the instruments and packed them away. At 2:00 a.m. another woman came in labor and I repeated the process. At 6:00 a.m., Hannah, a neighbor, came in labor and again I boiled everything, and set up the tray. She was still in labor when we loaded into the lorry that was to take us to Mano. Hannah sat there wailing, "Oh, Miss Ose, Oh, Miss Ose."

Finally, Miss Vesper quieted her. "Stop crying. I was delivering babies before Miss Olsen was born!"

All of the staff except Abraham accompanied me to Mano, he stayed in Tiama to help Miss Vesper. About four miles out of Tiama the lorry broke down. The driver got out and tinkered with the engine and finally got it started. Another three miles and the same thing happened, more repairs were made. A mile from Mano there was a third breakdown. I got out and started to walk to Mano. No one would believe that I hadn't missed that train on purpose. I took a small bag and started walking. When I reached the station I turned around to see that the hospital staff was behind me, carrying my luggage on their heads. I caught the train, complete with belongings!

At Moyambe there was a full compliment of missionaries to say good-bye and make sure that I was finally on my way. The trip went smoothly until we got to Rotifunk. A small stream ran through the eastern edge of town and was crossed by a small bridge. As the engine crossed the bridge, it developed a hot box. My coach had not yet crossed. Ahead at the station the missionaries were waiting, complete with food. Surely the repairs would take only a few minutes, but the minutes stretched into hours. One of the servants took the back road and brought food to me. Eventually, I left the train, walked to the mission compound, enjoyed a rest, used their toilet, and got a good supply of drinking water. Finally, the train moved into the station. I got back on board and went on to Freetown. Since I had missed the boat to Britain, it was decided that I should fly.

I took a flight similar to the one that Betty and Dr. Silver had taken a year earlier. I boarded at Freetown's airport at Lungi and found that I was the only single white woman on the plane. There were several couples who obviously were old acquaintances, and several single men, including a mining engineer who decided that I was going to make an ideal traveling companion. He sat in the seat next to me, and at mealtime, made sure we shared a table. He tried to entertain me with engrossing conversation. I wasn't sure how I was to separate myself from him. Fortunately, there was a friendly agriculturist who quickly told me how anxious he was to get back to England to see his wife. We spent much of the next two days together which gave me some escape from the amorous engineer.

The first night we stopped at Dakar, Senegal where the passengers spent the night in a lovely, beachside hotel. Dakar was hot and dry about 95 degrees, with only a slight breeze to help alleviate the heat.

While my room was comfortable, no drinking water was provided. I lay in bed a long time with a driving thirst. I was afraid to drink the tap water for fear of diarrhea, but I couldn't sleep because of the thirst. The debate and the thirst raged. I finally succumbed and drank the water with no ill effect.

During the flight from France to London, my engineer friend, a little the worse for liquor, perched on the arm of my seat, put his arm across my shoulder and asked, "Honey, what do I have to do to be a missionary?"

The thought of this inebriated Lothario as a part of the staid missionary community only provoked laughter. I told him he might try the Salvation Army where the strict discipline would be an advantage.

I spent ten great days in London visiting friends, with a special trip back to Greenwich where I had done part of my midwifery training. I spent a day at the Tower of London and viewed the Crown Jewels which I had neglected when I lived there.

In London, I chose the cheapest accommodations I could find, the YWCA, where I shared a room with two other women. One of my tasks in London was to spend the three pounds the baby clinic women had given me. I bought a cameo pin, something I had wanted for a long time. Apparently, one of my roommates had wanted one for a long time, too, since the pin disappeared from my luggage.

Finally, I left from Southampton and sailed to New York.

CHAPTER 21

Furlough

I spent a year in the United States. If I had thought that this was a year's vacation, that thought was soon dismissed. I was still employed and was expected, indeed assigned, to work and speak on behalf of the church. There were rather strict rules about fund-raising. We were expected to recruit both personnel and funds but were not allowed to ask for funds for private projects and, while traveling, were not allowed to accept any personal gifts over $10. Transportation, food, and lodging were paid for.

I spent the first month at home with my parents, but even that was busy with speaking occasions. My father was filled with pride and joy at my homecoming. My grandfather and stepmother seemed equally happy to have me at home, and my stepmother made great efforts to prepare the foods that I enjoyed; anything with apples, salads with lettuce, and pork roasts. I had lost a lot of weight during the three years, particularly during the last year when I was ill. Before I left Tiama, Abraham had said, "Your daddy no go sabe you, you dry-O!" Indeed, my father was dismayed at how thin I was. I was now 31 years old and my hair had started to turn gray. After four years away from home I was a different person, both physically and psychologically.

My parents were living in Richfield, Wisconsin where my father was the pastor of two EUB churches, one in Richfield and the other five miles away in Colgate. He asked me to preach at the Colgate church on my first Sunday at home, the church where I held my membership while I was away. Although I had only been a member of this church for five months before I left for London, it was always the church I remembered when I thought about going home. The members had been most supportive of me, sending gifts and writing frequently.

That first Sunday morning as I sat through the early part of the service, I was overwhelmed with tears. I was afraid I wouldn't be able to speak, but by the time of the sermon I was able to control the tears.

Missionaries tell similar stories about furlough experiences. If you are wise, you will make plans for some kind of intellectual refreshment either professionally, spiritually or both if possible. During that first furlough, I spent three months at Lutheran Hospital in La Crosse working in the laboratory. I was determined to be able to do some laboratory work at Tiama. I gained some knowledge and skills about blood and urine testing that I was able to use when I returned to Africa. The hospital provided housing and experience. In return, on alternate weekends, I worked as a staff nurse.

The other weekends I traveled to churches in the area. The senior technician in the lab usually took me in her car and frequently operated the projector when I showed slides. She said she got to know my speeches as well as I did, including my rather feeble jokes.

During the constant travel, I met wonderful, warm, friendly people who took me, as a complete stranger, into their homes, gave me a comfortable bed, and fed me inordinate amounts of delicious, wholesome food. I quickly gained back the pounds I had lost, but in general, I found the constant traveling unsettling. Despite friendly people, it was difficult to constantly make new acquaintances. I longed for some stability.

For example, my hosts almost never offered me the use of the bathtub, and I didn't usually feel that I could ask to use the tub or the shower if it hadn't been offered. I had to be content with washing at the sink. It became one of the family jokes. When I got home after a month of travel, my stepmother would ask how many baths I had taken. During my days at home, I had good use of the tub.

I was, and still am, amazed about Americans' ignorance about Africa. Television has not helped much since it usually only highlights wildlife and the remaining primitiveness of that vast continent. The truth is that even then, there were almost no wild animals left in West Africa. I had heard stories of leopards, elephants, and crocodiles, but even in rural Sierra Leone, I had never seen any. The large number of small countries and the vastness of the continent are puzzling even to those of us who have lived there. I keep an atlas handy and carry one with me when I travel. I frequently preface my talks with geographic identification. I don't think any generalization can be made about all of Africa. It is not even wise to say all Kenyans, or all Liberians or all Sierra Leoneans. Even to characterize all Mendes or all Manos is to run the risk of oversimplification.

People frequently ask certain questions. Americans (all Americans?) are convinced that Africa is overrun with snakes, but to deny the presence of snakes is to bring into question my credibility. People also have the idea that all Africans live in mud huts in tiny villages. When I describe or show pictures of modern, industrialized cities, they accuse me of using my imagination. Huge cities like Lagos and Nairobi

do exist. Nairobi is estimated to have a population of a million people while the population of Lagos, Nigeria probably is over four million. Most countries have at least one large city. Abidjan in the Ivory Coast, Harare in Zimbabwe, and Dakar in Senegal; and some countries have several large centers of population: Douala and Yaounde in the Cameroons and Kano and Ibadan in Nigeria.

The influence of the colonial powers put an indelible stamp on all of Africa. The artificial boundaries that were drawn up in Europe at the Conference of Berlin in 1885 separated people and languages. In many countries, the common or official language today is the language of the previous occupying European power. While British English is the countrywide language in Sierra Leone, the people to the north in Guinea speak French. The people to the south in Liberia use American

113

terminology. Each colonial power left a legacy of legal systems, educational organization, medical practice, transportation systems, and, to some extent, religious organization; for example, the Anglican church is the Church of Sierra Leone as well as the Church of the Province of Kenya. Guinea and the Ivory Coast are strongly influenced by the Catholic Church.

From April of 1955 until October, I spent my time traveling across the United States. My first experience was in the northeast where there were very few EUB churches. The meeting was in Quincy, Massachusetts. It was a two-day meeting, and I was scheduled to speak six times. In my inexperience, I attempted to do this. I wouldn't be so foolish to try this today. What in the world did I talk about?

My stepmother insisted that I had to be properly dressed. I had a quiet blue suit, gloves, and a small blue and white hat that I wore when I was speaking.

At this meeting, as it usually happened, I was housed with a family of the church and shared a room and bed with an officer of the national women's society. Although the information sent out about our visit requested that we have a private room or at least single beds, this was seldom provided. As a result, my sleep was disturbed as I tried to accommodate to unfamiliar bed partners. (Men were lucky. There was rarely, if ever, a man traveling from the office so men had private rooms and no bed partners.) Often there were hours of conversation at the expense of sleep.

My companion during this visit was a comfortable, friendly woman. At breakfast, my roommate suggested hopefully, "Since it will be an informal meeting, I don't suppose we need to wear our hats." Our hostess drew herself up regally and proclaimed, "We ALWAYS wear hats to church." Timidly, we complied.

I found later that in rural, midwestern areas, few women wore hats, and I stopped wearing mine. On one trip I left it behind on the train, perhaps not accidentally, and never replaced it.

During that furlough in addition to Massachusetts, I traveled to Pennsylvania, Ohio, and upper New York state. I took a long trip to Missouri, Texas, and California, all by train. After a conference in San Francisco, I had some free time and took the train north to Portland where I visited friends and relatives, then up the Columbia River Gorge, and on the way home stopped in North Dakota to visit cousins. The trip gave me a chance to see a broad expanse of the United States and satisfied my urge to travel and see new country.

In preparation for my return to Sierra Leone, I had hoped to be able to buy a car. Having a vehicle would allow me to transport women in complicated labor to the hospital. Secondly, it would give me some freedom to move about the country and would help in getting supplies. Many friends had encouraged this, and there were numerous offers of money for that purpose, but the mission rules forbade the acceptance of such gifts. We were not allowed to accept any gift over $100 from friends so I went to headquarters to plead my case, but the executive secretary was adamant. The rules could not be challenged. A stormy scene followed with accusation in both directions. I am always disgusted with myself when in such situations, I am reduced to tears which allows the discussion to deteriorate. I was crying in anger, but that didn't change anything. I left Dayton without permission to own a car.

PART II:

Romance
and Diamonds

NOVEMBER 1955 TO NOVEMBER 1958

CHAPTER 22

Changes in Tiama

In October of 1955, I made preparations to return to Sierra Leone. Gone was the euphoria of a new adventure. Although I had made up my mind to return, I was much more aware of the problems of loneliness, the frustrations of coping with the lack of supplies, and the struggle to understand and speak the local language. I boarded the train to New York beset with many doubts. I was tempted to get off the train and go back home, but I kept on the journey.

This time I was traveling directly to West Africa by cargo boat— it was probably my most pleasant trip. I shared the journey with two American missionary families, three French-Canadian priests, and a Sierra Leonean woman who was returning to Freetown to be married. They were a congenial group. We usually spent the evenings after dinner on the deck playing parlor games and having long, friendly discussions.

Once at a conference in Sierra Leone, a visiting theologian had remarked that the slow travel of the early days offered a distinct advantage to travelers. A walk of several days from one village to another allowed time for reflection. The absence of haste enabled people to be more deliberate in their decisions. Now this long sea voyage, both to and from West Africa, gave me a wonderful opportunity for rest, relaxation, and reflection. I think I appreciated this particular voyage for these reasons. It had been a hectic year in the United States, now there was time to think and plan for the coming three years.

The arrival in Freetown was different from the first time. In 1953, a new quay had been completed called the Queen Elizabeth II Quay. Freetown has one of the best natural harbors in the world. Now ships were able to dock at the quay and one could walk down the gangplank to dry land.

Tiama had seen important changes as well. The new dispensary was finished and stood on the land where the maternity building had stood. The new building had two rooms at each end and a long, covered veranda in the center where patients waited to be seen. The rooms at one end held the treatment and medicine room and the room where patients were examined and diagnosed. The rooms at the other end were used for the baby and antenatal clinics.

The old maternity building had been torn down and a new 12-bed facility was being built. During the construction, we used the antenatal room at the clinic for deliveries.

A new missionary residence had also been built on the same piece of land. Prior to its construction, there was talk of acquiring land outside the village for the residence. I was strongly opposed to the idea because I didn't want to live in an isolated area by myself. I enjoyed being in the middle of the town, close to neighbors and surrounded by all the sounds of town: drumming, dancing, singing, the Muslim call to prayer, the ring of church bells. Secondly, I thought the patients, particularly pregnant women, would be reluctant to travel outside the town at night to call me. I would be delayed in getting into town for deliveries and caring for sick children. Even as it was, I sometimes missed deliveries when I had to sprint the block from my house to the maternity unit. I would miss even more deliveries if I had to run seven or eight blocks.

The new house was a duplex, each side with two bedrooms, a large living room, and a bathroom. Space for a kitchen for each half was provided, but the second one was never equipped for use and became storage space. These rooms were separated from the house by

Tiama Dispensary.

Living room of the new missionary residence.

a covered veranda built over a large cistern, and a water tank was installed over the ceiling of the house. The water was pumped from the cistern to the tank with a hand pump so that there was running water in the bathroom and the kitchen. Across the front of the house was a small screened veranda which offered a lovely view of the town with the church off to the west.

The construction of these buildings was supervised by an American builder from Illinois. Legends abound about this man. When we get together for reunions, we still repeat "Pa Brown" stories. He was a big man, husky with a booming voice. He was supervising buildings at three stations: Moyama, Tiama, and Jaiama. The distance between Moyamba and Tiama was only about 40 miles, but it was another 150 miles to Jaiama. His major means of transportation was a motorcycle which he drove at reckless speeds. On occasion, he borrowed a mission vehicle which he used to transport building materials to the detriment of the vehicle. The heavy loads of sand, cement or roofing sheets were enough to break the springs or cause problems with the brakes of these small passenger vans.

It was obvious that Pa Brown had no amorous intentions of us single females. He was happily married to his wife, who was back in Illinois, and was the joyous father of several children. In Sierra Leone, however, he was alone. How could we house and feed him without offending the local customs? It was against the custom for any woman living without a husband to entertain a single man in her house. If she did so, the town buzzed with gossip about their suspected behavior.

Pa Brown made his headquarters at Harford School in Moyamba where he managed to engender some hostility. Since he worked irregular hours, he would be late for meals or expect breakfast before dawn. Some people found his booming voice irritating. He usually dressed very casually, rumpled shorts, open-necked shirts, heavy workshoes on his feet, but he was good-natured and good-hearted. He would carry small packages and letters from station to station or stop and shop along the way and purchase items that we asked for.

Housing in Tiama and Jaiama presented additional problems but the missionary in Jaiama and I both managed. At Tiama he used one of the bedrooms on the other side of the duplex. I rather enjoyed his visits, he was good company. He had spent some time in Nigeria doing a similar job, and had good stories about his travels. We always had stimulating conversation. He was easy to cook for and he broke the loneliness at Tiama.

The construction of the buildings at Tiama was under the supervision of a local contractor, and Pa Brown visited occasionally to make sure things were going properly. The local contractor and I didn't always agree, but since I was a woman and didn't know anything about building, I could safely be ignored.

I have mentioned that one of my eccentricities is my appreciation for tub baths. For years, I had tolerated the galvanized washtub, and I was determined to have a proper bathtub in my new home. I had even threatened to tow one behind the ship when I came back from the United States. The bathroom was planned to have a bathtub and a flush toilet. I made daily visits to the building site to observe the progress. One day, to my dismay, I discovered the bathroom was being built so the door from the bedroom opened into the middle of the wall where the tub was to be installed. The wall was already built up about two feet.

"You made a mistake." I protested to the contractor. "You've put the door right where the tub is to be placed."

"Oh no, Madame," he insisted. "The door must go on that wall."

"Yes, on that wall, but at the end of the wall, not in the middle."

"Madame, I know where the door is to be placed," he insisted.

"Let me look at the floor plan," I demanded. He pulled it out. "You see, here, the door is to be at the end of the wall, not in the middle."

We argued for some time, but I wasn't winning. The next day when I went to look at the building, the wall had been changed and the door was at the end of the wall, leaving space for the tub.

The new maternity building had a long central ward with eight beds. At the west end of the ward were two private isolation rooms. The delivery room was on the east end of the building. All three buildings: the dispensary, the maternity unit, and the residence were built of cement blocks and covered with zinc roofs called "pan" by the local people.

The buildings were located on a small hill that sloped down towards the center of town. The house was on the highest point of the hill which gave a good view of the town. The maternity unit was placed so the delivery room was elevated on the lower part of the hill. While this allowed good light in through the windows, it was tall enough so no one could look in the windows.

Although I was ignorant of construction methods, I watched the progress with great interest. One day, when Pa Brown visited, I voiced my curiosity about the roof on the maternity unit. It was about half completed. I had never seen a roof where the ends of bolts stuck up through the roof. Pa Brown was furious and immediately began to berate the construction manager. It seems that there were aluminum bolts and iron bolts. Pa had specifically bent some of the bolts. Instead of using the aluminum bolts, the contractor had used the iron bolts and not only that, he had reversed them so that the ends stuck up through the roof. Apparently there was a chemical reaction between iron bolts and zinc sheets causing an erosion of the zinc. All of the roofing already in place had to be removed and replaced, this time with the proper bolts.

One Saturday Pa Brown had made several trips between Tiama and Moyamba carrying supplies. Late in the afternoon, he stopped at my house. I encouraged him to have supper and stay, but he felt he had to return to Moyamba. To my surprise, about 10:00 p.m. he suddenly appeared at the door. About ten miles from town, the vehicle had broken down. He was close to the village of Lago and he went to ask the headman for a place to sleep for the night. The headman was very accommodating and asked Pa Brown, as was the courteous custom, which of his wives Pa would like to sleep with. Pa decided it might be better to return to Tiama and avoid the embarrassment.

Another Pa Brown incident took place in Jaiama where he was also supervising the building of a dispensary and maternity unit. Jaiama is situated in a very rocky part of Sierra Leone, and the church compound was dotted with large rocks. A particularly big rock was next to the medical residence and Pa Brown felt it needed to be demolished. He bored a hole in the rock and laid a dynamite charge. The rock splintered and several pieces flew over the house, including one large piece that crashed through the hammock where the watchman usually slept.

At one time, Pa Brown took a long holiday and rode his motorcycle across West Africa to northeastern Nigeria where he had also supervised construction for the Nigerian church. The distance is about 1,000 miles over rough country, some of it only crossed by bush paths. He made it safely there and back to our great relief.

CHAPTER 23

Smallpox

Upon my return in October 1955, there were several different missionary faces in Sierra Leone. Miss Vesper had finally retired, and the person in charge of the Jaiama clinic was Joy Thede who came from Missouri. She and her husband, a young seminary student, had planned to go as missionaries to Japan where Paul's parents had served. During their first year of marriage, Paul had been killed in an automobile accident. Joy was determined to continue as a missionary. The board sent her to England for midwifery training and she then came to Sierra Leone.

At Bo, Clyde Galow, a single male, was working at the Bible School. There had not been a single male missionary in our group for many years. Since there were plenty of single women at each station, the Africans decided which of "their" missionaries should marry Mr. Galow.

One day I was having a lively discussion with the staff about the criteria of beauty among white women. I was promoting Joy Thede as the personification of American beauty.

"After all," I said, "she has been married and the rest of us haven't."

"Oh," said Musu, "why don't you ask Mr. Galow to marry you?"

"It isn't that I don't like Mr. Galow, but I have no intention of marrying him," I said. "Besides, that's not the way we do things in America. Do you ask a man to marry you?"

"No," she replied. "We wait until the man asks our family for us."

"We wait, too, until he asks."

Before long the girl that Clyde was interested in arrived in Tiama. She was Gladys Fahner and they had been college classmates. From March until December of 1956, she and I lived and worked together. It was a harmonious relationship, and we are still the best of friends. We shared mutual interests, music, books, and handiwork as well as our professional interests. She was also a nurse-midwife as were several other missionary nurses. We had all trained at St. Alfege's Hospital in Greenwich, England, and Joy and I had lived with the same senior midwife while we did our domiciliary midwifery.

Clyde visited us in Tiama frequently. He, too, enjoyed music and had a good singing voice. One of our favorite pastimes was to sing together. We could all read music fairly well and did the old favorite hymns, but also experimented with modern gospel music and choruses.

John, the cook, didn't like Clyde. We could always be sure that when Clyde came we got poorly cooked food, burned toast, and the oldest linen, complete with holes, to cover the table.

During the missionary conference in August, Clyde and Gladys became engaged. The wedding was planned for the first of January 1957 in the Tiama church.

Between August and December I was assigned to relieve two other midwives at other stations. In September I went to Rotifunk while Metra Heisler was on vacation. In October I went to Jaiama while Joy had her leave.

The two stations offered widely different experiences. Rotifunk had a 40-bed hospital, several missionaries including Dr. Silver, and a large African staff. Jaiama, like Tiama, had a small dispensary and a 12-bed maternity unit. There was a missionary midwife in charge and a small African staff, headed by a wise and efficient midwife name Yumba Pettiquoi.

Both stations presented language challenges. The principle language used in Rotifunk was Temne which has no relationship to Mende. The hospital served a wide geographic area and many languages were used. Fortunately, some people could speak Krio so I could function using that. Occasionally, a patient came who was a Mende speaker and I could use my proficiency in Mende.

Jaiama was in the Kono district. The Kono language has a close association with Mende, and many people could "hear" that is, understand Mende, so that although I couldn't "hear" Kono, when I spoke in Mende people could usually "hear" me.

It was during this time that I saw my first cases of smallpox; the beginning of an epidemic that lasted 18 months and covered most of West Africa. There had not been a generalized vaccination program so most of the population was at risk.

Smallpox was a deadly disease. Historical accounts tell of great epidemics that swept across Europe and Asia with many thousands of deaths among the unprotected population. In the seventeenth century in England as many as one in every fourth death was due to smallpox. The epidemics in North and South America after the arrival of the Europeans were devastating to the local populations.

One account reports that the earliest case in the western

hemisphere was carried by a slave from Africa who came with the Spanish explorers.

Although vaccination had been practiced in Asia for hundreds of years, it was not known in Europe until Lady Mary Wortley Montague had her children vaccinated in Turkey in April 1717. She sent this information back to England, but it was not until 1796 that Edward Jenner started to use vaccination. Slowly, the process gained acceptance. Governments made vaccination compulsory and during the first half of the twentieth century, countries in Europe and North American were free of smallpox. But in the developing world, only small numbers of local people had been vaccinated, and the rest were vulnerable to the disease. In 1967, the World Health Organization (WHO) developed a world-wide immunization program. The last case of smallpox was seen in Somalia in October 1977 and in 1979, WHO declared global eradication of smallpox.

The disease had an incubation period of 11 to 14 days. The earliest symptoms were a sudden onset of fever, malaise, headache, severe backache, and total prostration. After two to four days, the temperature fell and a rash appeared which was followed by blisters and pustules. One of the characteristics was that the blisters were at the same level of development all over the body. The lesions were most prominent on the face and extremities but could cover the entire body. Often the lesions on the face would leave permanent, disfiguring scars. The patient was most infectious from three to eight days after the onset of fever. If death occurred, it could happen as early as the third day. Death rates were as high as 50 percent. There was no cure for the disease nor any means to prevent death. Analgesics could be used to relieve discomfort, but they would not stop the progress of the disease.

In 1956 I saw the first two cases of smallpox while I was working in Rotifunk. Two patients were admitted to the hospital. The staff had cordoned off one of the wards and the affected patients were confined to this area. The arrangement wasn't satisfactory, for within a few days the number of affected patients increased rapidly. The chiefdom health officer organized an area at the edge of town where there was an effort to isolate patients.

When I got to Jaiama the next month, there were increasing numbers of cases. Again the local officials attempted to isolate people who had smallpox, but with little success.

When I returned to Tiama in November of 1956, I was determined that Tiama would be spared so we started an extensive program of vaccination. The first problem was getting the vaccine which could only be obtained from one of the larger health centers. The EUB hospital in Rotifunk had a supply and was willing to share it with Tiama, but the vaccine had to be kept refrigerated. Today, WHO has a well-detailed and carefully thought out "cold chain" whereby a vaccine is kept refrigerated from the source until it is given to patients. If the vaccines are not kept chilled, they lose their effectiveness. We solved the problem of transporting the vaccine by using ordinary thermos flasks. One of the staff members, usually Francis Ngegba, took one day to travel to Rotifunk on the train and the next to return. Apparently, only once did the system fail when a man who had been vaccinated turned up several weeks later with smallpox.

The whole staff turned into vaccinators. The method used was to put a drop of the serum onto the skin of the left upper arm and then scratch it into the skin with a sharp needle. When the epidemic became more widespread, the government insisted that only trained vaccinators could do the procedure. Abraham Lavaly attended the required course and then did all the vaccinations. (See colorplate 4).

We made stringent rules. No one could be treated at the clinic, including the baby clinic, unless they were vaccinated. Smallpox vaccination leaves a very visible scar so that it was obvious if the patient had been protected.

I announced the rules one morning at the baby clinic where about 150 mothers had brought their children. Within ten minutes, the

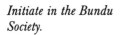
Initiate in the Bundu Society.

veranda was completely empty. We were undeterred. School children were forced to come for vaccination. Gradually, patients not only submitted to vaccination, but people began to request it.

Early in January, a group of adolescent girls were gathered in the "Bundu Bush." This was an enclosed area on the edge of town where the puberty initiation rites were performed. The area was off-limits to all men and usually to non-circumcised women, including me. On a few occasions, I had been asked to go into the bush to see and treat sick patients. Now the request came for me to come and vaccinate the girls. I agreed if I could bring my camera and take pictures. We came to a mutual agreement, and all the girls who were undergoing the initiation ceremonies were vaccinated. (See colorplate 5).

Requests for vaccinations started coming from the surrounding villages. Abraham was spending several days each week carrying out his task. In one village, a stubborn old man, the father of one of our teachers, refused vaccination. A few weeks later, he arrived at the clinic with a full-blown case of smallpox.

As a result of our vigorous program, only five cases developed in our area. One of the earliest was a teenage daughter of one of the teachers. The family rushed her off to Freetown where they hoped she might be given medicine to cure the disease. They were probably not received with welcome. Patients who traveled only hastened the spread throughout the country.

The very last case I saw was in March of 1958, a child of about nine months completely covered with pustules. The baby was severely ill, but eventually recovered.

The WHO deserves the credit for relieving the world of this dreaded disease. Since then they have focused their attention on eradicating several other scourges, notably polio and guinea worm. Their efforts to defeat malaria have been less successful.

CHAPTER 24

Clyde and Gladys' Wedding

Clyde and Gladys were to be married on January 1, 1957. Originally, they had planned to be married in the chapel at Harford School, but in Sierra Leone weddings could only be held in a church so they decided to be married in the Tiama church. The celebrations were a mixture of British, American, and Sierra Leonean customs.

Part of the American celebration was a wedding shower. We managed to surprise Gladys totally. On the morning of the shower several weeks before the wedding, Dr. Winnie Bradford arrived from Bo. Gladys was pleasantly surprised since Winnie didn't visit very often. Then some folks arrived from Harford School and she gradually realized what was happening.

Unfortunately for me, I missed the whole event when I developed one of my rare tension headaches and spent the whole day in bed trying to recover. My headaches tend to leave me totally incapacitated. Winnie gave me some sedation and went to join the others.

The shower was a huge success with most of the EUB missionaries in the country attending. As a joke, the shower gifts were canned foods with the labels removed. Pa Brown submitted cans of dog food. Gladys promised that when someone came to visit them, she would open a can and serve whatever it held, dog food or not.

Many people were involved in the wedding preparations. Gladys chose Joy Thede as her matron of honor while Clyde chose Jack Thomas, a missionary who shared teaching responsibilities with him at the Bible School. For their second attendants they each chose an African friend. We had long teased Musu about being married in the Tiama church, to which she always responded vehemently, "No one will ever get me to walk down that long aisle." But when Gladys asked her to be in the wedding party, she immediately agreed. I was to be the organist. Dr. Leader conducted the ceremony. The women involved in the ceremony wore dresses of identical material, a summery nylon, but of different colors. The dresses were calf-length with full skirts while the blouses had a bateau neckline and short sleeves. I made my own dress, blue, of course, while one of the missionaries at Rotifunk made the others.

Prior to the day, Gladys and I had discussed how to handle deliveries the day of the wedding. Of course, we hoped there wouldn't be any, but early in the evening of December 31, three women appeared in labor. Gladys offered to take care of the patients since I was supervising most of the activities the next day. Gladys went down and did two of the deliveries. The babies were a boy and a girl who were promptly dubbed Clyde and Gladys. Which became Cride and Gradys by the local people, (in many African languages, including Mende, the sounds of L and R are interchangeable). That left one patient still in labor. We asked missionaries Betty Beveridge and Metra Heisler if they would help us in case of an emergency. When they arrived, they took over the work in the maternity unit. It was a complicated delivery, and eventually, they had to call Dr. George Harris to deliver the baby with forceps.

That morning Clyde and Mrs. Leader, both of whom had great talents for arranging flowers, covered the altar and platform with local flowers and greens, including sprays of bougainvillea and poinsettia.

All things went well. Clyde had asked Mrs. Leader to represent his parents and Gladys had chosen Marge Hager who came from near her home in Michigan. Musu managed to walk the whole length of the aisle without mishap. Jack Thomas sang traditional American wedding music and the congregation sang some hymns. After the service everyone walked to the court barri in the center of town where we feasted on Jollof rice and wedding cake. (See colorplate 5).

CHAPTER 25

Put-To-Bed Women

In the Krio language there are very colorful phrases for pregnancy and childbirth. A woman who is pregnant is said to "get belly." When she delivers she is "put to bed." It can be compared to the phrases that we use in English when a delivered woman was said to be confined or lying-in when she had a baby. A famous maternity hospital in Chicago and another in Boston are still called the Lying-In Hospital, even though women don't lie in very long and certainly are not confined.

Since the beginning of time, babies have been delivered by midwives. We are sometimes called the world's second oldest profession. In most of the world outside the United States, babies are still delivered by midwives. In the developing world, where the midwives are often untrained, they are called Traditional Birth Attendants (TBA). The World Health Organization (WHO) has encouraged many countries to provide training for these people; almost always women.

In Sierra Leone, Dr. Milton Margai, who later became the first Prime Minister, was the first Protectorate person to be trained as a doctor. He began to use the existing social structures for disseminating knowledge about health practice. The secret society for women, the Bundu Bush, was the obvious place to start. In addition to encouraging educated African women to be the teachers in this enterprise, he also encouraged missionary women to visit the bush on a regular basis and talk about nutrition and childcare.

Most of the TBA's were illiterate, but a few of them could read and write. Gradually, I realized that one or two of the leaders in the local church were also local midwives. They had gained their knowledge during a long period of apprenticeship and were highly respected in the community. When they were unable to manage a delivery, the patient was brought to the hospital in hope that we could deliver the baby.

A local taboo forbade burying an undelivered woman. Someone in the village, probably a TBA, would cut open the abdomen and deliver the dead child. For this they charged a large amount of money. If they brought the living woman to us, it might be possible for us to deliver the baby even if it was dead or if the woman died. There was always the hope that we might be able to save both. In any case, our fees were only what we would charge for a normal delivery.

Both my equipment and supplies were limited. In particular, I had no intravenous fluids or any means of giving pitocin, a drug which is given intravenously which will stimulate contraction in the uterus both in labor and afterwards in the event of postpartum hemorrhage. I had none in stock and probably would have been too frightened to use it in labor since it can be very dangerous. If it causes contractions that last too long, it can deprive the fetal brain of oxygen, causing brain damage or death. If the delay in labor is due to obstruction such as a pelvis that is too small or a malpresentation of the fetus, the stimulation of the pitocin can bring uterine rupture which is usually fatal to both mother and baby.

We did have obstetric forceps and drop ether for an anesthetic. Abraham Lavaly had some knowledge of using both, and on rare occasions, I would ask him to come and help, but there was a strong aversion to having a man in the maternity unit. If I decided to ask Abraham for help, the women present were most reluctant.

"Can't you try a little longer?" they would ask.

During those years, my knowledge and skills improved, and I developed some strong opinions about how labor and delivery should be managed. More than once I turned to my obstetric textbook, read a procedure, attempted it, returned to the textbook, and looked for something else. It was only by God's grace that I didn't lose more mothers and babies. Certainly, this was not due to my great skills.

In one instance, the patient had a severe postpartum hemorrhage, and there didn't seem to be any precipitating circumstances. The placenta had come out easily and seemed to be intact. The labor had been pretty normal, and there was nothing to suggest an over-stretched uterus. I massaged the uterus and administered the medications I had to make the uterus contract, but the bleeding continued. It lasted about 36 hours, during which time I stayed with the patient. In retrospect, I am sure there was a cervical tear, a condition that sometimes happens with a rapid delivery. Uterine massage and medications are not effective in stopping this type of bleeding, but I had not been taught how to inspect the cervix, nor how to repair it. This is a relatively simple procedure, but again, it was something that I had neither the knowledge or the skill to manage. Eventually, the bleeding stopped and the woman recovered. I warned her not to deliver in the village for the next pregnancy since there might be a recurrence of the bleeding. Two years later she had another pregnancy and delivered at home. Again she hemorrhaged and this time she died.

In another instance, a young woman came with a prolapsed uterus. In this condition, the uterus descends through the vagina, and in this woman, it was partially outside her body. This condition is often the result of a complicated labor and delivery. There are several methods of treatment, including surgery, but there were few surgeons in Sierra Leone. Even if there had been one who was skilled in this procedure, the treatment would have been costly. She probably would not have been able to carry a pregnancy to term with this condition. Although she became pregnant several times after this, each one ended in spontaneous abortion.

Equally sad were the women who either could not conceive because of a previous pelvic infection or who had spontaneous abortions for the same reason. This happened to the wife of one of our teachers. She had a severely retroverted uterus where the uterus is tipped backwards toward the spinal column rather than bending forward in the normal position. In this case, the uterus was bound in place by adhesions from an old infection. The couple wanted a child badly. She finally became pregnant only to lose the pregnancy in a few weeks.

In most of Africa, it was of supreme importance for a woman to have a child. The child signified her status in the community; a childless woman was despised, rejected, and often the butt of ridicule. Sterility could be a cause for divorce. The woman was often sent out of the house, left to fend for herself.

One of the most difficult problems I had to face was what to do when there was a woman with an obstructed labor. For many years, the closest hospital was the government hospital at Bo, 60 miles away. The unpaved road was rough, and in the rainy season, very slippery. In the early years, the one big river we had to cross had no bridge but had to be crossed by a ferry that only operated during the daylight hours. While it was possible at night to wake the crew that ran the ferry, it was not easy.

Once the decision was made to transport a patient to the hospital, a vehicle had to be found to make the journey. There were only three or four vehicles in town, and they were large trucks. The rear of the truck was covered with a roof and the walls were partially covered with a removable canvas cover. It was very expensive to hire one of these trucks. If we decided to go during the night, we had to find the driver and persuade him to take us. This process often took several hours. During the day sometimes all the trucks were out of town, and we had to wait until they returned.

I remember a case of obstructed labor that happened to the wife of one of our teachers. Mr. Sesay, the school carpenter, a heavyset, placid, cheerful man, had married a young, slim woman whose cheerful disposition matched his own. Her pregnancy proceeded without trouble, but the labor was another matter. It progressed very slowly. I finally decided we would have to take her to Bo.

During those early years, Pastor Carew had a small, rickety paneled truck. I appealed to him to take Mrs. Sesay to the hospital. We put a mattress in the back of the van and the patient lay on that. Mr. Sesay and several friends rode with us in the back of the van with the patient. I sat in front with Pastor Carew. Some of the floorboards were missing and the dust rolled up through the floor. Pastor used to say that the van was a great leveler. When he and I reached our destination, we were the same color, a reddish-grey from the dust on the road.

It was probably midnight when we got to the ferry. The crew was on the other side of the river. We shouted and tooted the car horn and finally aroused them. The ferry was propelled across to us by men grabbing a rope that was strung across the river. The truck was loaded on the ferry and the process was repeated, carrying us to the other side. We reached Bo safely, the baby was delivered with forceps, and all was well. Two years later Mrs. Sesay came back with her second pregnancy, and as is often the case, she had a quick and easy delivery in Tiama.

On another occasion, I also took a woman to Bo. She had been brought to Tiama with an obstructed labor and I couldn't manage the delivery. She was in dreadful pain and cried all during the journey to the hospital. I had been reluctant to sedate her with morphine, due to the effect on the baby, but it was the only pain reliever I had. We managed to reach the hospital and the baby was delivered but the woman died within a few minutes. The incident made me very reluctant to transport patients unless I was convinced that they would survive the ordeal. The journey had only intensified the woman's suffering and the trip had been very expensive for the family.

One other journey to Bo was more successful. The labor had been long and slow. The cervix dilated to nine centimeters and stayed there for 24 hours. By this time, there was a bridge across the river. We got to the hospital about 10:00 p.m.

The doctor wasn't there but the patient was admitted. The head nurse in the delivery room was a Krio who piled abuse on my head. Her Krio speech was so rapid I couldn't understand everything she said, but I understood enough to know she had nothing but scorn for my knowledge and judgment.

"Why did you bring this woman here? She is fully dilated and will deliver soon," the nurse said.

"I don't think so," I replied. "She has been in labor for several days. The cervix is nine centimeters and will not dilate any further."

"You are wrong. There is nothing wrong with this labor."

We waited. About midnight the doctor, a lovely young English woman, arrived.

The doctor confirmed my findings. "This patient is only nine centimeters, but the baby is healthy and I think we will have a safe delivery. We will rest the patient and attempt to stimulate the labor in the morning." She turned to me. "How did you get here? Do you plan to go back to Tiama tonight?"

I was so tired, the thought of the journey home was more than I could cope with. "I'll try to find a place to stay tonight and wait to catch a lorry home in the morning."

"Why don't you come home with me?" she offered. "I have an extra bed and you can get some sleep."

I gratefully accepted. As I got into bed I said, "I am so relieved that the woman is safe. It takes a big load off my shoulders."

Later she told me, "I thought the load just passed from one bed to the other."

A few hours later the doctor delivered a live baby and all was well.

Physicians were reluctant to deliver a baby by cesarean section because of the lack of surgical facilities in the country and poor availability for repeat sections. Although it is sometimes possible for a woman to deliver vaginally after a section, it is not always possible. Since most sections were done because of obstructed labor, it was likely that the sections would have to be repeated with the next pregnancy.

Although this chapter deals mostly with the problems of labor and delivery, we were able to conduct many successful deliveries in Tiama. The attendance at the antenatal clinic and the number of women coming in for deliveries gradually increased. I felt that several factors helped this increase. First, we never lost a baby from infantile tetanus. Secondly, we were able to safely deliver some women who had difficult labors, but we also tried to be gentle and caring to the laboring women. (See Colorplate 6).

One day a 16-year-old was struggling with a long, painful labor. As she paced up and down the ward, one of the older women with her said, "If we had you in the village, we would beat you good and you would have that baby."

The young woman replied, "That's why I'm here."

CHAPTER 26

Vacations

One of the missionaries said about Miss Nora Vesper, one of the older missionaries, that the reason she was able to stay in Sierra Leone for over 30 years was that she took a nap every afternoon and a vacation every year. She, apparently like a few others who came to West Africa, had a natural immunity to malaria since I don't remember her mentioning being ill.

With this in mind, I tried to follow her example about naps and vacations. Most days I got my afternoon nap, or at least I laid down for a few minutes even if I didn't fall asleep.

But yearly vacations were more difficult to manage. Sierra Leone, unlike some African countries, Kenya and Rhodesia, for example, had very few natural physical attractions to lure tourists. Nor were there well-organized tourist facilities.

After my first vacation in September 1952, I quickly realized that visiting other mission stations was not a very satisfactory solution to the problem. In escaping from the difficulties at the home place, you were apt to be bombarded with the worries of other stations. Since I had arrived in Tiama in January 1952, I had been no further away than 12 miles to Mano. I was curious about the other mission sites so I traveled by train to Bo, the site of the newest EUB station.

The provisional headquarters of the government were at Bo. A large government hospital was located there as was the prominent Bo Secondary School for Boys. A number of well-stocked shops and a lively open-air market offered opportunities for shopping.

Several EUB churches had been established in the city, and the new Bible training school was being built. The school was situated on a small hill on the northern edge of the city. In December 1952, only one building had been completed, the house where the missionaries Charles and Bertha Leader lived. A large, multipurpose, two-story building was under construction with classrooms and a small auditorium for large meetings. Eventually, the compound contained six houses, a primary school, a church, and several other classrooms.

Initially designed to prepare evangelists and local preachers, the school offered a number of educational programs over the years, including courses in carpentry, masonry, and typing.

Fortified by Mrs. Leader's good cooking, I took the train down country where I spent a few days in Moyamba at Harford School, Rotifunk and then went on to Freetown.

I was met by the superintendent and his wife. I spent the next four days answering all her questions about the people and events up country. I was embarrassed and dismayed by being treated as a source of information about everybody's activities.

But I was finally able to see Freetown. It was an exciting city in those days. Big shops dominated the center of town–P.Z.'s was owned by a British firm and had the characteristics of a department store selling food, tools, sewing materials; Choithrams was operated by East Indians and competed with P.Z.'s.

The big open-air markets displayed fresh fruits and vegetables, seafood and meat as well as articles of clothing.

It seemed to me that you could buy anything in Freetown after shopping in Tiama where the purchases were limited to margarine and sugar. The Church Missionary Society (CMS) under the sponsorship of the Church of Sierra Leone, had shelves overflowing with books of every description as well as stationery, knitting patterns, crochet hooks and greeting cards–all on display in this wonderful place. In Little East Street, shops offered cloth, shoes, headties, and kitchen equipment. In all those years, I never visited the local markets. How could I have been so neglectful?

Just west of the main commercial area, perched on a small hill, was Fort Thornton the home of the British Governor General. Down the hill and slightly north was the enormous cottonwood tree where it was reported that slaves were penned between great protruding roots during the days of slave trading.

Freetown offered several delightful sites for vacation. On the top of Mount Aureol in the center of the peninsula was Leicester, a cluster of residences. Here the early missionaries had built a rest house, a big roomy affair. Built there for the same reason the British colonial authorities had built their residences on the side of the mountain at Hill Station, it was above the mosquito line and offered some protection from malaria. The house had been built to face the Rokel River at the point where it flows into the Atlantic. The view was spectacular. There was a great expanse of green on the mountain that sloped to the sea. Close to the house were the buildings of Fourah Bay College, soon to be called the University College of

Parliment House, Freetown.

Sierra Leone. Beyond that were the streets and buildings of Freetown.

One of the disadvantages of Leicester House was that it was inaccessible by road. A road ended about 500 feet below the house and then one had to walk the rest of the way. All supplies had to be carried up this path to the house. Usually the house was only occupied by people on vacation, but it was also used as a residence when there was a shortage of missionary housing in Freetown. In the 1970's a road was made to the top of the mountain and the house was used more frequently.

Then there were the beaches of Freetown on the western end of the peninsula. It has been said that Freetown has some of the finest beaches in the world. The long expanse of sand is followed by a gradual slope of the ocean floor. The undertow was very slight so that it was safe to swim in this part of the Atlantic. Only scattered houses and villages were situated along the beach. I presume that sun-bathing and swimming were not common recreations for the early missionaries so the house was built at Leicister. But increasingly, we chose to spend a vacation at the beach. A house was purchased at Hamilton Beach close to the shore which gave opportunity to spend time in the sun and sand. Later the use of malaria prophylaxis allowed people to spend time along the water with less fear of becoming ill.

I took my next vacation in March 1954 and traveled to Jaiama in the Kono district on the far eastern border of the country. Jaiama was not on the train line but was about 50 miles north of the end of the line. You traveled to Pendembu and then made the rest of the trip by car or lorry. If you were fortunate, you could catch a ride with a friend. If not, you took your chances on finding space on a crowded lorry. I was lucky and caught a ride with a friend.

The CMS had a bookshop in Bo as well as in Freetown. The manager was an energetic Englishman by the name of Ted Stapleford. Ted was living on the Bible school compound so we all knew him well. In addition to the bookshop, Ted ran a traveling book-van. It was a large truck outfitted in the back with shelves and book racks. Books of all kinds were for sale. Some of them were religious in content, including Bibles, and there was printed material in several languages. In addition, the van carried common, non-religious items that were scarce in small towns:stationery, pens, thread, needles, and crochet hooks.

Ted was taking the van to the eastern province, and I went along as a passenger, but I had to "earn" my way. I started out by selling the crochet hooks and thread and did a thriving business. Very early in the trip, a man bought a Mende primer.

Then he said, "But I can't read."

I had done some work with teaching people in Tiama to read, using the Laubach method which uses simple drawings and phonetics. Most of the local languages had been put into print around the turn of the century using a phonetic system. In the early stages, therefore, it was possible to teach someone how to read without understanding the grammar or even the meaning of words. The man brought the primer, and he and I sat down on a stone alongside the road and started to read.

This scene was to be repeated at almost every town we visited. People were eager to learn to read, and materials were available, but there were few people ready to teach reading. Laubach's motto was "Each one, teach one," so that the person who had learned to read was encouraged to teach others how to read.

The journey ended at Jaiama where Miss Vesper was the missionary in charge of the clinic and maternity unit similar to the one at Tiama. I had met Miss Vesper in 1945 when she was visiting Wisconsin as a missionary speaker. Although at that time I was planning to go to China, Miss Vesper inspired me with her vibrant witness and stories of fascinating adventures. She told of making health visits to remote rural areas where there was no modern medicine. In her concern for orphaned infants, she started a fund used to purchase dried milk to feed these infants. Contributions to the fund continued long after she retired and it was one of the funds that never lacked for money.

At Jaiama, the church operated a large primary school as well as a church. A young missionary couple with three small children also lived at the station.

I spent several days with Miss Vesper, then traveled north to Kayima with missionaries Jim McQuiston and Jack Thomas. Les and

Nimiyama Falls.

Winnie Bradford were living in Kayima. Their first child, Dorcas, had been born in November of 1953.

Kayima was at the end of the road on the far northeastern edge of Sierra Leone, close to the Guinea border. Les had been accepted as a missionary so the EUB could keep Winnie as a doctor. But once they were married, the couple decided that Les was the missionary and that they should be stationed where he could work most effectively, developing agricultural projects. They settled in Kayima where Winnie practiced medicine in a minimal way, limited by the lack of physical facilities, auxiliary help, and medications.

It was good to renew my friendship with the Bradfords and Dorcas was an additional attraction. Their house was on the south edge of town which had no electricity and only a limited water supply. Winnie had established a small clinic in town, and we walked there every day to see patients.

One of the physical attractions of the area was a rather large waterfall, the Nimiyama Falls, about five miles away from Kayima. There was no road to the falls so the three men and I walked on bush paths. Few people lived in this area, and I don't remember seeing any other villages. The path led through long stretches of uncut forest, called by the local people, a bush. Although the Africans rarely use the term, it was indeed a jungle. Les had used his time in Kono to good advantage and had a vast store of knowledge of local flora and fauna, including the names of most of the trees and flowers that we saw that day. He spotted a rare green mamba, a small but very dangerous tree snake, high in the branches of a tree. At one point, we waded through a stream where the water was as high as our waists.

At last we reached the waterfall, created when the Sewa River dropped some 30 feet. The placid, slow-moving stream turned into a torrent as it fell through the rocks with plumes of spraying water. It was worth the long walk to see this magnificent sight. Jim and I stayed at the top of the falls but Les and Jack climbed to the bottom where the falls became the lower reaches of the Sewa.

I had been told that if these falls were harnessed, they would provide enough electricity for the whole of Sierra Leone. I also thought it would be a great tourist attraction if accommodations would be provided.

I finished my visit with the Bradfords, spent a few days with Miss Vesper, and started home. Ted had long since gone back to Bo so I took public transportation, a crowded lorry. By some good luck, I got to ride in the cab with the driver.

The first hurdle to overcome was getting out of diamond territory. The area was controlled by the Sierra Leone Selection Trust (SLST) which had a monopoly on all diamond mining in this part of the country. There was limited access to diamond territory since only one road led into Kono. Widespread illicit mining and a brisk trade in diamond smuggling were a threat to the operations of SLST. When the lorry reached the boundary of the diamond area, all the passengers were made to get off and submit to a search of themselves and their luggage. The police exempted me and I sat in the cab of the lorry, waiting for the search to be completed.

The next snag was the ferry. It crossed the river south of Bunumbu. Normally, it operated during the daylight hours, but we got there after dark. We sat at the river's edge until the ferry crew could be roused on the other side of the river. Eventually, someone convinced them to come and carry us across.

As I sat in the dark lorry waiting for the ferry, there was a lot to think about. The mission had a rule that single women could not own and operate a vehicle. Presumably, it was too dangerous. I wondered if I would have been in any more danger driving a car under my own control than I was sitting in the lorry in the middle of the night. At last we crossed the river, and I got back to Bo to spend the rest of the night before going on to Tiama.

In 1962, while again living in Tiama, I took another vacation to Kono. This time I had three passengers with me–Esther Megill from

Rotifunk, one of the Harford teachers, and the wife of my African Pastor in Tiama. We also went to visit the falls. By now a road had been built close to the falls, and we were able to drive to within a few feet of the top. The area was uninhabited and the forest still uncut. What a wonderful place for a retirement cottage.

During my second tour, I was able to take a vacation outside of Sierra Leone. Don and Lilburne Theuer, who were then running the mission office in Freetown, invited me to go to Guinea with them. We were to fly from Freetown to Conakry, hire a car, and drive into the mountains to Dabola. In addition to the adults, one of the travelers was their daughter, Marlyn, about 18 months old.

The flight from Lungi airport to Conakry, about a 45-minute trip, went without incident. Guinea was a French Colony, and the contrast with the austere British colonialism was evident immediately. Conakry was laid out with broad, tree-lined streets and graced with lovely houses set on expansive lawns. There was a delightful, comfortable French hotel with great French cooking. We ate heartily.

Our first problem came the next morning when the rented car arrived. It was a very small French model. All three adults were rather tall, with Don being over six-foot. We had carried a generous amount of luggage, too. In the middle of the hotel lobby, Lilburne and I repacked the suitcases and were able to leave two behind in the hotel.

Don and Lilburne Theuer loading our vehicle in Conakry, Guinea.

We started for Dabola. The road was wide, paved and comfortable. Unfortunately, the hearty meals we had enjoyed the previous day returned to haunt us, and Lilburne and I developed severe diarrhea. There are no convenient service stations lining African roads to provide relief for such problems. Several times Don stopped the car while Lilburne and I headed for some convenient bushes. Don and Marlyn seemed to have avoided the problem.

About noon we stopped at a small restaurant with two bathrooms which Lilburne and I occupied. Don and Marlyn ate well. We started out again, only to continue our occasional stops. We eventually reached Dabola.

It was a beautiful place with the hotel perched on a high hill, providing a panoramic view of the surrounding mountains. We spent a quiet week reading, chatting, and recovering from our gastric ordeal.

One of Don's efforts that week was to try and teach me to play cards. During my childhood, playing cards was considered a sin only equal to dancing, smoking, and drinking liquor. When I lived alone in Tiama, I often wished I knew how to play solitaire to help while away the time. But I could never, and still can't, tell the difference between clubs and spades. By the end of the week, Don decided it was a hopeless cause, and I went back to Tiama reduced to playing six-handed Chinese checkers with myself.

Perhaps my most interesting trip was a visit to the city of Bonthe on Sherbro Island, a fairly large island on the Atlantic. Pastor Carew had to go for a supervisory visit for the church and invited me to go along. We took a lorry from Tiama to Mattru, a distance of about 50 miles. Mattru is on the Jong River which is the southern end of the Teye River that flows through Tiama. The Jong eventually empties into the Atlantic. At Mattru, we got into a small, motor-powered launch to make the trip to Bonthe. The trip took about four hours on the open sea.

At first glance, Bonthe looked like the remnant of nineteenth century England. Before the road and railroad were built in Sierra Leone, much of the country was approached from the sea. Both large ships and small boats carried goods and passengers along the coast. Earlier this included a heavy traffic in slave trading.

A large number of traders had settled in Bonthe, both Krio and Europeans. In 1900, half the trade in the territory was carried on in Bonthe. The island was administered as part of the Colony as opposed to the Protectorate, and was influenced by the presence of Krios, just as Freetown was. It has retained its Victorian charm. The streets were wide and shady; lined with great tall trees, mostly mangoes and breadfruit. Of course, there was no traffic since there were no motor vehicles

Residence in Bonthe.

on the island. Most of the houses were built of cement block and resembled houses in Victorian Britain. Spacious lawns surrounded each house and included flowering bushes such as hibiscus, alamanda, and bougainvilleas as well as small garden plots with paw-paw, pineapples, and yams.

The Krios brought their churches with them—Anglican, Methodist, and Baptist. The church buildings, too, resembled English parish churches. The UBC had also come to Bonthe, and the American-style building was a large, cement block structure. Its worship area was in the old Akron-style building so popular in American churches at the turn of the century, with the altar and pulpit in one corner of the sanctuary and the pews curved around in a semi-circle. (See Colorplate 6).

The African pastor and his wife, Rev. and Mrs. Gorvey, made both of us feel very welcome. Mrs. Gorvey was a high school graduate of the local secondary school and, I soon found out, a wonderful cook. In fact, my major impression of that weekend was being served four cooked meals a day. As soon as we arrived we were given tea and biscuits. Early every morning a wake-up cup of tea was delivered to my room. At noon we ate Jollof rice which included generous pieces of chicken and fish. Slices of plantain fried in palm oil made a delicious side dish. All of this cooking was done on a three-stone fire in a small kitchen behind the house.

The parsonage was a large, two-story building that resembled the other buildings in town. My bedroom was almost as big as my side of the duplex in Tiama. Each day a young child carefully swept my room as well as the rest of the house and grassless front yard.

By 1961 at the time of my visit, Bonthe had lost most of its economic importance. The harbor had silted up, and produce for the rest of the country was now shipped to Freetown by rail or road.

The parsonage family included two lovely little boys about five and seven. They offered to act as tourist guides, and we wandered through the town past shops, the once busy port, and through the market.

On Monday morning, Pastor and I got into the launch and went back to Mattru. These little boats are a bit fragile, and for someone who has a great dread of water, it was not altogether a pleasant experience. I was glad to know that I was going home.

CHAPTER 27

The Knight in Shining Armor

With Gladys gone I was not only lonely, but again I carried the responsibilities of the clinic by myself. During the next 12 months I was involved in one of the more interesting experiences of my time in Sierra Leone.

One night I had a patient in obstructed labor and decided to take her to the hospital at Bo. We had the usual problems of getting a lorry and driver. Two of the staff, Musu and Francis Ngegba, went with us as did several relatives. Musu and I sat in the cab with the driver, the patient lay on a mattress on the floor of the lorry, and the relatives sat on benches on either side.

We hired a local lorry to go as far as Mano, and then I asked Mrs. Hamud, the Lebanese trader, if her lorry and driver would take us to Bo. She agreed, but the driver was not very happy about it.

It was raining, and the dirt road was very slippery. The driver, with a show of bravado, drove with great speed. Several times the truck slid along the road. I asked him to go slower which only encouraged him to go at great speed. Finally, six miles from Bo he stopped the lorry and refused to go any further because I was "abusing" him. It was now about 2:00 a.m. If we delayed until daylight, I was afraid we would lose the mother or the baby, or both. I decided I would walk to Bo and get help. Once I got to the hospital they would probably send an ambulance out to get the woman.

I started walking. Musu, tears streaming down her face, walked with me.

"Please Ma," she pleaded. "Don't do this."

"But Musu," I responded, "if I don't get this woman to Bo, she may die."

"But Ma, this road is dangerous. There are thiefmen and evil spirits. They may come to hurt us."

"Musu," I insisted, "I am going for help. If you want to stay with the lorry, you go back."

I kept on walking. We had not walked very far when the driver

147

brought the vehicle alongside of us and picked us up. He apparently had decided that allowing me to walk to Bo would not only hurt his reputation, it would probably cost him his job.

We got the woman safely to the hospital. After she was admitted, the doctor in charge asked if I had a place to stay for the night.

"I will go out to the mission compound and stay," I replied.

"Will the lorry driver take you?"

"I wouldn't ride with that driver to the gate of the hospital," I responded.

"We will send a hospital car to carry you out to the mission compound," the doctor offered.

So Musu and I went out, woke up the Leaders, and got a place to sleep.

In the morning at breakfast there were two other guests—a woman and a Dutch doctor, named John Sustring. The doctor, in charge of the government hospital at Moyamba, was a tall, courtly man who had worked both in Indonesia, and in my hometown of Milwaukee. Much of our conversation that morning was spent in relating our adventure of the previous night.

After breakfast, Musu and I stopped at the hospital to find out that the woman had been safely delivered. Then we caught a lorry back to Tiama.

A few days later, I received a letter from Dr. Sustring, asking if he could write to me. Of course, letters were always welcome, and one often carried on an extensive correspondence with a seldom-seen friend in another part of Sierra Leone. Two weeks later, a second letter came, this time with a proposal of marriage. I was flattered and dumbfounded. My initial response was that while it was romantic, I couldn't imagine marrying a man based on one encounter that lasted an hour and two letters.

But the man was not to be discouraged. He continued to write frequently and occasionally drove to Tiama on a Saturday. We began to explore areas of mutual interests. We both liked classical music, and we shared a Christian commitment. Our interest in the health profession was a common bond. I had been very lonely after Gladys left, and the companionship and letters were most welcome. He was generous and often brought small gifts. I am sure that not many courtships are carried on with gifts of apples and cheese. There is little that is so flattering to a woman or such a boost to one's self-esteem as an honest declaration of love as well as a proposal of marriage.

But I was not ready to make a commitment. I was still determined to continue my missionary responsibilities, and I wasn't going to leave

Tiama without a nurse again. Eventually, John decided that he would apply to the Board of Missions to come to work for the Evangelical United Brethren Church. It was the ultimate concession, and I felt I could no longer refuse to marry him. We both wrote my parents and made the announcement to the missionary community. There were mixed reactions.

My father and my home church were delighted. My father never really forgave me for not marrying and the church immediately began making wedding plans. My father was to come out for the wedding. My stepmother, LaVile, began looking for a wedding dress, blue, of course. I still have it.

Some of my missionary friends were delighted. Clyde and Gladys, for example, rejoiced. But others, including Dr. Silver, felt I was making a serious mistake. The teachers at Moyamba who knew John well also had mixed reactions. A few of them were pleased that I was happy. Several others didn't like John and felt he was not a good choice for me. And one or two had determined that they wanted him to marry them and were jealous.

Despite my euphoria, I still had major doubts. John, like many Europeans, had deep contempt for many things American—table manners, food, classical music. While Americans often treat this sense of superiority with much humor and usually ignore it, it is not a very good basis for a marriage. Although John was about 20 years older than I, I felt that wasn't too much of a problem. After all, my father was 18 years older than my stepmother and they had a very happy marriage.

In addition, John had strong views about the role of women. One day he was at my house for a meal along with several other guests. Before we ate, I offered grace. Later he remonstrated with me, saying that offering prayers was a man's responsibility and that I should have asked him to pray.

One day he said, "Of course, after we are married you won't work in the clinic or at the hospital any more. You will be a housewife."

"But what will I do all day?" I asked. Housekeeping duties have never been high on my agenda.

"You will sit in the living room and sew a fine seam," was his answer.

That sounded pretty boring. It certainly couldn't compare to the thrill of delivering a baby.

I puzzled over this since one of the things he professed to admire about me was my ability to function in this remote rural clinic and my independence was a sore spot. Once, as we were traveling to Freetown in his car, he persistently gave me instructions about how to drive. Finally, I stopped the car and said, "When I drive, I drive, and when you drive, you drive, but don't tell me how to drive." There was a long silence for the rest of the journey.

Then there were our religious views. I have always had a rather liberal view of the Gospel. As part of a vigorous and effective African congregation, I did not feel an obligation to have any authority in the local church and was content to participate in the activities that were assigned to me. I was a midwife, not an evangelist. One day John asked me if I were really a Christian, and did I believe in the Bible.

I began to look at other areas where I thought we might have conflicts. One day, for example, he informed me that he was really lowering his standards by leaving government service and becoming a missionary doctor. I was also concerned about our having to share money management. Although I have never handled my own finances very well (and still don't) I had been managing my own money for over ten years. I wasn't quite ready to submit this matter totally to another person. St. Paul's injunction that women obey their husbands didn't look particularly attractive to me so I made some suggestions.

"I think there are some matters we should look at before we are married," I proposed.

"What do you have in mind?"

"Well, who handles the money? Who is responsible for the household? I don't think we should solve these now, but it would be a good idea to talk about them," I suggested.

John was dogmatic. "We will just take any problems we have and bring them to the Lord in prayer."

Privately, I thought, we needed to warn the Lord we were coming.

My doubts persisted. Gradually, I figured out the biggest obstacle confronting us. John didn't like Africans. Even my staff complained that he didn't know "how to greet," meaning that he was less than polite when dealing with them. He was aloof and unfriendly. He felt Africans were inferior. One of his comments was that God couldn't have made Africans because they were so ugly.

My house had always been open to both local people as well as to visitors of all nationalities. We ate together, worked together, and it was not unusual to have Sierra Leone guests use my spare bedroom. One Saturday afternoon, John and I were sitting in my living room when an elderly woman came to my door. Sometime earlier, her daughter had died in childbirth, and she had come with her grandchildren to live in Tiama. We had fed her baby grandson, and sponsored the older girl in school. It was common for her to visit me. I invited her into the living room, and we visited for a few minutes. After she left, John said, "After we are married, we will not allow such people to come into our house."

I think it was the last straw. I had visions of the two of us holed up in our little house, talking only to each other with no social contact with our neighbors. It was going to be a lonely life. Of all the differences between us, this would be the greatest.

A few days later when he came to visit, I told him I wanted to break off the engagement. He was angry and tried to convince me otherwise. He wanted to know why I had come to this decision, but I refused to give him any reasons, feeling that there were too many problems to even begin to unravel. His unwillingness to discuss any difficulties only compounded the matter. Finally, he drove off to Moyamba.

The weekly mail for the United States left Tiama on Monday morning and I usually wrote my weekly letter on Sunday. I decided not to write this news until the next weekend. But John, who had been corresponding regularly with my father, wrote that night. When his letter arrived, my father was furious.

"What is she doing? Doesn't she have any sense?" he exploded. (I learned this from him later.) "I will write at once and tell her what I think about this and that she is making a big mistake."

LaVile urged caution. "You don't know why she has done this. Wait until you hear from her," she said.

I wrote a full, long letter giving my reasons for discontinuing the relationship. I must have given a good argument since both Dad and LaVile wrote back that I had made the right decision.

On the following Monday evening, a car arrived in my yard carrying my best friend, Florence, from Harford School in Moyamba. I was surprised and delighted. It was the first time that anyone from Harford had come to visit. We talked about a number of things.

Finally, I said, "I broke off my engagement to John on Saturday."

"Yes, I know," Florence replied. "As soon as John got back to Moyamba on Saturday, he came and told us. We have all been worried about you all weekend. Are you all right?"

I told her what had led me to the decision and that, indeed, I was fine. The decision had been carefully thought out, and I had not done this rashly or in anger. She drove back to Moyamba satisfied.

I have never regretted the decision I made. I tore up all the letters and threw away all the pictures; and my African friends continued to come and visit me at my house.

Many months later while I was living in Jaiama, there was a postscript to the story. John was transferred to Princess Christian Hospital, a maternity unit in Freetown. One night when he was working in the delivery room, a woman, carrying a very sick baby, burst into the delivery room. He told the woman to leave and wait outside, and putting his hand on her shoulders, escorted her out of the room. He was quite within his rights, as it was not medically acceptable to have sick children in the room where a delivery was being conducted.

But it is against custom in many parts of Sierra Leone for a man to touch a woman without her consent. The sick baby died, and the woman took John to court. He was very upset. Eventually, he was acquitted, but before the verdict was given, he left the country and went to Britain. All of this was published in the local newspaper. By the time I read it, he was gone. I felt badly for him. He was a competent physician and didn't deserve this treatment. I would have written and expressed my sympathy, but he was already out of the country and I didn't know where he had gone.

Perhaps it was just as well, since I am not sure he could have accepted my sympathy.

CHAPTER 28

Holidays

Holidays away from home and familiar surroundings present unique problems since so often the holiday celebrations are associated with family traditions or local customs. When living abroad, you can simply ignore a holiday which I frequently did. July 4th, for example, was the day that came after July 3rd. Only twice did I observe the American Thanksgiving; once because I was in Freetown with other Americans, the second time in 1962 when the Peace Corps volunteers organized a dinner in Tiama.

But Christmas could not be ignored. Numerous studies have been done to show that Christmas can be a very lonely and depressing time for people without families or for those separated by long distances. I had decided that I would never spend Christmas alone.

I have written about my first Christmas after Winnie's wedding when a friend came back to Tiama with me. The next year I went to Moyamba where we had a party on Christmas Eve and the next day drove to Shenge, a small village on the Atlantic Ocean. It was here that the United Brethren Church first started its missionary work. Among the many attractions is a beautiful white beach fringed with palm trees. There is a sheltered cove, ideal for swimming and sunning. I enjoyed both and managed to get a first class sunburn, one of the few I had in Africa.

Most of the trappings usually associated with Christmas were absent. Of course, there was no snow. In Sierra Leone, Christmas comes at the height of the dry season. Traditional holiday foods were simply not available or were hard to get. I usually gave a Christmas party for the clinic staff at which I served lots of rice and stew and included either Christmas cake or mince tarts. Since there were no evergreen trees, on occasion I had a small artificial tree and usually decorated the house with some representative of the nativity scene. Gifts were rare and gifts from overseas had to be mailed in August or September in order to arrive at the end of December. Usually we exchanged gifts among the staff; fruit or a chicken to me from them while I tried to give appropriate things such as articles of clothing or a calendar. Christmas cards and letters from the United States arrived over a period of a long span of time, starting in mid-November and continuing until sometime in February. My birthday is at the end of March so the end of the Christmas mail mingled with early birthday cards.

Most of all, I missed the music. In the United States in December, there is usually a wealth of both professional and amateur concerts, including, of course, the annual presentation of "The Messiah." Advent music at church begins on the first Sunday in December, and I had usually been a member of the church choir. The rehearsals of Christmas music began early and the season culminated in a special presentation of hymns and carols.

All of this was missing in Sierra Leone. Christmas carols, if sung at all, were sung only on Christmas Day and were few in number; since they were unfamiliar, they were sung badly.

In 1957, my resolve not to spend Christmas alone in Tiama hit a snag. From September on, a number of orphans whose mothers had died in villages surrounding Tiama, were brought to us. In the developing world, raising infants on breast milk substitutes was a hazardous undertaking. The water was unsafe, sterilizing bottles was a complex process, and powdered milk or formula were prohibitively expensive. While this was true in 1957, it is still true in 1996.

Further, wet nursing was not acceptable for the local community. Mothers considered it abhorrent to breast-feed a baby that was not their own. The idea may have been related to the custom that sexual intercourse was taboo while a woman was breast-feeding. If a mother extended her period of lactation, she also extended her period of abstinence from sexual intercourse, and her ability to become pregnant again as well. It is also true that successful breast-feeding requires that a woman is fairly healthy and has an adequate nutritional intake, not always an easy requirement for an African woman.

We solved the problem of the cost of bottle feeding by using money that had been contributed by the women in America who gave to the Nora Vesper milk fund. This was always a popular project and never lacked money. The other problems presented greater difficulties. To solve them, we admitted the orphans into the hospital and fed them until we felt they were well established on milk and had gained adequate weight. This process usually took about three months. Our water supply, while not sterile, was taken from the hospital cistern and was relatively uncontaminated. We soaked the feeding equipment in a chlorine solution which provided adequate sterilization and did away with having to boil the equipment.

By November of that year, with four orphans to feed, all the staff was involved. As Christmas approached, I began to have doubts about my being able to leave for the holiday. I really couldn't ask the staff to be responsible for three hourly feedings while I was gone for four or five days. With reluctance, I decided to stay in Tiama. I approached the season with depression. But having to stay turned out to be a real blessing for I realized how much of our Christmas celebration is unrelated to the real meaning of the event. As usual, there was a solemn service at church on Christmas Eve. I then came home and reread the Gospel account of Christmas and listened to Christmas music on the radio.

In the morning I didn't feel well, not an uncommon occurrence, but a good excuse for a late morning in bed and a leisurely day.

To my great delight, about noon, the McNabs arrived from Njala. They were Scottish, and he was the agricultural officer at the nearby station. They were committed Christians. Together we had a quiet day of joy and celebration. We shared our Christmas meal and our Christmas cheer. Although I never spent another Christmas alone at Tiama, I remember that one with quiet satisfaction and contentment.

When the secondary school opened in Tiama in 1960, I was involved in some of their activities, and at Christmas we decided to do a pageant. Many Africans have a gift for story-telling and acting and since it is not hard to portray the Gospel in action and words, I asked for volunteers from the students to play the parts. The boy who asked to play Joseph was named Mohammed. I asked him whether he felt there was some conflict in the portrayal, but he didn't feel any. It was easy to gather appropriate costumes; both men and women often wore flowing garments for special celebrations and these seemed adequate to depict the biblical story. The program proceeded with the traditional scriptures and as many carols as were available in the Mende hymnal. The schoolroom was full to overflowing, and the audience seemed to enjoy the portrayal of the Christmas story.

After 1960 when the Peace Corps volunteers came to live in Tiama, we celebrated the American Thanksgiving with the traditional trimmings. Somebody was able to buy a turkey, and I made pumpkin and mince pies. In addition to the three volunteers living in Tiama, several other Americans joined us.

At Christmas time in 1962, I stayed in Tiama and invited several other people: a couple from New Zealand who were living in Njala, a Canadian family working with our mission, and a British girl who was teaching at one of the secondary schools in Bo. Each nationality contributed something traditional from his or her own holiday feast. The man from New Zealand was especially fond of American fried chicken so that was part of my contribution.

I was grateful for the new friends who shared the holidays, but I also learned that new holidays were part of the African celebration.

CHAPTER 29

A Time to Move

At the end of 1957, a new missionary was due to arrive in Sierra Leone. Joy Thede, who was stationed at Jaiama, was to go on furlough at the end of June 1958. The executive committee proposed that Betty Esau, the new midwife, should go to Jaiama. As I have said, Jaiama was at the far eastern end of the country, about 350 miles from Freetown. Although there were good medical facilities closer to Jaiama than there were to the clinic at Tiama, Betty would be without transportation. A big hospital, sponsored by the diamond mining company, was about ten miles away from Jaiama at Sefadu. Betty would be farther away from supplies both medical and personal, and much more isolated from the missionary community. I protested about stationing a young, inexperienced woman in such a remote area, and my protests were heard. The only other solution was to station Betty at Tiama and send me to Jaiama. I couldn't complain since I had helped to create the situation.

I was due to go on furlough in October 1958 which meant that I would be in Jaiama for six months. I had been thinking about going to graduate school to work on a master's degree in nursing education while on furlough and had even started to make inquiries about the possibilities. To do this, I would extend my term in Sierra Leone for another six months in order to arrive in the United States just prior to the opening of the fall semester in August. Once I found that I was going to Jaiama, those plans were canceled. If I had to leave Tiama, I wasn't going to stay in Jaiama any longer than I absolutely had to.

Betty came to Tiama to spend two months with me for orientation. This woman has always inspired me with her courage, persistence, and dedication as a Christian. She was the second daughter in a family, born with a physical handicap which had presented many problems in her childhood. Betty's parents loved her very much and much of that love was expressed in their protection of her from a hostile world. As a result, she didn't have some of the therapeutic help she might have had. She was quite shy and lacked self-confidence. Near the end of her high

157

school years, a teacher helped her have some corrective surgery. Then Betty startled her family by announcing that she was going to enter nurse's training. Having successfully accomplished that, she went to college to get a degree. That finished, she determined to go to the mission field. At each step, her family tried to discourage her, but she persisted.

Like most of the EUB missionaries that went to West Africa, she went to London to do her midwifery and then came to Sierra Leone. We had two good months together. Because she was friendly and eager to work, the staff and patients readily accepted her. I had been in Tiama for six years, most of that time as the only missionary, and had established my own routines. Betty told me later that if just one more person had said, "Oh, but Miss Olsen didn't do it that way," she might have been led to violence.

Each morning we opened the clinic with a short Bible message and prayer. I never did become fluent enough in Mende, however, to be able to do this without an interpreter. Each member of the staff was expected to take his or her turn in leading prayers. After Betty had been there a few weeks, I suggested that she lead the morning prayers. She protested that she wasn't able to do it, but I knew that after I left, the staff would expect her to give the leadership. She spent time on preparation, carefully wrote out what she would say, and managed very well that day. She eventually developed both skill and self-confidence to be able to speak extemporaneously. She felt a similar reluctance upon returning to the United States on her first furlough when she was expected to speak in church and to women's groups. Again she overcame her difficulties. In fact when I was in Kansas in 1963, I heard a number of people mention what an effective speaker Betty was and how well she represented both the church and Sierra Leone.

In April 1958, I went to Jaiama where Joy Thede and I had three interesting months together. Joy was true to her name, as years ago I had heard one of our tutors in England characterize her, "Joy by name and joy by nature." I admitted to myself that I had always been jealous of her. She was friendly, attractive, and seemingly without vanity. During the three months we were together, my jealousy turned to friendship and admiration which has continued throughout the years.

Jaiama was in the heart of the Kono district of Sierra Leone. The UBC in Kono had been started in 1910 by the missionaries Rev. and Mrs. J. Hal Smith. The Smiths stayed in Kono until 1915 when the Rev. Smith accidentally shot himself.

Much of the growth of the church in Kono was due to a Sierra Leonean, the Rev. D. H. Caulker, who had come from the Sherbro area. He came to Kono about 1911 and stayed for almost 100 years. He died in Kono at the age of 113. Paster Caulker was a remarkable person. Not only did he become fluent in the Kono language, he was able to speak some 17 other languages. He was able to attract local people to the church, but also preached to people of varying ethnic groups outside the district.

In 1984, several of us went to visit him. He was unable to walk and his eyesight was greatly diminished. We asked him to pray for us, and in perfect English, we were blessed by this dedicated man.

Jaiama was a small town just outside the boundaries of the official diamond territory. The church compound at the southern end of town included: a small church building, dignified in its simplicity; a large primary school and boarding home, several residences, the dispensary, and a maternity building. The latter two, similar in design to those at Tiama, were at the bottom of a small hill next to the road that crossed the town.

The two missionary residences were at the top of the hill and about a block apart. At this time, since the only missionary present was the medical person, the other residence was used as the parsonage for the African pastor and his family. The medical residence was an immense building which when occupied by a single woman, made her feel like a small goldfish floating in the ocean.

Medical residence. Jaiama, Kono District

Along the western front of the building and on part of the southern end, was a large covered veranda. Part of the veranda was screened which made it a pleasant place to sit in the evening, protected from flying insects. We frequently ate our meals out there, enjoying both the lovely view and cool air.

Inside was a large living room with a fireplace. Evenings in the rainy season, and again in December tended to be cool, and we enjoyed having a fire. The house included a large dining room complete with a large table. Although I never did have more than seven guests at any one time, the room would have accommodated three times that many. A wide hall connected the living room with three big bedrooms, a bathroom, and there were additional rooms for storage. The kitchen was separate, but connected to the house. The main part of the house had a full story attic which served as housing for the watchman. The house was surrounded by flowering shrubs, mango and palm trees, and an abundance of flowers.

The household staff included three people: a yardman who kept the extensive grounds in order, a cook named Sakati, and a watchman named Kangwanakwa.

Sakati was older than John Brewa, my cook in Tiama, and even more rigid in his habits. While John was willing to experiment and learn to cook American-style, Sakati was reluctant to try new things. He was a good cook, and like John, not only managed the cooking and shopping but also did the cleaning and laundry. Before coming to work for me, John had not previously worked for an American woman. In contrast, Sakati had worked for a series of American women and took our fancies as a temporary nuisance. Soon another woman would come with her own idiosyncrasies.

Sakati had an unusual ability to break dishes. When I returned to Sierra Leone in 1955, I had brought with me a gift from my church in Wisconsin; a complete eight-piece place setting of Japanese china, decorated with delicate sprays of apple blossoms. I enjoyed the lovely addition to my table and was pleased, when I had guests, I could set an attractive table. The staff at Tiama had been warned about not breaking the new dishes.

"The first person to break a dish will be in big trouble," I threatened.

"Please, Ma," John had replied, "We know who will break the first dish."

And, of course, I was the one who managed to chip a piece off the creamer when I hit it with another dish.

I moved the dishes intact to Jaiama. Within six months, however,

Sakati had managed to break six of the eight cups plus a few other pieces. So much for my pride!

Kangwanakwa was a tall, well-built man; friendly and pleasant. Many years before, one of his legs had been amputated, but he managed good mobility with a single crutch. I am not sure how quickly he would have moved if there had been a real emergency, but at night it was comforting to know that he was up in the attic, present if there was any trouble.

The excessive foliage around the house presented a few problems. The staff had warned me about snakes, but I ignored their words. I had seen very few snakes during my stay in Sierra Leone, and I didn't think Kono was any different. One Sunday noon, Joy and I had returned from church with a Sierra Leonean friend. I went to the bathroom and as I closed the door, I heard something fall off the hook on the back of the door. But as I turned to look at the "belt," it moved. I solicited the help of our visitor who managed to grab the snake and throw it outside.

Several weeks later, I had guests for dinner including Ted Stapleford who was making one of his tours with the book-van. The other guest was a young British District Commissioner from nearby Sefadu with whom I had become good friends. The living room contained an old, upright piano that had long since ceased to function, but which none of us who subsequently lived there felt we could remove. As the three of us sat chatting after dinner, another snake left its home behind the piano and started across the living room. Gallantly, the two men came to the rescue and evicted the snake.

That was it. The next morning I assigned the yardman to clear some of the bushes and growth around the house. I never saw another snake.

CHAPTER 30

Chiefdom Affairs

Jaiama, like Tiama, was the center of the chiefdom; in this case, the Nimi Koro chiefdom. It was a very wealthy chiefdom, said to be the wealthiest in the country since the chief, a young man, was allotted some of the revenue from the diamond licenses.

Chief Dudu Bona used his wealth to good advantage. He had acquired a fairly large number of wives, probably about 20, which did not begin to compare, however, with a previous chief, Chief Matturi, who reportedly had 100 wives. Unlike many chiefs, Chief Bona used liquor sparingly. He had used some of his money to construct several cement block houses near his large compound. The buildings were light and airy, and he was able to rent them to people needing housing in the village.

Chief Bona and the mission staff maintained a cordial relationship. He was anxious to continue these friendly, working partnerships because it was to the advantage of the people in the area to have the schools and medical work maintained. He was concerned that the church might close some of the work so he went out of his way to be kind and friendly.

A strong male secret society existed in West Africa called the Poro Society. This society was present both in Sierra Leone and Liberia, and was related to the Wunde Society that existed in the Kori chiefdom. The society was particularly strong in the eastern edge of the country. A fearsome devil of this society appeared on rare occasions. Women were prohibited from looking at this devil on pain of death. I wanted very much to see the devil and was not concerned about the threat.

One of the elderly leaders in the society had been treated as a patient at the dispensary. I think he had a rather serious heart condition; and whatever treatment we gave him did not make him well, and he died. Some of the funeral ceremonies were open to the public, and I asked one of the local evangelists to go with me to see the ceremonies. A large crowd of people had congregated, and were singing and dancing to the accompaniment of traditional drumming. I knew the

Poro devil was expected to appear during the ceremony. We observed the happenings for some time, but the devil did not appear. People had been drinking heavily and the scene became threatening. I finally realized that as long as I stayed, the devil would not appear. I also realized that although no one would harm me, I was putting the evangelist in danger so we went home.

Chief Bona heard about my interest in the devil and a few days later sent a note that he would have a devil in his compound and that I was invited to come and see him. I would be allowed to take all the pictures I wanted. I accepted his invitation. It turned out not to be the Poro devil, but one of the "entertainment" devils. He was completely covered with raffia clothing and had a large, but not very fearsome mask on his head. He danced and did acrobatic tricks while I took pictures. I never did see the Poro devil, but there was at one time, an authentic mask in the Public Museum in Milwaukee so I had to be content with looking at that. (See Colorplate 7).

I had one other interesting experience with the chief. One of the women living in his compound was an elderly midwife. Our face-to-face contacts had always been very cordial, but both Joy and I were aware that she viewed us as rivals. When women in labor were coming to the hospital, she would often detain them until it was too late for them to walk to the hospital, and then she would manage the delivery.

One of the chief's young wives was due to deliver early in August. She went into labor and delivered while I was in Freetown. She didn't deliver in the hospital, but had her baby in the chief's compound. Among the people who worked at the hospital was Yumba Pettiquoi who was skilled as a midwife and shared the midwifery responsibilities with me. I had great confidence in Mrs. Pettiquoi and knew she could handle normal deliveries adequately and was quite capable of taking care of emergencies. (See Colorplate 7).

When I came back from Freetown, the chief's wife brought the baby to the dispensary, but I refused to see it.

"You found someone to deliver you in the village," I told them. "They can now take care of your baby."

My stand had an immediate effect. Chief Bona was at the dispensary within minutes.

"Why did you refuse to see my child?" he demanded.

"Chief Bona, you know how hard we have worked to have women come to the hospital to deliver even for normal deliveries. If your wives don't come, we will have trouble persuading other women to come for care. If the women in your compound want to conduct deliveries, then there is no need for the hospital to stay here."

"I suppose you are right," he agreed. "I need to set an example and have my wives come to the hospital."

The palaver was over and we parted friends. He named the baby Lois. From then on, his wives came to deliver at the maternity unit.

CHAPTER 31

Diamond Mining

The first diamond was discovered in Sierra Leone in 1930. Two years later prospecting rights for diamonds in the whole country were granted to the Sierra Leone Selection Trust (SLST), an arm of the De Beers Corporation of South Africa. All of the top management in Sierra Leone were white South Africans.

For many years, SLST had a monopoly on all mining and selling of diamonds. The diamonds were found in alluvial deposits (deposits in sand and gravel) along rivers and streams, mostly in the eastern and southern provinces. The stones were so close to the surface that it was sometimes possible to pick up a stone out of the gravel along a path or road. Both gem stones and industrial diamonds were mined. Most of the diamonds were quite small, but in 1972, the third largest diamond ever discovered anywhere was found in Sierra Leone.

The SLST used mechanized equipment to mine diamonds. The thin, top layer of soil was removed and the underlying gravel was transported to washing plants. In 1957, the gravel was carried in small carts, each about the size of a large barrel which ran on a track that was laid to the edge of the mining area. Later as a more extensive area was mined, the gravel was carried in larger dump trucks. A conveyer belt carried the gravel to the top of a four-story separation plant. There, water washed over the gravel, carrying away the loose soil, and the gravel then passed over a series of sieves. The heavy diamonds and stones fell to another belt that was covered with a thick layer of grease, and the diamonds adhered to the grease.

When we visited the mine in 1958, men stood next to the belts and picked the diamonds. Since smuggling was a continual problem, the workers changed their clothing before going into work and were stripped and searched after they had finished.

Thousands of people flooded into Kono. Young men from all over the west coast of Africa came to make their fortune by finding the one big stone. These men found places to live in many of the small Kono villages, including Jaiama, but others settled in the bigger towns. The

Cart carrying gravel.

Separation plant in Koidu.

Gem quality diamonds.

tiny villages of Yengema and Sefadu became big, dusty, filthy towns because there was no organized system of water supply or sewage disposal any place in the district.

Most of these men mined illicitly, digging for diamonds in fields that had been used for farming. The terrain was covered with holes, 10 to 20 feet in diameter and 6 to 10 feet deep. The bottoms of the holes were covered with water. The illicit miners used the same techniques to "wash" the stones that the SLST used, but on a smaller scale. Their tool was a small wooden box which was covered with a screen on the bottom. A layer of gravel was put in the bottom of the box on top of the screen. Standing ankle deep in water, they would wash the gravel until the loose dirt was gone. They would then turn the sifter upside down, dumping the gravel onto dry ground. Any diamonds in the gravel would now be on top of the residue.

Because diamonds are easily concealed and smuggled, SLST made great efforts to control access to diamond territory and smuggling, but it was an impossible task. In 1955 the Sierra Leone government and SLST reached an agreement that restricted the operations of the company to an area of about 500 square miles. The following year, the Alluvial Diamond Mining Scheme was introduced. This allowed private contractors to take out a license to mine a particular area outside the SLST territory. The owners of the license were free to hire laborers to mine in their area. Diamonds found in this territory were to be sold to the government buying office. However, this policy stopped neither the illicit digging or smuggling.

Diamond territory was prohibited territory, so anyone traveling in that area had to have special permission. Vehicles were stopped, and the occupants and their belongings searched. As missionaries, we were scrupulous about avoiding any suspicion of diamond smuggling. As a result, we usually were exempt from such searches. On one occasion in 1961, I drove my Volkswagen bus to Jaiama and had as passengers three other women including a Sierra Leonean. When we reached the checkpoint, the guards simply waved us through.

Sometimes the checkpoints were carelessly watched. Jaiama was just outside the prohibited area. One night I took a laboring woman to the government hospital at Sefadu. When we got to the checkpoint, there was an unmanned roadblock consisting of two empty oil drums and a few sticks. We moved the drums, drove through, and then replaced them.

There was a bizarre story told about two young men from Oklahoma who decided to come to Sierra Leone to make their fortune in diamonds. They had read about the rich fields in Kono, boarded a plane, and flew to Sierra Leone.

During the flight, a fellow passenger asked, "How did you get visas?" "Do we have to have visas?" they replied. "We thought you just had to have a passport." Included in their luggage were two rifles. By some quirk, they got through customs at Lungi airport, rifles and all. One man was given a 30-day visa and the other a three-day visa. They took the train to Bo, still 50 miles from any diamonds, and there their adventure was interrupted. They were arrested, their rifles confiscated, and they were thrown in jail. Since there was no American embassy in Sierra Leone, the EUB business manger in Freetown, Don Theuer, handled the problems of American citizens. Don went to Bo and was able to get them released from jail. They were thoroughly disgusted—their money and rifles were gone and they hadn't seen a diamond. They flew back to Oklahoma.

The "strangers" in the district were of varied backgrounds, and many of them were very wealthy. Unlike Tiama and Rotifunk, financial support of the Jaiama dispensary was not a problem. The income at the dispensary in the six months that I was there was more than I had collected in Tiama in three years. We were able not only to meet all of our expenses, but helped support the other two stations.

The wealth of the strangers in the area was often exhibited by the clothing and ornaments the women wore. Women of Fulani and Mandingo origin wore great, flowing outer garments of dazzling materials. I often cast covetous eyes on that lovely clothing, and I was interested in taking a gown back home with me. One day a woman wore an exceptionally beautiful dress, a sheer overgown embroidered with medallions of blue velvet and gold thread.

"Where did you buy that material?" I asked. "I would like to buy something like it."

"My husband bought it in Mecca," she replied.

Not only did I not buy this material in Sierra Leone, I didn't find anything comparable to buy.

The wives of the miners wore marvelous accumulations of gold jewelry. Heavy gold earrings hung down from their earlobes; so heavy that they were attached to a band over the head to help support the pieces. The ear pinna, the large portion of the ear, also had a series of small gold earrings. A large gold choker was worn around the neck and in the center was another large ornament under the chin. A gold chain supported a similar large ornament on the woman's chest. And, of course, there were gold rings and bracelets.

This abnormal wealth created problems for us at the clinic. The local Kono people did not always share in the uninhibited wealth. In fact, many of them were still earning their living by farming. We needed to keep the prices we charged at a level they would pay and still utilize our services.

However, because our prices were so low, we attracted a large number of patients that could afford to pay much more. Often they had no physical problems but came to be "sounded" and perhaps to buy some medicine. Injections were a popular item. We solved this by selling injections of Vitamin B_{12} which was harmless, could be beneficial, and had an immediate systemic effect described as a tingling all over the body.

The biggest problem came in the prenatal clinic which we held once a week. Many of the pregnant women came only to have an examination with no intention of coming to deliver at the hospital. Attendance reached 60 women every week. Each examination took time with the result that the women who intended to deliver in the hospital were not getting the care they needed. We attempted to make a selection and charge the outsiders who only wanted to be examined while not charging the women who intended to deliver locally.

Occasionally, one of these strangers did deliver at the hospital. One of these women was beautifully dressed and adorned with all of the gold jewelry. When we were ready for discharge, her husband came to pay the bill.

"How much do I owe you?" he asked as he pulled out a large roll of bills from his pocket.

"The charge is 60 shillings (about five dollars)." I replied.

He laughed uproariously. "IS that all? That's not very much."

It wasn't very much. He put the rest of the money back into his pocket and proudly carried his new son out the door.

CHAPTER 32

New Friends

It was fun working with Joy as we shared the responsibilities and work, but there was one disastrous occasion when we had a case of obstructed labor which we tried to resolve by applying obstetric forceps. As we attempted to extract the baby, one blade of the forceps broke. It only made a tiny sound, but in our ears it sounded as loud as a clap of thunder. We put the woman into the Jeep and transported her to the hospital at Sefadu where she was safely delivered.

But the reverberations were greater than the sound of the cracking forceps. The doctor at the Sefadu hospital reported us to the government medical services for malpractice and demanded that we lose our midwifery licenses and be deported. All of this was unknown to us until much later. The church medical committee defended us, and we were able to avert both the denial of licensure and deportation. Much later, Dr. Renner, the Sierra Leonean who was chair of the conference medical committee, told me of the incident and assured me that we had their full support.

Joy left in the middle of July. I missed her very much, but was satisfied that I had only three months before I could return to the United States. Part of my consolation was that I had a car to drive. One of the missionaries lent me a Jeep to be used during those months. It had been sold to a man in Jaiama who would take possession when I left. The steering wheel was on the left side of the car in a country where traffic traveled on the left. On the whole, the vehicle was in good repair and I experienced few problems. However, in six months I had 13 flat tires. Although I knew how to change a tire, I only did it once. The rest of the time some chivalrous man offered to do the changing and I cheerfully accepted the offer.

Before I arrived, Joy had used the same car. It was still unusual for any woman to drive a car (we knew of no African woman who drove), and African men felt that Joy was a bit reckless in her driving. Also, they felt it wasn't very safe for a woman to travel alone. Considering the itinerant population in Kono and the general lack of law and order, they were probably right to be concerned for our safety. Shortly after Joy left, the pastor and one of the church leaders came and asked me not to travel alone. It was a request that was easy to follow because it is not difficult in Africa to find passengers. In fact, it is extremely rare to start out without passengers for as soon as the community knows that a vehicle is going somewhere, people will appear who had planned to travel that day anyway.

My one big weekly excursion was to go to Sefadu to get the mail. Mail from the United States came in late on Saturday afternoon so I went early on Saturday evenings. One evening I had as a passenger the headmaster of the primary school.

As we left Jaiama, he said, "You know, Miss Olsen, it is a very shameful thing for a man to sit in a car and allow a woman to drive."

A bit startled, I said, "Mr. Koroma, if you want to drive, I will be glad to let you."

"Oh," he said, "I don't know how to drive!"

The hospital staff in Jaiama included two very experienced African midwives: Mrs. Yumba Pettiquoi and Mrs. Titi Matturi. Mrs. Pettiquoi, who had been with the mission for many years, was a quiet woman with a sweet smile. I appreciated her wisdom, her vast experience, her unending patience, and her quiet humor. She was past childbearing years, but had adopted an abandoned orphan. His mother and twin brother had died in childbirth, and Mrs. Pettiquoi had raised him with love and much care.

Titi Matturi also had extensive experience and more education than Yumba. She was also pregnant with her fifth child. In August I delivered her baby. She was a small woman and the baby weighed nine pounds. During the delivery, she reverted to the delivery position of the local women, squatting, and pushed the baby out.

There were several young people on the staff. Since it was much more difficult to hire people in Jaiama than in Tiama, due to the economic prosperity in Kono, I had brought two people from Tiama with me, a young male dispenser and a young girl who worked as a nurse.

After Joy left, I had my most dramatic crisis in Kono. It started on a Sunday morning when I was seeing those few patients that needed emergency care.

In many parts of the developing world, a disease exists called schistosomiasis. The causative organism affects humans, but in order to survive it also must develop in an intermediate host, a small snail that lives in shallow streams and ponds. The snail can only live at certain altitudes, and the Kono district was at the right altitude.

The organism breeds in the snail and is then expelled into the water. When people stand in the water, the organism invades their skin and gets into the blood stream. Eventually, the organism circulates to the bowel or bladder. The infected individual then passes blood either in the urine or stool. There are many other complications usually chronic, debilitating, and sometimes life threatening.

In areas like Kono where streams are used for bathing and washing clothes, nearly everyone is infected with schistosomes. The local people call it "red gonorrhea" since the urine is often tinged with blood.

The disease can be prevented and cured. However, when the patient goes back to the stream, he may be easily reinfected. At that time in 1957, the treatment was long and difficult, requiring 18 injections given on alternate days so that the full course of treatment took six weeks. The medication itself can give some uncomfortable side effects and contains lithium and antimony. Side effects include gastric disturbances, cardiovascular irregularities and neuromuscular effects. The medication itself could be fatal due to these systemic effects.

Because the medicine created so many problems, I made sure that I kept careful control of all the medicine. When a patient was to receive an injection, I would bring out a single dose for that treatment.

On this particular morning, there were two or three patients scheduled to receive the injection. Helping me and giving the injections was the young girl from Tiama.

As usual we had several other patients, including several babies. One of the babies had an infection and required penicillin which I ordered. A few minutes later I looked up. The baby was gone, the ampule of medicine was gone, and the man needing the schistosome treatment was still sitting there. My helper had mistaken my instructions and had given the medicine to the wrong patient.

We hurried after the mother, brought them both back, and admitted them to the maternity ward. There was no antidote for the medication, and within 24 hours the baby died. I was devastated, for indeed, we had killed the baby.

The next day about noon a group of about 50 men climbed the hill to my house led by the father of the baby. They wanted reparation. They insisted that we should pay them money. I was equally insistent that my own personal finances as well as those of the clinic had little to offer. Failing that, they suggested both the nurse and I should go to jail. That was a possibility I couldn't deny.

The men left in anger but without violence. A few hours later the court president and one of the men from the church came to talk about it. I told the whole story, including my own feelings of guilt and despair. They assured me that I would not be fined, go to jail, or be sent out of the country. The next morning Chief Bona came to the clinic and again reassured me that we would not be held responsible and that the whole matter was an accident. I was relieved, but the whole incident had been very upsetting. After I closed the clinic that afternoon, I headed out of the village in the car and drove to the top of one of the highest hills in the area. I loved the view over the northern plains with the mountains in the distance. I cried until there were no more tears. After it was dark, I drove home.

To get to my house, I had to drive through town. Within five minutes of my arrival, the pastor and another church member were at the door. Knowing how upset I had been, they were afraid I might have harmed myself. Their second fear was that I might have gone to confide in the young British District Commissioner in Sefadu who had become a close friend. If the matter came to the attention of the government, there would be more trouble. I had done neither. Again, it was good to know that the community was concerned about my welfare and shared my concern about the matter.

CHAPTER 33

Making Friends

During my stay in Jaiama I developed a close friendship with two young Sierra Leonean couples, all of them teachers at the local school. The women were Tabitha Williams and Tuzylene Bangura. I had known both of them when I lived in Tiama.

Tabitha was the daughter of one of the prominent businessmen in Tiama. She was the only daughter of her mother who had made great sacrifices to educate this girl. Her efforts were well rewarded. Tabitha was not only a lovely person and dedicated Christian, she was also an excellent teacher.

At one point when I was still living in Tiama, we had a long conversation around the time she was finishing her course at the teacher training institute.

"Do you plan to come back home and teach in Tiama?" I asked her. I knew that she would be helpful both in the work of the church and with the women.

"I am going to ask to go to some other town rather than Tiama," was her reply.

"But why? I am sure your mother would be very happy if you were living at home."

She was firm in her response. "If I stay here and live at home, all my money will go to my father, and it will all be spent on liquor. I want to live away from home where I will have more independence."

Tuzylene came from a strong Muslim family. However, her parents had sent all the children to school, and Tuzylene, while at Harford School for Girls, had become a Christian. I am not sure why she asked to go to Jaiama, but she also was a conscientious and effective teacher.

The two women became close friends with two young teachers on the staff. Donald Wonnie was a Sherbro from Bonthe Island. He and Tuzylene eventually were married and returned to Tiama to live. David Caulker, a Sherbro by inheritance, had been born and raised in Kono. He was the only grandson of the Rev. D. H. Caulker, who had helped to establish the church in Jaiama. David's father had disappeared when he was a child, but he was lovingly raised by his remarkable mother and grandparents.

The five of us spent much time together. Some of them were frequent passengers on my Saturday evening trip to Sefadu. David and Tabitha were engaged to be married in August in Tiama. Several of us planned to drive there for the occasion.

As soon as school was out, Tabitha traveled to Tiama. David and several of us were to come down country just before the wedding, traveling in my Jeep.

It was four months since I had left Tiama and I was anxious to go "home." I was driving, and evidenced my desire by driving faster and faster. After we left Bo one of the men said, "You really aren't safe to drive. You are going faster and faster." I moved over to the passenger seat and let him drive.

I have mentioned Tabitha's father. Pa Okora Williams was a prominent man in Tiama, and had been one of the first persons to attend school after the first school had been established. After Tabitha finished her education, her father started negotiations with the chief of the adjoining chiefdom; who already had over 30 wives. The two of them were in the process of deciding the bride price for Tabitha. The friendship between Tabitha and David was developing into a permanent relationship. David's mother, Dindi, came to Tiama to talk about the wedding negotiations. Pa Williams was adamant in his refusal to agree to the wedding between David and Tabitha. But Tabitha was equally insistent that she would not be a wife to the chief and that she wanted to marry David. Mama Dindi, Tabitha's mother, and Tabitha refused to change their minds. Her father had already accepted part of the bride price from the chief. The women persisted and finally won. The money for the bride price had to be returned; and her father refused to have anything to do with the wedding celebration.

The wedding was a joyous occasion. After it was over, we drove back to Jaiama. I had only two months left before I could leave for the United States.

CHAPTER 34

Return to the United States

I was scheduled to leave Jaiama and Sierra Leone in October 1958. The missionary who was to relieve me arrived on a Thursday. The mission superintendent, Dr. Lowell Gess, was driving to Jaiama and was to take me down country on Monday.

My colleague arrived and although she usually was not critical, began finding innumerable problems. Maybe she hadn't wanted to come to Jaiama any more than I had. Anyway, the accounting system wasn't right, the clinic was poorly organized, and the house was dirty. I was overwhelmed. The situation was made worse when I had an attack of malaria on Friday night. In addition to my physical discomfort, I was frustrated and tired. The past three years had presented many challenges including adjusting to the new setting in Kono. The discouraging remarks increased my sense of futility. I was ready to leave Sierra Leone and go home. I woke up on Saturday morning resolved to leave as soon as possible. I went to the parsonage first. Pastor Smith was taking a shower.

I shouted through the closed door, "I'm leaving this noon with the Jeep."

He shouted back, "You can't do that. There is a farewell party for you this evening."

"No," I insisted. "I am going as soon as I finish the clinic."

I went to the new owner of the Jeep. "Will your driver take me to Freetown? Then he can bring the Jeep back."

He, too, tried to reason with me. "But why leave now? Isn't Dr. Gess coming to get you?"

"He is, but I am going today."

When I got back to the house, Pastor Smith was there and tried to reason with me, but my mind was made up. I was packed and ready to go. I went down to the clinic and saw the patients who were there. The malaria did nothing to improve my temper or my patience, but I finished my tasks.

I left as I had planned. I stopped at Sefadu to say goodbye to Barry

McClosky, the assistant district commissioner who had become a friend. Unfortunately, he was out traveling with some of the district police to track down another group of police who had been reported for doing illicit diamond mining.

Just after we had driven through Sefadu, about 15 miles out of Jaiama, we met Lowell Gess.

"Where are you going?" he asked with surprise.

"I'm fed up with Jaiama and I just want to get out of there."

"But I will be going back on Monday," he argued. "Can't you wait that long?"

But my mind was made up and nothing he could say would persuade me otherwise. We drove to Bunumbu where we had the first flat tire. The driver changed the tire, and we drove on to Bo where we spent the night. Here we had the second flat tire. Then we drove to Tiama where we had the third flat tire. As I have written, in the six months that I drove the car, there were 13 flats.

At Tiama, of course, I stopped to have a long visit with Betty Esau. Tiama was home, and there were old friends to greet. But by this time, I was beginning to feel ashamed of my hasty retreat and my ill manners toward my friends. As we sat eating the noon meal, I confessed that I was particularly sorry for the way I had talked to Dr. Gess. I decided when I got to Freetown, I would offer my apologies.

Within a few minutes, he drove into the yard and joined us at the table.

I immediately began my apologies. "I'm sorry for the way I acted. Please accept my apologies," I began.

He was most gracious with his reply. "Of course, I accept your apology. I am sure you were under a lot of strain." "Besides," he added, "I didn't think the house looked dirty."

Dr. Renner, the African senior pastor in Freetown, used to say missionaries who were irritable and unreasonable just before they had finished their tour of duty and were ready to go on leave, were "end of tourist." It applied to me.

The rest of the trip to Freetown was without incident.

The mission executive committee, at that point, gave the missionaries a choice of flying home or going by ship. I had opted for sea travel and wanted to land in one of the southern ports of the United States. The travel agent in Freetown had arranged for me to travel on a Delta Line ship, an American line. I was to board the ship in Monrovia, Liberia and would travel to New Orleans. I flew to Monrovia and waited ten days for the boat to come.

Monrovia, like Freetown, was a rather sleepy little town. While Freetown bore the influence of the British colonial presence, Monrovia gave evidence of the effects of the American freed slaves who had settled there in 1820. The houses were built in the style of those found in the American south. The government buildings resembled similar office buildings found in American state capitols. In fact, the government was modeled after the United States organization with an elected president, a supreme court and a two-house legislature.

I found a room at the Hotel France, a small, seedy building in the center of town. The menu in the dining room never varied from day to day. For the evening meal, we were served steak and french fries. At noon, hamburgers were supplemented with tomatoes and okra. I explored the surrounding streets, but the small shops were poorly stocked. I walked, I knitted, and I read. I quickly exhausted my small supply of reading material so when I boarded the ship, I had nothing left to read.

A missionary friend in Sierra Leone knew someone in the Lutheran mission in Liberia, and I was able to contact the mission compound. On Sunday morning one of the men came to pick me up and take me to church. At the end of the service, he offered me a room at the Lutheran guest house. I accepted at once. The compound faced a long stretch of sandy beach that is a part of Monrovia's south shore, and I spent some of my time walking along that lovely tropical beach. The mission house had a wealth of books which I enjoyed. But more than either of these pleasures was the constant flow of people, mostly Americans, who came to stay at the guest house while they conducted their business in Monrovia.

After I got to Monrovia, I found that I was to be the only woman on board the ship. I was tempted to fly back to Freetown and arrange another passage, but decided that this was going to be another good adventure.

The ship finally came into port, and I was able to board. There was one other passenger, a Southern Baptist doctor who had been looking at various mission hospitals in West Africa, deciding where he would like to work. He was traveling steerage to save money.

The ship had a long middle deck with a short upper deck on one end where the galley, lounge, and several cabins were located; one of which was mine. On the middle deck was an unusual cargo of 150 rhesus monkeys in cages that were being carried to the United States for use as laboratory animals. I was immediately warned that I was not to walk on the main deck, both because of the monkeys which the officers were afraid might bite me, but also because of the unreliable crew. Some of the crew had been arrested further down the coast for dealing in drugs, and the officers were concerned for my safety. A frequent pastime during ocean travel is repeated walks around the deck, but now I was confined to the very short hike across the upper deck.

The officers were kind, and everyone did his bit to keep me entertained. The Baptist missionary and I played Monopoly everyday with innumerable variations on the game. The radio man and I played three games of Scrabble every evening. The two of us were pretty well matched and it was a pleasant way to spend the time. He also had some books which I borrowed.

Halfway across the Atlantic, the galley ran out of coffee. Since the cargo included coffee beans, the cook was able to roast and grind some from the hold.

Then I got sick. After my bout of malaria in Jaiama, I had only taken a partial dose of chloroquine. I hated taking the medication since the side effects, increased nausea and disturbed vision, were almost worse than the symptoms of malaria. The sensitivity to light and blurred vision were upsetting, but even worse was the disturbed sleep and frightening nightmares that always followed the medication. Now I had a return of the fever. I took the initial dose of medication and resolved to finish the full course this time. I decided I wouldn't get up for breakfast. About 10:00 a.m. I got up to see if I could get a cup of tea. My cabin opened onto the main lounge. There sat all the officers discussing who should knock on my door and find out what the problem was. I assured them it was nothing serious and I would take care of myself. After that I made sure I was present at the table for each meal. I did my necessary laundry in my room. Since the offer had been made, I occasionally made a cup of tea in the galley.

We landed in New Orleans. My parents were there to meet me, and we drove home to Milwaukee. This furlough included some soul searching about whether I should return to Sierra Leone. I was aware of the many challenges, loneliness, and frustration when I had complicated cases I couldn't manage.

I felt at this point in my career I needed to look at advanced education and pursue my plans for a master's degree. I extended my furlough for six months during which time I worked as a staff nurse in a hospital in Winona, Minnesota. I finally decided to return to Sierra Leone. The satisfaction of the tasks were greater than the frustrations. I returned in April of 1960.

PART III:

Wheels Make a Difference

CHAPTER 35

An "Eggciting" Trip

I was to fly back to Sierra Leone. I don't think there were any direct flights from the United States at this time, although there were later. I was scheduled to fly from Milwaukee to Paris and then to Freetown, a trip that usually lasted about 24 hours. However, a strike in Paris by baggage handlers necessitated changes in the schedule.

Today, in the 1990's, it is common for teams of volunteers to visit and work for short periods at the site of a mission institution, but in the 1950's it was uncommon for lay people to volunteer their services. One very active volunteer in Sierra Leone at that time was a wealthy businessman from Ohio. His mind teemed with ideas for projects. Implementation of the projects usually involved a considerable effort on the part of the local people including the missionaries.

His most recent idea was for someone to carry hatching eggs to Sierra Leone where they would be used to start a booming poultry business. He convinced me to carry the three dozen eggs on the plane.

The first snag was getting the eggs. I phoned many places in Wisconsin until I finally found a hatchery that would supply the eggs. They arrived just a few hours before I was to fly out of Milwaukee. They were carefully packed in a wooden case about 15 inches square.

The next problem arose when I checked my luggage. The airline would not take any responsibility for the eggs. I would have to carry them as on-flight baggage all the way.

Due to the strike in Paris, the schedule was changed so that I had to make several additional stops. I changed planes in New York and then had to stay overnight in London. Dutifully, I carried the eggs to the hotel and back to the airport the next morning. We flew to Paris where I had to change planes and go through a baggage inspection.

"What do you have in the box?" the inspector asked.

"Eggs." I replied.

He didn't understand what I said and called for a second man. We repeated the routine. A third man was called and repeated the question.

183

"I am carrying eggs," I repeated.

He started to laugh and told the others what was in the box.

"Would you like to have them scrambled?" he suggested.

"Perhaps we could have an omelet," his friend suggested.

The third man asked, "Are they boiled?"

"No," I replied, laughing with them, "they are fresh and I hope that eventually they will be hatched."

We flew to the next unscheduled stop in Conakry, Guinea, just north of Freetown where we spent the night. The trip to the airport in the morning took me through the back streets and alleys of Conakry. The taxi driver explained that President Sheku Toure was traveling to the airport and all main streets were closed to regular traffic to ensure that the roads were open and safe for the President. This closure of roads when the government head is traveling is a common procedure all over Africa.

At the airport I had more problems. I was asked to declare all my money. I was carrying a fairly large amount, mostly in travelers checks, some for other people, and some for my own supplies to be purchased in Freetown.

"Why didn't you declare this money last night when you came in?" the inspector demanded.

"Nobody asked me to," I replied. "I would have been willing to declare it."

"Since you didn't declare it, you will have to leave it all here in Guinea."

I put up as many arguments as I could. "But I need this money to buy food and pay for transportation when I get to Freetown."

"It is the law," he insisted.

"If someone had told me about the law, I surely would have obeyed it. I will be in great difficulty if you take all my money."

Reluctantly, he agreed to let me keep the whole amount.

The large entry hall of the airport was completely empty of anyone except the customs officials and myself. Suddenly we heard the sound of sirens and approaching vehicles. The President was arriving. He walked through the empty airport accompanied by Chinese bodyguards carrying machine guns. It was only occasionally that I was aware of how conspicuous a Caucasian can be in a country totally inhabited by black Africans. This was one of those times. There was nothing I could do but stand quietly and smile. President Toure smiled back and nodded to me.

The President left the airport first on what was an internal flight. Soon afterwards we took off for Freetown. One of the passengers on the plane was Dr. John Karefa-Smart. Dr. Karefa-Smart, a physician, had been born in Rotifunk. At one time he had worked on the medical staff at Rotifunk and was now a minister in the Sierra Leone government.

The airport at Lungi, the major airport in Sierra Leone, is on the north side of the Sierra Leone River that flows into the Atlantic. Freetown is on the south side of the river. The trip from the airport to the city includes a trip by bus to the riverside and then an hour's ride across the river on a large ferry.

When we landed at Lungi and reached the river bank, there was a government launch there to take Dr. Karefa-Smart across the river to Freetown. He generously offered to give me a seat in the launch, which of course, I accepted, still carrying the egg crate. As we climbed aboard the launch, I watched a commercial firm load several thousand day-old chicks onto the ferry to be carried to Freetown. Carrying three dozen eggs may not have been the most futile effort I have ever made, but it comes close.

I carried the eggs to Tiama where Les Bradford, the agricultural missionary, came to get them. He put them in an incubator, but nary a chick hatched.

There was one more mishap before I reached Tiama when I took the train from Freetown to Mano. While I was arranging the luggage on the train, I foolishly put my purse on the small table in front of the open window. A smart young thief outside the train grabbed it and ran away with all the money I was carrying. Fortunately, I had left my passport in the Freetown office. In addition to the money, I lost all my American identification and had to wait until I returned to the United States three years later before I could replace the other documents.

CHAPTER 36

The Changing Scene

A number of changes had occurred during the two years since I had left Tiama. Old Chief Gbappe had died and a relatively young chief, also called Gbappe and a relative of the former chief, was now in authority. He had been educated at the elementary school level and previously had worked for the railroad. He was a friendly man, and he and I had a pleasant working relationship.

A new secondary school had been built and was now enrolling students. The first class started in September, 1960. A fine set of buildings had been erected including dormitories for boys and girls, although only a small proportion of students were girls. The school had a faculty of three, all Sierra Leoneans.

There had also been changes at the church. Mr. Thomas, the organist, and also headmaster of the primary school, had gone to England on a study course and I was asked to play the organ. It was a large pump organ, and a remarkable instrument. Bishop Warner had purchased it in Paris and had it sent to the Tiama church. It was powered, as were small parlor organs, with foot pedals and because of its size, it took a good amount of energy to keep the sound loud enough to accompany congregational singing. I attacked the music with a speed unusual for the congregation. More than once Pastor Carew would stop the singing and say to the congregation, "You know Miss Olsen is at the organ. Let's try to keep up with her."

Pastor gave me some additional responsibilities; in particular, directing the choir. Most of the members were students at the secondary school. Donald Wonnie, one of the teachers, had a fine baritone voice and Mr. Lenga, also on the faculty, sang tenor. Both of them had some experience in reading music while the students had to be taught to sing by rote.

Later I was asked to teach a Sunday School class of 60 teenage girls. This was a real challenge! There were no prepared materials so I had to devise my own. I suspected that one of the reasons I had been asked to teach was to give the girls an opportunity to hear English, or at least American, spoken. The venture was not terribly successful as the girls often did not understand me. Like many African girls, they were quite shy. Not only did they not answer my questions, but I was unable to encourage them to disagree with anything I said. One day, in exasperation, I said, "If I told you the moon was made of green cheese, you would all agree, wouldn't you?"

"Yes, Miss Olsen," came 60 voices.

For me personally there were several welcome changes. I bought a Volkswagen Kombi bus. The bus had three rows of seats, two of which could be removed. A fairly large space behind the rear seat allowed plenty of room to carry supplies. However, the bus came with minimal equipment: for example, there was no gas gauge. Since there was no gas station in Tiama, I had to keep careful track of when I filled the tank and how many miles I had driven so that I didn't run short of gas.

The bus served several purposes; the main one was to carry passengers to the hospital when a patient had an obstructed labor. Second, I could carry supplies including medications from Freetown and Bo. It also enabled me to carry out a long time dream to start clinics in some of the surrounding villages. And, of course, it allowed me to do some personal travel and see parts of Sierra Leone and even Liberia that I had not seen before.

Another change was that a generator had been installed on the hospital compound. Because it had limited capacity and was expensive to run, we used it only for a few hours in the evening. Since Sierra Leone is so close to the equator, sunset and sunrise occur at about the same time all year round. We would turn the generator on about 6:30 in the evening and turn it off about 10:00. The watchman usually turned it on, but several of us were able to start it. We had expected to use it at night when there were deliveries, but that presented problems. The only light bulb in the delivery room was directly over the delivery table. The windows had no screens so that if we opened the windows, soon we had a multitude of bugs, many of them falling on the patient, on the person doing the delivery and worst of all, on the baby. If the windows were closed, it was hot and we still had bugs. I soon returned to using the kerosene lamp during the night.

Second, the noise of the generator would be heard all over town. If I turned it on during the night, in the morning a stream of visitors came to ask why we had used the lights.

In addition, I bought a radio. At the start of each term, the mission board gave us $50 as an outfitting allowance which we could spend on anything we thought we needed. I spent the entire amount on a Phillips radio that ran on batteries and had an attached record player. It gave me endless hours of delight. I was able to tune in to the international broadcasts: the World Service of the British Broadcasting Company (BBC), The Voice of America (VOA), and the American Armed Forces Network. In addition, many of the West African countries had a national broadcasting station, such as the Sierra Leone Broadcasting Service (SLBS), and Liberian Broadcasting Company (LBC). A Christian station in Liberia (ELWA) carried news, religious programs, and good musical programs. The BBC had a wide range of programs: classical music, drama, and of course, extensive news broadcasts. On the VOA and the Armed Forces Network, I listened to news from the United States and also heard American baseball games.

I had augmented my "Messiah" set of records with a number of classical records. A shop in Freetown carried a wide selection and I was able to add records to my collection each time I traveled to Freetown.

I also acquired a piano. It came from one of the couples who lived in the mission headquarters in Freetown. They went back to the United States and did not return to Sierra Leone. I had met the wife while I was on furlough.

"What are you taking back to Tiama with you?" she asked.

"I would like a musical instrument, maybe a piano, but I can't afford it and the cost of shipping is more than I could manage."

She quickly offered, "Would you like to have ours? We are not going to have it sent home."

"I would really appreciate it."

Before I got back to Tiama, the piano had been delivered and placed in the unused side of the duplex. Not only did I enjoy playing it, but I had two students, neither of whom became very good pianists. Since the only instrument in town was the one at my house, they had very little opportunity to practice and the supply of printed music was limited.

There had been changes in staff at the dispensary. Abraham Lavaly was no longer working there. During my absence, he had been accused of having more than one wife. The church had always had a strong stand against polygamy and would not employ a man with more than one wife. Rosaline had also left and was happily married to a Nigerian man who worked for the railway. Her husband was reasonably well educated and very stable financially. I was pleased that she was established in a comfortable and pleasant relationship.

Gradually, we increased the size of the staff. The hospital at Rotifunk had developed a midwife training program and two of the graduates were sent to Tiama. Tator Bagrey, in particular, was a tremendous help and managed about half the deliveries. The staff was now large enough so that there was always a nurse on duty and we didn't have to send for somebody at night when a baby was being born.

I was particularly proud of a small metal incubator that I had brought back. It was heated with hot water bottles and came equipped with a small tank of oxygen. We only used it once when we had a pair of premature twins. I placed the incubator in one of the unoccupied side rooms and attached the oxygen. In this way, the incubator was separated from the small kerosene lamps that the mothers used for night lights. When I came down to the hospital during the evening to check on the

Tator Bagrey's bridal picture.

babies, one of the mothers had brought her lamp and put it next to the incubator so "the babies won't have to be afraid of the dark."

It was probably just as well that the oxygen cylinders ran out of oxygen and we were not able to have them refilled. We later learned of premature babies who were blind as a result of long exposure to oxygen. It was also expensive, and there was always the danger of fire.

I had also brought floor tiles to cover the floor of the living-dining room of the house. All the floors were cement and not very pleasant looking. No matter how often the floor was swept and scrubbed, it never looked clean. Apparently, while I was still in the United States I had written that I was bringing the tiles. Before I reached Freetown, the executive committee passed a rule that no missionary could lay her own tiles. Apparently, the men on the committee felt that women were incapable of such a complicated task.

So I waited. Several months went by and no one came to lay the tiles so I took the matter into my own hands. I read all the directions and decided I could manage it. The household staff moved all the furniture out, and the floor was cleaned with a lye solution. The center tiles were to be laid first in a straight line in the center of the floor. The tiles were applied with a thick black tar. If too much tar was applied, it seeped through the cracks between the tiles. If there was not enough, of course, the tiles didn't stick to the floor.

I think if I had known how much hard work it entailed, I might not have started. In addition, the floor was not evenly laid and the walls were not exactly straight so the tiles didn't always lie evenly.

With my first effort, I had the first two rows laid. The next morning I was down at the clinic seeing patients when Clyde Galow, the current mission superintendent, arrived unexpectedly.

"I knew I would get caught," I confessed. "I'm doing something I'm not supposed to be doing."

He didn't seem too surprised. "Now what?"

"Nobody came to lay the tiles, and I have waited several months so I am doing it myself."

"I suppose there's not much I can do to stop you now. How is it going?" he asked.

"It is a lot of work, but I have started and should be finished by the end of the week," I replied.

I did finish it and always appreciated a floor that gave some color to the house.

CHAPTER 37

Pulling Wunde

Secret societies play an important role in West African society. The two largest and most powerful in Sierra Leone are the Poro for men and the Bundu for women. The Bundu Society is called Sande in Liberia and in parts of Sierra Leone.

The Mende people in the Kori chiefdom were a section of the Mendes called Kpaa Mende. The male secret society here was the Wunde Society. Although it has some similarities to the Poro, there are differences.

If I seem vague about some of this material, it is because they are secret societies. I gained my knowledge of the Bundu Society during my experiences of taking care of young girls and pregnant women. But gaining knowledge of the Poro and Wunde was much more difficult. Members who disclose the secrets are threatened with tribal excommunication or death. Some material has been written about the Poro but I found only one published article about the Wunde and that had no relationship to what I saw of the Wunde society in Tiama.

At one time, boys were initiated into the Wunde Society every year, but by the 1950's, the ceremony was held only infrequently. The initiation is termed "pulling Wunde." It had happened in Tiama in 1955 while I was on furlough in the United States. Then in January 1961, there was another initiation.

One of the most thorough descriptions of the Poro Society was written by Dr. George Way Harley, a Methodist missionary doctor in Liberia. The Mende claim that Poro originated among their people but it extended to the Temne and Sherbro; and in Liberia among the Vai and Mano.

The Poro has no central organization, but operates locally through independent "lodges." After a man is initiated into the local Poro, he is free to participate in any group where he is visiting.

Several authors, including Harley, say that ritual murder and cannibalism are a part of the initiation ceremony, although the governments of Liberia and Sierra Leone, the colonial British government particularly, were able to control some of these activities. However, during the recent wars in both countries since 1990, it is rumored that some of these practices have returned.

Male circumcision does not seem to be a part of the Poro-Wunde initiation, but the boy must be circumcised prior to the initiation. Female circumcision, on the other hand, is an integral part of the Bundu initiation. Harley claims that the excised male foreskin and female clitoris are boiled together in a soup and fed to the initiates.

Most of the ceremonies of the Poro/Wunde Society are held in a sacred bush, an area at the edge of town which is surrounded by a thick fence of trees and bushes. The entrance is carefully guarded, and no woman or uninitiated man may enter the bush. In the center of the bush is a secret burial ground where the dead chief is buried. After the announcement of the death, burial will be delayed for several days while the appropriate ceremonies are carried out.

Formerly, initiates went into the Poro/Wunde bush for several years for the training period. Gradually, the time was shortened so that by the 1950's, the period was about four weeks. When the boys entered the bush, scarification marks were made on their bodies: on the neck, back, and breast. After the initiation period as the boy was prepared to leave the bush, he was given a new name.

Addison describes the members of the Wunde Society as "expert in lying in politics, competent in war, cunning in finance, ruthless, and utterly unscrupulous." A publication of the Sierra Leone government says, "the society teaches orderliness, bravery, and facing danger without fear." Fire is the chosen symbol of the society. In addition, the members are taught civic duties and responsibilities, care of their children, and regard for old age. (See colorplate 8).

There were five degrees of membership: leaders, firemen, peacemakers, representatives of strangers, and candidates for training. The peacemakers wear women's clothing and a plumed head dress.

I had been told that Wunde initiation would be held in January, and was aware of the event by persistent drumming every night. I was told the final event would be held on a Saturday afternoon and that I could observe this part of the ceremony. Two seminary students from the United States were visiting me, and together we went to the site of the ceremony which was being held in a small village west of Tiama.

We were part of a large crowd of women and children seated near the river. One of my most vivid memories of the event was the absolute silence that was maintained by this crowd of women. There was no talking or whispering, even the babies and children were kept quiet and motionless.

I had taken my camera with me hoping that I could take pictures. I approached a number of men and asked for permission, but each time was flatly refused. Finally, I asked Abraham Lavaly, and he grudgingly gave me permission.

The peacemakers, dressed convincingly in women's clothes, were the first to arrive, filing quietly around the village. As they walked around, the women began to clap their hands in rhythm. This clapping continued throughout the ceremony. Next came the warriors carrying shields and spears. Then the initiates came running through the village. They wore only loin cloths, and white clay was daubed on their bodies in a seemingly random fashion. The boys ran, shouting, to a small structure in the center of town, on open building covered with a thatch roof. The warriors and boys, emitting fierce yells, circled around and through the building with great energy. This went on for about an hour. Then the boys ran down the road, past the women to the small stream that separated the town from Tiama. As they ran, the crowd threw pails of water on the boys. Some women ran to the riverside and brought back more water. Three times the boys made the dash to the river and back to town. In the final dash, the older men carried a young boy on their shoulders, running and shouting. This boy was carried through Tiama to the Teye River where he was immersed in water.

The initiation ceremonies clearly mark the passage from childhood to adulthood. While I have no explanation for many of the

Peacemakers of the Wunde Society.

activities, I was struck by the use of water. Water has symbolic significance in many religions. For example, almost all Christian churches use water as a symbol of cleansing and forgiveness. The United Brethren Church practiced adult baptism by immersion, and some of my most lasting memories of Sierra Leone were the services when 50 to 60 converts marched through town to the riverside to be immersed in the Teye before they became members of the church.

The Poro and Wunde Societies controlled the political life of the local community, but also had influence in national politics. Both societies were also at the center of military life in the country. Although military influence was somewhat controlled by the government, the political influence of the societies was still strong. Rumor had it, that the candidates for national offices in Sierra Leone, including the presidency, came to the Kori chiefdom to seek the endorsement of the Wunde Society. In Liberia, Presidents Tubman and Tolbert sought the sanctions of the Poro Society to strengthen their power. President Doe, not a member of the ruling Americo-Liberian society, but a member of the indigenous Krahn group, had his authority increased by his participation in the Poro activities and relied on the strength of Poro rituals when he was in power at the head of the government in Liberia.

I continue to wonder if the resumption of fighting in Liberia since 1989, and in Sierra Leone since 1992, has utilized the organization, powers, and skills of the secret societies in their efforts to gain and maintain control of their country.

CHAPTER 38

The Peace Corps Arrive

The presence of the United States Peace Corps volunteers was a lively influence in the town after their arrival in 1961. President Kennedy had initiated the Peace Corps in 1960, and these eager young volunteers soon established themselves all over Africa.

The first volunteer in Tiama was a farmer from Montana, Dan Kyle. Dan had recently graduated from the University of Montana with a degree in agriculture. In addition to his academic knowledge, he had skills and knowledge gained from years of working on the family ranch. We were fortunate that he was our first volunteer. He possessed numerous practical skills, had a lot of common sense, and worked very hard. When he first came, he lived in a room at the secondary school and took his meals with the African principal, Frank Anthony. Adjustment to food in another culture is often a most difficult task, but Dan didn't do too badly. The only thing that seemed to bother him were the small portions of meat that were served, having been used to the large supply of beef on his father's ranch.

Dan and I became close friends. At least once a week he came down from the school compound to have a meal with me. He was also an excellent cook himself. He was the middle son of three boys and was the one who had assumed some of the cooking chores at home.

He was also a good mechanic and skilled in repairing things. Occasionally he made a few mistakes, but I easily forgave him. At one point for example, he trimmed some of the trees on the hospital compound, but in the process the branch of a tree fell across the wires leading from the generator to the house, breaking them. Eventually, he was able to reattach the wires and restore the electricity.

Steve, who came from Utah, was the next volunteer to arrive. He, too, was a recent college graduate. He was the exact opposite of Dan. While Dan was rather quiet and not effusive, Steve was exuberant and voluble. Like most of us, Steve had decided that to live in Africa one should be as African as possible. He took great delight in visiting the surrounding villages and enjoyed sharing the meals that were offered to him. As a result, probably because he was not being careful about his water supply, he developed a chronic diarrhea. I attempted to treat it, but without success, and finally insisted that he go to Freetown to consult the Peace Corps doctor. The doctor used more aggressive treatment, kept Steve under surveillance until he was cured, and was sure there were no adverse reactions from the medication.

Both Dan and Steve had the appetites of the healthy young men they were. It was a joy to cook for both of them since they enjoyed the food, were willing to try local food, and finished dinner never leaving any leftovers. Although Steve didn't have the ability to cook and prepare meals that Dan had, he was able to manage in the kitchen when he needed to. By the time Steve arrived, the volunteers had their own apartment, which included their own kitchen.

One evening I came home from out of town about supper time and Steve offered me a meal. It was leftover spaghetti, and the sauce included fresh mushrooms. We both ate heartily. When I got back to my house, George Harris, one of the doctors from Rotifunk, had come for the next day's clinic. He slept in one of the bedrooms on the other side of the duplex.

During the night I became very ill and began to vomit profusely. I managed to get to the bathroom. Then there was a second episode and George appeared at the bathroom window asking if I needed help. But I thought the nausea would quit and I didn't need help. After a third round of explosive vomiting, George came in and gave me a sedative to stop the vomiting.

In the morning I was too ill to work. At mid-morning, Steve appeared. He too had been ill all night. Apparently, he had retained his food longer than I had and was plagued with severe diarrhea all night. We commiserated with each other and put the blame on the mushrooms.

Not all volunteers were able to adapt to the rather simple life in Sierra Leone. Two volunteers arrived independently of each other. After a week in Tiama they each decided not to stay. Perhaps it was that Tiama had little to offer in the way of entertainment, or they found the diet too limited. In any case, both of them left and were probably sent back to the United States.

There were never any female volunteers in Tiama, but there were a fair number in the country including several at Njala. Apparently, some of them had their eyes on Dan. I soon began to get requests asking if some of the young women could come and spend a weekend with me. I soon had a series of female guests, and while Dan was always courteous and friendly, there was no ensuing romance.

Sometime later a third volunteer arrived. He was as different from

Dan and Steve as they were from each other. He came from a wealthy family in Ohio where his father was an executive in a large industrial firm. Jim found life in Tiama to be very trying. Unlike Dan, he was totally devoid of mechanical skills. Unlike Steve, he didn't make close friends with the local people. He had problems adjusting to the local food. He refused to eat bread or meat produced locally, eating only imported meat from Freetown. Although Jim would eat meals at my house, he refused to eat bread that I had bought from the local baker.

The four of us continued to spend time together. They still came to my house once a week to eat, and occasionally, I went up to the school compound to have a meal with them. On very special occasions, they would borrow my Volkswagen bus to go someplace. Once when I had to take a patient to Rotifunk to the hospital and was very tired, Steve drove both the patient and me to the hospital.

Jim lasted six months. Although none of the three was a trained teacher, they were all assigned to teach in the secondary school. Sierra Leone youngsters are like all kids the world over, and enjoyed misbehaving in class. I'm sure they didn't get away with much with Dan, but Jim was another matter. The students were extremely mischievous, and he had problems maintaining discipline. Finally, one day in desperation, he slapped a student.

The African principal, Frank Anthony, had strict rules about discipline. Contrary to practices in many schools in Sierra Leone, teachers were not allowed to administer corporal punishment. Any case of misbehavior had to be taken to the principal. There was a hearing and if there was any punishment by flogging, Mr. Anthony administered it himself. This usually consisted of two or three lashes with a cane. I doubt if there was any physical pain involved, but the ignominy of being punished by the principal was an adequate deterrent.

Jim's offense was the final straw, and he was transferred to Freetown. After a brief stay, he left for the United States.

Both Dan and Steve stayed their full two years. Dan did a great deal with agricultural projects. One of his most successful was raising pineapples; big and sweet, the pineapples averaged nine pounds apiece compared to the local pineapples which were often not more than two pounds.

When Dan left there was a great farewell celebration in his honor. School and community alike sang his praises. He had won both respect and love.

After he returned to the United States, we kept in touch for a long time. He went back to school for more education and later sent pictures of his wedding and then of his children.

CHAPTER 39

Exploring Sierra Leone

Taking advantage of the dry season in February 1961, I decided to explore the northern part of Sierra Leone. I first drove north to Magburaka. Since there were few, if any, hotels outside of Freetown and Bo, it was customary to ask a local missionary for a place to stay. My first stop was with Marion Birch and his wife Marilyn, missionaries with the Wesleyan Methodist Church.

Marion and his twin sister, also named Marilyn, had been born and raised in Sierra Leone, the children of missionary parents. He was fluent in several of the local languages, and he and his wife were now working as evangelists. One of their projects was the development of tapes in the local languages to be used in Christian broadcasting. As a piece of equipment, they had a small electric organ. During my short stay, to my delight, I was allowed to spend some time playing the organ.

I stayed one night. The next morning I planned to drive north toward Kabala, a town just south of the Guinea border. While we were eating breakfast someone came to the door to report an accident. A man had climbed high into a palm tree where he was tapping the tree to collect palm wine, a local alcoholic drink. He had fallen from the tree and impaled himself on the stump of a tree on the ground. The tree had pierced the abdomen.

"Lois, could you take this man to Magburaka to the hospital?" Marion asked.

"I guess so," I answered with some reluctance. "What do we do with the wound? Should we try to bandage it?"

"How could we do that?" Marilyn asked. "The less we move him the better it will be."

I asked, "Do you have anything like morphine or Demerol that we could give him to ease his pain?"

Marilyn thought it over. "That would cause trouble with his breathing and we don't know if his lung is injured."

Marion had the final word. "I think you should take him as quickly as possible. He is probably bleeding and the sooner you get him to the hospital, the better. Perhaps, they can save his life at the hospital."

The man was lifted into the back seat of the Kombi. The injured man couldn't speak any English, only Tenme, which I couldn't speak. A friend of his who could speak a little English came along and sat in the front seat with me. The injured man was in terrible pain and kept muttering to himself.

"What is he saying?" I asked my passenger.

"He says he is dying," was the reply.

I, too, thought he was probably dying and just drove a little faster.

He was still alive when we got to the hospital. Miraculously, none of the major blood vessels had been cut, there was minimal bleeding, and the doctors were able to repair the internal damage. When I stopped on my return trip two days later, he was recovering. When I asked what we should have done, the doctor suggested that a clean bandage would have kept out the dirt and reduced the amount of infection.

I drove north to Kabala. This town was near the northern border next to the Republic of Guinea. The landscape is characterized by large hills, unlike the rather flat land around Tiama. A group of American missionaries had established a school of missionary children at Kabala. The school was on top of a high hill with a breathtaking view of the surrounding countryside.

Most of the teachers were American. Jane Eberle was the EUB representative at the school. I had a good visit with her. Most of the students were children of missionary parents of all denominations. A few

Volkswagon Kombi.

African children were also enrolled. I knew several of the missionary children including two from the Bradford family as well as several others who were parts of the EUB family. It was good to have a chance to visit with them.

Education for missionary children always presents a problem. Some children are sent to local schools where instruction in the early years is done in the local languages. The American children pick up the language very quickly. Classes are often very crowded. I have seen first grade classes with 100 children, for example. There are limited supplies of books and teaching materials. Many schools still don't have electricity so that such modern teaching aids such as videotapes and computers can't be used even if the school could afford them.

Some missionary parents teach their children at home, particularly in the lower grades. But this denies the children the social contacts they need to have with children their own age as well as lessening the effect of group learning. If the mother has professional responsibilities, she may find it difficult to have time for both teaching and preparation.

Americans are often reluctant to send their children to boarding schools. They dislike being separated from their children for long periods and sometimes feel there are unwelcome influences in the boarding schools. Sometimes children are sent back to the United States to continue their schooling. In a school like the one in Kabala, the curriculum is developed along American lines, thus preparing the children for entry into the local school system when they return.

No matter what decision is made, it is one that is made with great difficulty. If the children are separated from their parents, it can be traumatic. On the other hand, the bond that develops between children in such a boarding school is very strong, one that usually lasts their whole lives.

CHAPTER 40

Taking Health Care
to the Villages

One of my continuing frustrations was my inability to gain fluency in the Mende language. I could manage medical conversations fairly well but was not able to do much beyond that. The mission council in Sierra Leone did not seem to feel that language competency was either necessary or desirable. However, the handbook for missionaries issued by the mission board in the United States stipulated that instruction in the local language could be provided. I had spent a year at Yale studying Chinese that had obviously not prepared me for Africa, although that year had provided some help in how to study a language and had given some knowledge of phonetics.

During my first two terms in Sierra Leone, I had spent some time with two local teachers, Pastor Wolseley, the assistant pastor at the church and one of the local teachers, S. K. Carew. At that time, there were no current Mende grammars or dictionaries. The two men were very helpful as I struggled to learn the complicated grammar. Mende is a tonal language, and not only did I have trouble hearing and reproducing the tones, but my broad Wisconsin accent interfered with some of the pronunciation. One of my candid Mende friends commented that I could only say two phrases well.

When I returned from furlough in 1960, I decided the way to learn a language was to totally immerse myself in a village where little English was spoken. Clyde and Gladys Galow agreed to come to Tiama for a few weeks while I went to study Mende in Lago.

Lago is about ten miles north of Tiama on the edge of the Kori chiefdom. The village had a large primary school with several teachers who were the only people in the village fluent in English. There was also a large, multi-purpose building in the center of town where meetings were held and which housed the local congregation for Sunday church services.

The building also included two small rooms. I was able to move into one of these for a place to sleep. I carried a small kerosene stove for heating water, a small supply of food, a mosquito net, drinking water, and a supply of medicine. I soon realized I couldn't figure out how to put up the mosquito net so I didn't bother. The windows had no screens, but the mosquitoes didn't seem to be a problem.

I quickly developed a routine for the days. In the morning there were early visitors, the village headman and some of his friends with whom I shared morning coffee. Their English and Krio were limited but I was able to pick up some words and phrases in Mende. When the visitors left, I ran a little clinic distributing some of the medicines I had brought. My chores over, I would walk to where the women were cooking. I knew enough Mende to ask the names of objects. Gradually, my vocabulary increased, accompanied by some knowledge of the grammar. One of the themes at Yale had been "Listen and repeat, listen and repeat, the only way to learn a language is to listen and repeat." I was putting this wisdom into practice. I had the best teachers, willing to correct my pronunciation.

The first week went well. Then I paid for my neglect of putting up the mosquito net by developing a raging case of malaria. The villagers sent word to Tiama, and Clyde and Gladys came to get me.

Long afterwards, Clyde would tease me about my learning experience in Lago saying that my main lessons had been not to sleep without screens and a mosquito net.

The week's experience and the friends I made were the open door to starting a clinic in Lago. I had always dreamed of developing a series of village clinics. It was ten miles to Lago, just the right distance. It was too far for the villagers to walk into Tiama but a reasonable distance to take the Kombi. There was a good road to the village and there were not other medical facilities for quite some distance.

We went out on Fridays. Usually three of the staff went with me, and we carried all the medicine we thought we would need. We used the same building in which I had slept while I was there, using the small room for prenatal examinations and the big room for the rest of the examinations and treatment. We treated people who were ill or injured and developed a large well-baby clinic. Eventually, over 100 women brought their babies to the clinic each week. The income barely covered the expenses, however, and no one on the staff was paid anything for the trip. As in Tiama, all medicine used for prevention and treatment in the baby clinic was distributed free of charge. We also gave free treatment to school children and the teachers. Although we obviously couldn't conduct deliveries, we frequently brought pregnant women who were close to their delivery date back to Tiama.

We didn't carry food along, instead I paid one of the local women to cook for us each week. During the first few weeks, I was given a room in which to eat my dinner while the staff ate together. I usually ate alone in Tiama and wasn't willing to repeat the performance in Lago so we soon shared our meals.

Lago was on the northern edge of Mende country; just beyond the village lived the people who spoke Temne. We began to have a fair number of people who attended the clinic who could only speak Temne. We had trouble communicating. I offered five pounds to the first person on the staff who could manage the clinic in Temne. To my surprise, I picked up enough Temne so that I was able to do the communicating myself.

After we had operated the clinic for about two years, one day, the headman and a group of elders came to see me.

"We have decided that we should charge you rent for the use of our building," they said.

I was dumbfounded. "We really don't have any money to pay the rent," I replied.

"But you make a lot of money from the medicine you sell," was their response.

"But we don't charge anything for all the medicine that is given to the babies in the baby clinic. It costs us something to pay for the petrol to drive out here," was my answer.

"Your staff gets extra money for coming here," was the next argument.

I was really dismayed. "No they don't, and we pay for the food we eat."

We were unable to come to any agreement. After a few weeks, we canceled the clinics. The staff was relieved that they didn't have to do the extra work that the clinic entailed.

To my surprise, we began to get delegations from other villages, asking us to visit their town and start a clinic there.

This was near the end of 1962. I was making plans to go home in the middle of 1963 and I wasn't sure I wanted to start another clinic for only a few months. I wasn't sure if my replacement would want to continue a village clinic.

Several groups offered to let us use a building rent-free. They also offered places to sleep for me and the staff and would provide food. I discussed it with the staff, but we all were reluctant to start in a new place.

A few weeks later, a group of men came from Lago.

"We want you to come back to Lago with the clinic."

"But I told you we can't pay any rent," was my reply.

They looked a little shamefaced.

"We won't charge you rent. The women in the village are very upset because their children are not getting care. There is no one to examine the pregnant women and no one to treat the sick people."

I was reluctant.

"We made a mistake," they apologized. "We really do want the medicine."

So we went back and continued the clinic until I left for the United States. The person who replaced me did not have a car and the clinics were discontinued.

We had attempted to start a clinic in another village about ten miles south of Tiama, but somehow we were never able to maintain a consistent schedule of visits. Frequently, we had to cancel the proposed trip. Eventually, we gave up the project.

But the concept was good. I would like to have developed a series of clinics. Many years later when I lived in Kenya, the hospital managed 17 clinics which were visited once a month. It was highly successful promoting health care for mothers and infants and was instrumental in reducing both maternal and infant morbidity and mortality rates.

CHAPTER 41

More Put-To-Bed Women

Gradually, the number of women attending the prenatal clinic and the number coming to the hospital for deliveries increased. Most of the women from Tiama came for deliveries and increasingly, women from the surrounding villages also walked in for care.

Among those we took care of were Tuzylene Wonnie and Tabitha Caulker. Tuzylene and Donald Wonnie had moved from Jaiama to Tiama where Donald was teaching at the new secondary school. Tabitha Williams Caulker was still living in Jaiama where Gertrude Bloede delivered her first child. She came back to Tiama to have her second baby. Her mother was still living in Tiama.

I was grateful for all the uncomplicated deliveries and rejoiced with the families when a healthy child was born and joined the other members of the household.

However, not all experiences were trouble-free. Occasionally, I transferred patients in labor to Bo or Rotifunk. Other women were advised to go to better equipped facilities during their pregnancy when I thought there was going to be a problem.

One of these times was during the pregnancy of Teacher Lamboi's wife. He had married one of his students. I had delivered the first baby with no problems. Within weeks of that pregnancy, she was pregnant with the second child which was a violation of the local taboos. Most Mende women, in fact, many African women, abstain from intercourse for months after birth. Some have no intercourse until they finish breast-feeding which may be as long as 18 to 24 months. Often menstruation does not resume until breast-feeding is deliberately stopped, or has decreased to one or two feedings a day.

The young couple was severely criticized for their impetuosity. When it came time to deliver the baby, we ran into problems. I was able to deliver the baby, but the placenta was retained. By good fortune, this happened while Dr. George Harris was in Tiama on one of his visits, and he was able to extract the placenta.

The next time the Lambois waited the required two years for a baby. Fearing a repeat of the retained placenta, I was unwilling to attempt the delivery. About a month before the baby was due, Mrs. Lamboi went to Bo to stay with relatives. As the day of delivery approached, she developed an attack of malaria. As often happens, the malaria precipitated the labor. Not realizing that she was in labor, she delivered in the house. There was also a retained placenta with the accompanying hemorrhage. Before she could be taken to the hospital, she died.

For months I wondered if I could have prevented the death if she had stayed and delivered in Tiama. Perhaps, but if she had died "in my hands," my guilt and grief would only have been intensified.

At another time, I carried Rosaline Scott to Manjama near Bo where Winnie Bradford was managing a small clinic. Rosaline had worked in the Tiama clinic since 1955 but after her marriage to a young man from Nigeria, she was content to function as a wife and mother. Her husband was a delightful person and had a good position working for the railway. In her first pregnancy, Rosaline was pregnant with twins. There was a history of twins in the Scott family as Rosaline had twin brothers. She was a tall, thin girl, and the diagnosis of twins was made early in the pregnancy. The pregnancy went well, but when the expected time of delivery came, she didn't go into labor. I was not willing or equipped to induce labor, particularly with a first baby and a uterus distended with twins. Two weeks after the due date passed, we went to Bo and drove to Manjama. Winnie had more courage than I did, but we were also within a few minutes of a well-equipped government hospital at Bo. Winnie induced the labor with intravenous syntocinon and without untoward effects, a boy and girl were soon born.

Then Musu had a baby. She had worked as a nurse in the clinic since 1953, almost seven years. She was now about 20 years old which was very old for a Mende woman to be unmarried and childless. She told me that whenever she went home, the village people would ask, "Where is your child?"

"I don't have any," she would respond.

"Then where is your husband?" would be the next question.

"I don't have a husband, either."

Several young men had been friendly and made the appropriate gestures which she had refused.

One evening when a local woman came to visit me, we started to talk about Musu.

"I wonder when she will get married," I speculated.

"You know she isn't normal," the woman told me.

I hadn't noticed there was anything wrong with her. "What do you mean?"

"Well, she doesn't menstruate," the woman replied.

I wasn't sure of that and really doubted if it were true, but the woman continued.

"Not only that, but she can't have relations with a man, and she can't get pregnant."

All of this was disproved when Musu became pregnant. Whether it was to deny the rumors or as a result of community pressures, she succumbed to the sweet talk of a much older man who lived outside the community. He was a civil servant, relatively well-educated with a wife and family. Marriage to Musu was out of the question. If he ever acknowledged paternity, he made no promises of support or help.

Musu was on the pudgy side, and I didn't detect the pregnancy until it was fairly far advanced. The rest of the staff were aware of the situation and helped Musu keep it a secret. Eventually, of course, even I could see that something was coming.

The labor was long and difficult. It was not unusual for Mende women to have labors that lasted five to seven days. Dr. Silver always maintained that these long labors were related to the poor protein diet. The lack of protein was related to poor muscle function so that the expulsive efforts of the uterus were ineffective and labors tended to be long and painful.

Musu followed the pattern, and it took five days before she gave birth. It was a trying time. She was in the hospital for all five days. I stayed with her most of that time so sleep became a precious commodity. As I tried to get a few hours sleep, she would wake me, saying accusingly, "You pretend to be asleep, but you aren't." Was it her apprehension that prolonged the labor? By now she had seen many deliveries and knew that it could be both painful and frightening.

Finally, on the fifth day she delivered a little boy. There was a surprisingly short second stage, only 20 minutes. He was a small child only five and one-half pounds, but healthy.

Later Musu had a second child and eventually married a local farmer who seemed to appreciate her cheerful disposition and industriousness.

One day a young Temne woman from a distant village was brought in. She apparently had been in labor for several days, five or six. Again it was a last desperate chance that we might be able to deliver the baby before they both died. The first obvious problem was that the woman had a full bladder and could not urinate. This sometimes happens when the baby's head is in the vagina, pushing the bladder up into the abdomen and compressing the urethra so that the woman is unable to pass urine. It is essential to empty the bladder to give more room for the baby to come through the birth canal. I was able to pass a catheter and empty the bladder. Within a few minutes, the baby's head appeared and the baby was born.

But this was not the end of the problems. The prolonged pressure of the baby's head against the anterior wall of the vagina had caused the tissue to become infected, and there was now an open hole between the bladder and vagina. This is called a vesicovaginal fistula and is very common among the very young girls in West Africa who have a long, obstructed labor.

The woman was now unable to control her urine. There was a constant dribble of urine out of the vagina which resulted in a continuous disagreeable odor. Soon the other women in the ward were complaining loudly about the smell. There was also an ethnic problem. The girl was Temne and could speak no Mende while the rest of the women were local people who had little tolerance for non-Mendes.

Vesicovaginal fistulas are sometimes treated surgically, but like other surgical procedures, there were few surgeons in Sierra Leone that would do the repair, plus it was very costly. The surgical repair also limited childbearing since the surgical site was apt to break down during subsequent deliveries. Some surgeons would only attempt the repair after the woman was past her childbearing age.

The only other option was to hope that the fistula would heal spontaneously. After several days, the family took the girl home. When she returned several months later, the fistula had closed and she was without problems.

As the attendance at the clinic and maternity unit increased, so did the number of difficult cases. In one of my letters home, I wrote of a month in which we had 16 deliveries, 11 in one week. It was also a week in which 11 babies, six months of age or older, had died. This happened in March, the end of the dry season, when water supplies were low. It was in March that we often saw cases of typhoid and measles.

As one would expect, if the women on the hospital staff are young, they are probably going to get pregnant and have babies. I have already talked about Musu and Rosaline. A third young married woman was Susanna, wife of one of the teachers at the secondary school. Both she and her husband were concerned because she had been unable to get pregnant. A series of investigations were started. The doctor started with a sperm count which was met with serious objections by the husband. He protested that, of course, it couldn't be his fault, she was responsible. Second, he felt that masturbation to produce the sperm was distasteful and unnatural. Eventually, he was convinced to produce a specimen, but the sperm count was normal. We began investigations on Susanna. She had adequate ovulation with normal, patent ovarian tubes. After a long time, she became pregnant to their great delight.

Within a few weeks, problems appeared in the pregnancy. Her blood pressure went up and she developed edema and albumin in the urine. While this complication is not uncommon in late pregnancy, it is always an ominous sign and even more so in early pregnancy. We put her in bed, rested her, and sought advice from one of the mission doctors. This happened just before I was to go home on leave. After I left, her condition worsened and she was sent to Rotifunk for care. Eventually, her condition became so serious that a cesarean section was performed in an effort to save both her life and the life of the baby, but both she and the baby died. The baby was too premature to survive, and Susanna apparently had a kidney disorder that was aggravated by the pregnancy and caused her death.

Later in 1962, we saw even more difficulties. There were three maternal deaths in a period of six weeks, a terrible time for me.

The first person to die in labor was a young girl, one of several wives of Chief Gbappe. She was a pleasant, plump girl, about 16 years old. During the latter part of her pregnancy she developed mild signs of preeclampsia. It didn't seem too serious.

Preeclampsia is a condition which occurs only in human pregnancy. It occurs more frequently in very young women. The cause is unknown. As mentioned in the case of Susanna, it usually appears during the last three months of pregnancy.

If the condition is allowed to continue, it may progress to eclampsia which is the presence of convulsions. In this state, it may be fatal to both mother and baby. The final cure is delivery of the baby and placenta, although bed rest may help to alleviate some of the symptoms.

I debated about sending the chief's wife to the government hospital at Bo for delivery, but decided that her symptoms were so mild, I would try to let her deliver in Tiama. The first stage of labor proceeded easily, but the second stage was another matter. She pushed for over an hour, and there was only fair progress. Suddenly, she convulsed. We were able to deliver the baby, but within a few minutes the woman died.

I was crushed. Chief Gbappe had waited outside the maternity building through the whole experience. He accepted the death with a typical degree of fatalism. "Now God" is the local expression. While it might have been God's will, I felt that it didn't absolve me from my mistake in judgement or my inability to prevent the death.

The second maternal death occurred a few weeks later. In retrospect, I don't know what caused the death. I had delivered several previous babies for this woman, although this time she had twins. There was no hemorrhage and no sign of shock. After the delivery, her condition rapidly got worse and she died. Dr. Jim was present and attempted resuscitation, but was not successful.

The third woman was brought in unconscious from a far village. She, too, had convulsions. The baby was dead, but undelivered. We were able to deliver the stillborn fetus, but within a few minutes the woman died.

The first death had been most upsetting, but the combination of the three deaths was overwhelming. Even if death seems inevitable, as it did with the third patient, one relives the experience endlessly. What could I have done differently? If we had better equipment, more medication, could we have prevented the deaths? Certainly someone with more experience than I had would have prevented at least one death and perhaps all three.

After I got a car, I did transport some patients to the hospital; sometimes to the government hospital at Bo and sometimes to the EUB hospital at Rotifunk.

One afternoon I took the wife of one of the young evangelists to Bo. He and several women from his village went with me. The patient was admitted and assured of a safe delivery so the group who had traveled with me decided to stay at Bo with the patient.

I started home just about dusk. When I was about 20 miles from Tiama, my headlights began to flicker. The Kombi has an engine in the rear of the car. I stopped the car and looked around. To my horror, I saw a wisp of smoke coming from the engine. I got out, ran to the rear, opened the engine door, and saw that the engine was on fire. The battery had a cover that had jolted loose which set a spark and started the blaze. I grabbed dirt from the road, threw it on the battery and was able to put out the fire. Of course, the power was gone and I was stuck with a dead engine.

There was very little traffic on that road, and it could be hours before another car came along. Fortunately, one came fairly soon and I sent a note to Tiama asking someone to come and rescue me.

I was stranded at the foot of a small hill at the top of which was a small village. Soon the villagers came down to see what the problem was. They urged me to come and sit in the village, but I was reluctant to leave the car. Three little boys came down and discussed the situation at length.

I heard one of them say in Mende, "She ought to be afraid!"

"What should I be afraid of?" I asked.

They whispered, "The spirits!"

At last help came. Pastor Carew came with his Landrover and brought Dan Kyle along. With the help of the villagers, they pushed the car to the top of the hill, left it in the village, and took me back to Tiama. A few days later somebody brought a new battery back to the car and brought the car back to Tiama.

CHAPTER 42

Strangers Arrive

Visitors or "strangers", in the local terminology, were always a welcome interruption to the quiet in Tiama. One of the earliest visitors was the return of a local boy, the son of a woman from Tiama and a Scottish government official. When the Scot returned home, the woman married a local man. But the boy's father continued to send financial support, and George was able to complete his education. He then traveled to the United States for his college degree.

On his return to Tiama, there was an enormous celebration in the village. In addition to day-long dancing and drumming, there was a special program in the evening in the court barri. George, Pastor Carew, and I were invited to sit on the stage. Lengthy speeches of welcome were made by the various chiefdom officials. George had an appropriate response.

The major event of entertainment was a snake charmer who appeared with an 18-foot boa constrictor. The boa constrictor is non-poisonous, but kills its prey either by swallowing it whole or by wrapping itself around the victim and causing death by constriction. Several times I saw dead constrictors, but this was the only time I saw a live one. As the man held the snake, he allowed it to advance and retreat to the great amusement of the crowd.

While in the United States, George had married an African-American woman and they had one child. Several weeks after his arrival in Sierra Leone, his wife and child came to join him in Tiama. They lived with his mother and her husband. The house was spacious, but of course, had no electricity or running water. Adjustment to kerosene lights and an outhouse, as well as the lack of running water in the house, was difficult for the family.

Then the wife found that she was pregnant and began to look for a place to deliver the baby. The government hospitals in Freetown and Bo offered very primitive services for childbearing. She went to several church facilities but they insisted that their only facilities were beds in the main wards where there was no privacy. She had no assurance that a physician would deliver her, but she would be attended by a local midwife.

At this time in the United States, nurse-midwives were very scarce, and it was rare, and usually unacceptable to have a midwife conduct a delivery.

For a long time I thought about offering my services. Since the first delivery had been uncomplicated, it was unlikely that there would be problems with this baby. This was before I had my car so I was aware of what kind of problems we would have in getting her to the hospital in an emergency. But I finally decided to offer my help.

"Estelle, I would be willing to deliver your baby if you want me to. I would do it at my house so you would have some privacy."

"Thank you," she responded, "but we have decided to go back to the United States for the delivery." I knew George's mother would be very disappointed not to be able to be present at the birth.

George had tried to find work in Sierra Leone, but at this point, he had only been given vague promises so the family went back to the United States. In the meantime, he was hired by a nongovernmental organization that owned a large piece of property outside of Freetown. The building included school facilities and land for agricultural projects. The building had been unoccupied for some time, but George was hired to reopen the school.

The family came back to Sierra Leone including the two children. The obstacles of the job were enormous. The building was old and had not been maintained in good condition. The water system was not functioning. The school was far enough away from Freetown that supplies and personnel had to be transported to the site but public transportation was not available. Students were reluctant to enroll in a school that had no reputation or a well-established curriculum.

George stayed several years, growing more and more frustrated. His wife's initial enthusiasm for Africa diminished and she became very bitter. Finally, they gave up the project and returned to the United States. I kept in touch with them for several years and visited them in the United States. I regretted that Sierra Leone had lost someone with so much potential and expertise.

In the 1990's the United Methodist Church, as well as other denominations, have large programs for volunteers to go to developing countries to help with various projects. Usually, these were efforts at construction: putting on new roofs, repairing windows and doors painting and plastering.

Today, a complicated system has been developed for organizing volunteers. They raise their supportive funds for travel, housing and food, and are also asked to raise substantial funds toward the work they are going to do: paint, plaster, wood for doors, glass for windows, metal roofing, etc.

In the 1950's, however, no such organization had evolved and we rarely got volunteers. The most unforgettable volunteer to come to Sierra Leone was an industrialist from Ohio, Micky Foster. Micky had been inspired by his pastor who had been an EUB missionary in Sierra Leone. The pastor introduced him to Abraham Saboleh, a Mende who was studying agriculture at Ohio State University. Saboleh was a warm, friendly person, always courteous, and a committed Christian. Micky opened up his home, his heart, and his purse to Saboleh. Saboleh soon made Micky's home his American home.

Micky's interest in Sierra Leone was intensified so he decided to come out to help. He was as generous to the missionaries in Sierra Leone as he had been to Saboleh. Micky was the successful owner of a large industrial plant in Ohio and was able to use his construction and managerial skills in various places in Sierra Leone.

He was a short, stocky man who bristled with energy. His business was well-established and apparently, the administrative staff was able to function independently, allowing him to spend long periods away from the plant. His wife did not seem to share his enthusiasm for African travel as she never came with him; or perhaps, he didn't invite her. At one time, he did bring along his ten-year-old grandson.

He spent several weeks with me at Tiama. My best memory of him is on an Easter weekend. On Saturday night I had taken a patient to Rotifunk to the hospital. Although I had worked all day, about midnight I decided I needed to transport the patient. One of the nurses went with me. I stayed at the hospital until the patient was safely delivered and then at 6:00 a.m. we started home.

Easter at the Tiama church was a day of great celebration, and the church was always filled to the doors. There was usually a choir procession and many joyous hymns. Micky had come for the service, and I didn't want to miss it. But my fatigue was more than I could overcome. About halfway from Rotifunk to Tiama, I could no longer stay awake. I stopped the car and lay down in the back seat. After 15 minutes of sleep, I was able to go on to Tiama. When I got home, I crawled into bed and gave Micky strict instructions that he was to wake me in time for the service. About an hour before the service was to begin, he knocked on the door. The cook had failed to arrive, but Micky had prepared a big breakfast including scrambled eggs, bacon, and toast. Afterwards, we went to join the service.

As I have mentioned, once the bridge over the Teye was completed, the most convenient road from Freetown to Bo ran through Tiama, and many people stopped at my house; some just to say "hello" and have a drink of cold water; others joined me in my meal or brought lunch with them and shared their food.

One family that did this fairly often was a Seven-Day Adventist missionary couple who lived in Bo. They followed a strict vegetarian diet so didn't usually share my noon meal. But in return for coming into the house, the wife would often bring a loaf of her homemade bread which she made from bran cereal. It was delicious and a welcome relief from the continuous diet of white flour bread that we bought in Tiama.

One day a car stopped and a young Englishman came to the door. Chris DeLinde was working with the British Council in Bo. He had heard that I came from Wisconsin and wanted to meet me. While he was in Britain, he had met a girl from Wisconsin and wanted to meet more of us from the "badger state."

I had never met the woman but knew of her family. Her father was a professor at the University of Wisconsin-Madison and an authority on British history. Chris and I talked at length about Madison and the university.

Chris was voluble and energetic; filled with enthusiasm for many things: history, travel, and food. He had spent several years in India before coming to Sierra Leone.

He stopped at my house frequently. One day he bounded onto the veranda and told me he had just talked on the telephone to his American friend who was living in Chicago. I was amazed at the ability to telephone to the United States. Transatlantic telephone calls were something new, and I wondered if I could call my parents from Freetown.

In August the missionaries all came to Bo for our annual mission conference. Chris invited Elaine Gasser and me for lunch. Elaine, whose home was in Baraboo, Wisconsin, was currently teaching at Harford School in Moyamba. Chris promised a truly American lunch. While the food was delicious, it was more British than American and included some very tasty smoked salmon.

A few weeks later, Chris planned to travel to Chicago and Madison. When he found that my parents lived just north of Milwaukee, he made plans to visit them as well. He and his friend, Karen, stopped at Richfield and offered to carry something back to Sierra Leone for me. My stepmother sent a roll of summer sausage and a block of Swiss cheese with caraway seed which was one of my favorite foods.

Chris and Karen went to Madison, then back to Chicago. Chris flew home to Britain and then to Sierra Leone, carefully carrying the cheese and sausage. He stopped at Tiama and told me excitedly about the whole trip. His best news was that he had proposed marriage to Karen and she had accepted. He was elated.

The sausage had traveled well, but alas, the cheese had not done as well. I wondered what the custom officers had thought as the luggage, with this reeking bundle, passed under their nose. It was inedible and had to be discarded.

About two months later, Chris stopped for the last time. He had received a long letter from Karen; she had broken the engagement. He was very sad and I felt it cruel of her to build up his hopes and then destroy them. He had decided to leave Sierra Leone and go back to India. I missed his cheerful visits and hope he found happiness in India.

Occasionally, distinguished visitors came through. Stanley Mooneyham, the well-known agricultural missionary, stopped and spent a weekend in Tiama attending church services which were recognized throughout the country for the enthusiastic worship and participation of the local people.

One day someone brought the famous African-American author, James Baldwin. I was not aware then of his dislike for missionaries which I learned later on when I read some of his books. Whatever his personal feelings were they were not apparent, and we had a short, pleasant conversation.

Another occasional visitor was John Hargraves who at that time was a professor at Fourah Bay College. He became an authority on Sierra Leone history and customs and continued to publish material on the country after he returned to Britain.

Frequently, traveling church representatives stopped, sometimes for just a few minutes and sometimes for much longer stays. One of the latter was the Rev. Stanley Forkner. The church in the United States had organized a team of pastors to come to Sierra Leone on a preaching mission. Each pastor was assigned to a specific church and the Rev. Forkner came to spend a week in Tiama. One of his major projects was a daily Bible study with the people who spoke English in the community.

He was terribly frustrated by the African attitude toward time (so was I, usually). The afternoon meetings were to start at one o'clock. In those days, both clocks and radios were a rarity in Tiama. About an hour before any activity at church, the bell would be rung, and then rung again when the meeting started. I had learned to wait for both bells which were rung for a rather extended period.

A little before one o'clock, Rev. Forkner would be ready to leave for church which was just across the street from my house.

"You are too early," I would say. "The warning bell hasn't rung."

"But it is ten minutes to one," he would protest.

"You and I are the only ones who know that. When the group is ready, they will ring the bell."

"It is time to go," he insisted. "I am going to the church."

About 20 minutes later he was back. "There is no one there."

"That's right," I explained patiently each time. "The first bell has just been rung. If you go when the second bell starts, you will be in plenty of time."

The system worked well and gradually he learned to adapt, but the system was hard on time-conscious Americans.

Occasionally, important government officials stopped in Tiama. I have mentioned how thrilled we were at the dispensary when the Prime Minister, Dr. Milton Margai, stopped. Sir Maurice and Lady Dorman also came to visit the town. He had been the British Governor General prior to independence in 1961. After independence, Dr. Margai asked that he continue as Governor General of the new country. I remember that during their visit they were gracious and kind. They were escorted on a tour around the town to view the most important buildings.

Later Sir Henry Lightfoot-Boston, the first Sierra Leonean Governor, paid an official visit. The community gathered in the court barri where numerous speeches were given.

I had just been through a bout of amebic dysentery which had left me very weak, but I was determined to see the Governor. I managed to walk the three blocks to the meeting and sat near the back. As the Governor and his party left, everyone stood. I was the only white person in the crowd, and I was also about a foot taller than almost everyone else. Again I was aware of how conspicuous I was. I did not go unnoticed, and the Governor smiled and nodded as he left the building.

As I reread my letters from Sierra Leone today, I am reminded of the loneliness of the first three years there. As the years passed, the letters tell of a steady stream of visitors who brightened my days.

After independence, a number of experts came to Sierra Leone to offer assistance to the new government. Some Americans came through the United States Agency for International Development (AID), and some came as an extension of universities in the United States. Others were sent by UNESCO, the United Nations Education Scientific and Cultural Organization. A number of these people were stationed at the agricultural station at Njala, only six miles from Tiama, and I came to know some of them very well.

The first white American couple came from DeKalb University in northern Illinois. They were followed by two African-American couples sponsored by USAID. Mr. Rice was involved in the administration of the Teacher's College at Njala, and Mr. Johnson had been an agricultural extension agent in Georgia. I got to know the Johnson's better than I knew the others. They had brought their three daughters, age 9 to 18 with them, two of whom were enrolled at Harford School at Moyamba. We exchanged meals and visited each other frequently, and the Johnson's often came to church in Tiama.

One Easter Sunday morning stands out. The church was completely filled, with some people standing outside looking through the windows.

I was the organist and choir director. We had managed to organize a rather large choir which included college and secondary school students home on their school break. As was the custom, they proceeded down the aisle from the back of the church. One of the young men had decided to embellish his dress with a bow tie that flashed red and green lights. As this spectacle came down the aisle, I nearly fell off the organ bench. I looked over at the Johnson's where Mr. Johnson was holding his sides, convulsed with laughter as the tears streamed down his face.

Later both the Rice's and Johnson's left Njala and moved north to Makeni. We maintained the friendship and I spent at least one weekend with them in their new home.

From left to right: Dan Kyle, Peace Corps volunteer; Lois; Steve, Peace Corps; three faculty from the University of Illinois

The Brown's came from New Zealand. His field of expertise was arithmetic, and he had come to develop a new arithmetic teaching program for Sierra Leone. Again we became good friends; I have written about the Christmas we spent together.

During their stay in Sierra Leone, the Brown's decided to visit Liberia. Sierra Leoneans still drove on the left side of the roads while the Liberians drove on the right. The Brown's were not aware of this, and shortly after they crossed the border, they were in a serious accident. Both of them had broken bones and had a slow and painful recovery.

Finally, a team of university professors came from the University of Illinois at Champaign/Urbana. They were able to establish a relationship between the University of Sierra Leone at Njala and the University of Illinois. They offered scholarships at the University of Illinois for a number of students, and several of their faculty spent time at Njala acting as classroom lecturers and advisors, particularly in the field of agriculture.

CHAPTER 43

Independence

Sierra Leone became an independent country on April 27, 1961. This was part of the wave of independence movements that swept all of colonial Africa starting in 1957 when the Gold Coast became Ghana. Within a few years, the three remaining colonies that had been British West Africa: Nigeria, Sierra Leone, and Gambia were granted independent status.

As a whole, the movement towards independence in Sierra Leone was a gradual process and relatively peaceful. Shortly after World War II, Africans were admitted into the legislative and administrative bodies of government, beginning with the Protectorate Assembly founded in 1946. This group had elected and appointed members and had some authority over matters in the provinces. In 1951, an Executive Council, again with some African members, assumed administrative decisions. Dr. Milton Margai became Chief Minister in 1954. Gradually, independence was becoming a reality.

With the approach of independence, there was much rejoicing. However, not everyone was pleased with the process and there were some minor disagreements. One of the demands was for elections prior to independence. The Kono people, living in the diamond territory, wanted assurance they would derive maximum benefits from the diamond industry. Struggles for leadership positions developed and a number of opposing political parties were organized.

Just prior to the independence celebration, some of the political leaders were accused of threatening violence to wreck the celebration. The Governor General declared a state of emergency; 43 people were arrested and detained in prison including the leader of one of the opposition parties, Siaka Stevens. Several years later, Mr. Stevens peacefully became the Prime Minister of the country and held that post for almost three decades.

Much of the credit for the peaceful and joyous transition from colony to independence must be given to Dr. Milton Margai. A quiet, unassuming man, he was able to achieve much of his success without ostentation or bravado. Smith Hempstone, a Chicago newspaper reporter who has written extensively on Africa, characterized Dr. Margai as "a wisp of a man." *West Africa* magazine described him as "quiet, cool, and cautious, though he can be decisive and even ruthless."

He was most often seen wearing the traditional blue-and-white, hand-woven, country-cloth gown, even when he was among those dressed in suits and ties or even top hats and tails. In one picture, he is emerging from the colonial office in London a year before Independence, flanked by his brother Albert and Siaka Stevens. Both men were dressed in suits and ties and are wearing smiles of victory. Dr. Margai stands in the center, wearing a long white gown, with a look of sorrow and patience on his face; he is not smiling.

Dr. Margai never lost concern and rapport with the indigenous people of the Protectorate. He spoke several local languages and was able to communicate with the peoples of many ethnic groups. He had a deep appreciation for and encouraged local customs. A part of the independence celebration was a demonstration of local dancing. The program was two-and-one-half hours long and included dances from many groups; among them were those of the masked "devils," the clowns of Sierra Leone society who often performed graceful and highly athletic exercises.

The performance ended with 500 Wunde men, the secret society of the Kpaa-Mende people. Their group included chiefs of the area as well as all classes of the organization. At the very end, Dr. Margai himself went and joined the dancers.

One of his greatest contributions to Africa was his effort to develop a peaceful association with other African states. He, with President Tubman of Liberia, was the initiator of the Organization of African Unity, the continent-wide association that works toward harmonious relationships throughout all of Africa.

Several months after independence when Queen Elizabeth visited Sierra Leone, she paid tribute to Dr. Margai's ability to lead his country peacefully, characterizing him as "wise, experienced, and devoted."

The major event of independence took place in Freetown. Just before midnight on April 26, the Union Jack was lowered and the green, white, and blue flag of Sierra Leone was raised. The crowd greeted the old flag by singing "God Save the Queen" and welcomed the new banner with the new national anthem.

The national anthem was based on the hymn tune "Old Hundred." The tune was adapted by John Akar who later held positions as head of the Sierra Leone Broadcasting System, and later as Ambassador to the United States. The tune is very singable with a reasonable range and meaningful words, stressing unity, peace, and loyalty to the government of the people.

My letter in April of 1961, to my parents gives a full description of the events in Kori chiefdom:

> *I don't know if I wrote that there was a hint of trouble earlier. The A.P.C., the All People's Congress, had threatened, among other things, to kill Dr. Margai, the Prime Minister; to call a general strike, and to blow up things like the electric stations and railway. When there was an initial effort at violence, 17 people were arrested. As things went on, more were arrested so that by the middle of the week about 45 had been arrested and were in custody while others were taken in and examined. It is ironic that with all our pride as EUB's Dr. Margai, two more ministers, and both Willie Fitzjohn and Richard Caulker (our representatives in Washington and London), are all graduates of the Albert Academy (the EUB high school in Freetown); all are EUB's and so is the leader of the APC who is also an Albert Academy grad and EUB.*
>
> *I have listened to a good share of the events that happened in Freetown over the radio. But since we had a lot going on here, I didn't always hear things the first time, but many of them were repeated. The big night was Wednesday night when the flag-raising ceremonies were held all over the country. Our week started here on Tuesday night. The Carews had a dinner for Mrs. Anthony and invited me, too. Then on Wednesday evening, the Anthony's had a dinner at their house. At 10:30 p.m. we all met at the football field where there was a blazing, big bonfire. About ten minutes to midnight we sang "God Save the Queen". Then the chiefdom police lowered the Union Jack. This was followed by a prayer, after which we sang "Lead, Kindly Light", the favorite hymn of Dr. Margai. The police then raised the new Sierra Leone flag: green, white, and blue stripes; and we sang the new Sierra Leone anthem. Of course, at this point there was a hitch when the flag didn't quite get up. We sang the national anthem anyway and about 15 minutes later, they finally got the flag up. This was followed by traditional dancing.*
>
> *On Wednesday, there were all sorts of games and races for the kids; this continued on Thursday afternoon. Thursday morning there was another ceremony at the field. Abraham Lavaly read the proclamation from the Prime Minister, first in*

Abraham Lavaly taking the salute on Independence Day.

*English and then in Mende. Then Pastor and Frank Anthony
(the principal of the high school), made speeches and we sang
all three verses of the national anthem. All the school kids
marched through the town. On Friday afternoon, a comic football match was played.*

*Saturday afternoon was the garden party. They did much
better than I expected. It was held in Abraham's compound
which is shady and has lots of grass and flowers, unusual for
an African compound. They served roasted meat on skewers,
bread, coffee, and soft drinks (at least to me), and hard liquor
to others. I ate with the Lebanese. Last night there was a social
dance at the court barri.*

*Today (Sunday), we had a service of Thanksgiving at
church. The kids sang a new hymn composed by the Minister
of Communications.*

*The women dressed in "ashobis" for many of the occasions.
These are dresses of the same material and color and made in the
same pattern. Someone gave me a special dress for the occasion,
a two-piece dress cut in traditional fashion and made of wide
purple-and-white stripes. A striking feature of all West African
independence celebrations were colorful cloth designs produced
commercially. Sometimes they feature a map of the country or a
picture of the President, the new flag, or a member of the Royal
family, who came from Britain for the celebration.*

I closed my letter home as follows:

> *Oh, I forgot the most fun of all. The village had collected money from everyone (except me) and with it bought treats for the school kids, killed a cow, and shared it. They gave me two pounds for the "missionaries." This included the Carew's, the Anthony's, and me. Since Mr. and Mrs. Anthony went to Freetown on Thursday, I invited the Carew's and their kids to an American picnic last night. We had the time of our lives. We went down to the sandy bank along the river. I took wieners and some potato salad, marshmallows, a poppy-seed cake, cookies, and as many trimmings as I could muster. Pastor built a fire, and I initiated the kids and Betty into the art of roasting wieners and marshmallows. The kids ate until their eyes and tummies just bulged. And I enjoyed it immensely. I don't know when I have had such fun!*

CHAPTER 44

The Queen Comes to Call

November 1961 was also the visit of Queen Elizabeth II and Prince Philip to Sierra Leone. It seemed to me there was greater excitement in the country over the visit of the royal couple than there had been over the independence celebration. The Queen had been scheduled to visit in 1959, and extensive preparations had been made at that time. However, she found she was pregnant and cancelled the visit. The local comment was there was no reason why she couldn't have had her baby in Connaught Hospital or Princess Christian Hospital in Freetown. Those of us who knew about the two government-sponsored hospitals wondered if she would have been charged sixpence to use the bed pan as was asked of the local people. Anyway, the visit was rescheduled for November 1961.

As with independence, the major events took place in Freetown, but both the Queen and her husband visited all three of the Provincial capitols. The royal couple met all 150 chiefs in the country, attended the agricultural show in Kenema, visited the diamond mines in Kono, and talked to hundreds of local people.

Tiama and Kori chiefdom were a part of the Southern Province where Bo was the Provincial headquarters. All of the missionaries had received invitations to attend the meeting in the Bo Town Hall where the Queen and Prince Philip were to preside. Several other large public gatherings were also held in Bo. As all of my staff wanted to attend, I closed the clinic and offered to take them with me.

We were to leave Tiama at 6:00 a.m. on the day of the big event. The men who were to go with me, stayed on the compound and woke me at 2:00 a.m., asking if it weren't time to leave. I sent them back to bed, but at hourly intervals they repeated the process. Finally, at 5:30 a.m. I decided to get ready. We were just about to get in the car when a breathless woman appeared at the doorstep.

"A woman in labor is walking into the hospital," she announced.

"Where is she?" I asked.

"She is coming on the road from Pelawahu."

We organized. "Tator, you get ready for the delivery," I ordered. "I will drive down the road and see if I can find her. We won't leave for Bo until she is delivered."

I drove for a mile in the direction the woman had indicated, but saw no sight of the patient so I turned around and came back. When I got to the hospital, she and her companions had arrived. Fortunately, she was ready to deliver. Tator delivered the baby and I assisted. By 6:30 a.m. everything was finished. Mother and baby were fine so we started out for Bo.

The reception at the Bo Town Hall started at 10:00 a.m. We missionaries sat together in two long rows, and I was fortunate to sit on a center aisle seat. The front rows were allocated to the chiefs, some of whom had brought five or six wives. The front rows were a blaze of color with the chiefs' colorful robes and the women dressed in bright *"ashobis"*.

At the appropriate time, her Royal Highness came down the aisle with her husband following, accompanied by the Provincial officials. The Queen sat on the platform while a series of prominent people were presented to her. She was then given traditional gifts including some beautifully woven country cloths and carved ivory.

In the afternoon, a *"durbar"* was held on the athletic field. The term *"durbar"* was borrowed from India and meant a presentation to the ruler by her subjects. Fifty-two chiefs of the Southern Province were

Official Kori chiefdom delegation for the Queen's visit. Paramount chief M.S. Gbappe III seated in the center, speaker Abraham Lavaly on the chief's right.

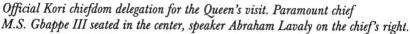

Dr. Mabel Silver (left) and Mrs. Bertha Leader on their way to the royal garden party.

presented to the Queen. Each chief was carried in a covered hammock, preceded and followed by dancers. The dancers presented a display of some particular aspect of local life in the chiefdom: mining diamonds, casting fishing nets, tapping palm trees for palm wine, and mudding a house. Raffia-robed devils accompanied the dancers. The Kori chiefdom had a presentation of the girls of the Bundu Society. As at the time of independence, the Wunde dancers also performed and again, the Prime Minister joined in the dance.

As each chief stopped in front of the Queen, he got out of the hammock, walked to greet her, and was given a medal of recognition.

The day was blazingly hot with the temperature over 100. The royal couple sat under a canopy with the Prime Minister and numerous other dignitaries. We stood with about 2,000 people on one of the surrounding hills with a great view of the magnificent ceremonies.

At twilight, a garden party reception was held at which certain local people were presented to the royalty. Three of our missionaries were so honored: Dr. Silver, and Dr. and Mrs. Leader. Dr. Silver and Dr. Leader had previously been honored by the British government with the award of the MBE (Member of the British Empire). Very few Americans had been given this honor within Sierra Leone.

CHAPTER 45

The Healing Touch

When the bridge was completed and the road to Rotifunk was finished, we were able to have better communication with the major EUB hospital. The hospital had increased their personnel, including several American doctors, and they were able to give us more help. Since the distance to Rotifunk was about the same as the distance to Bo, I usually took the complicated cases to Rotifunk.

By 1960, the hospital at Rotifunk had made a number of improvements. Several buildings had been constructed to house patients as well as several houses for hospital staff. Betty Beveridge, who had been a senior nursing sister in London and a working colleague for those of us who had done our midwifery training there, organized and administered a midwifery training program. After graduation, some of the midwives were assigned to outlying maternity units. Two midwives came to Tiama, both of whom were reliable and competent.

A series of new doctors joined Dr. Silver at Rotifunk. As to be expected, they came with varied abilities and mixed motives. The first of these was Dr. James, a bit on the erratic side. He had evangelistic zeal that overshadowed his commitment to physical healing. He was apt to view a hundred patients sitting on the veranda of the hospital waiting for treatment and announce that the Lord had sent him to preach. He would then head out to the village to spread the word, leaving Dr. Silver to take care of the patients. At the end of the year, the medical board decided that he might fit into another situation with greater ease so he moved to a hospital of another Christian denomination where he seemed to make a better adjustment.

With the increased number of doctors at Rotifunk, physicians began to visit Tiama once a week. It was also easier to transport complicated cases to the hospital and to utilize the laboratory facilities at Rotifunk.

During my first furlough in 1955, I had learned to do some laboratory tests but my knowledge and skills, as well as my equipment, were limited. I was able to test for hemoglobin and for some time was able to run a test for syphilis. However, as the facilities at Rotifunk improved and transportation became easier, it seemed more advantageous to send blood samples to the hospital for testing. At Tiama, we were never able to test for malaria or vaginal infections, and it would have been helpful to be able to do these examinations.

Once a week we would draw blood to test for syphilis from the pregnant women and then someone, usually Francis Ngegba, would carry the serum to Rotifunk. The round trip was a two-day journey. He traveled to Mano by lorry, caught the train to Rotifunk where he stayed the night, and returned the next day.

On one particular day, I had spent the morning collecting samples and labeling them; only the blood serum was sent to be tested. I had allowed the blood to clot, removed the clots, and intended to prepare the serum for transportation, first taking time to go to lunch. When I came back to the clinic, Rosaline, being unusually efficient, had thrown out the serum and washed the tubes. I was furious. When she came back from lunch, I said very quietly, "Just go home."

The next morning when she came to work she said, "My, but you were angry yesterday. You didn't even shout at me."

In addition to Dr. James, we eventually had three more doctors. The first was Lowell Gess, who with his wife Ruth, had previously served in a remote area of Nigeria. He was an excellent surgeon and had gradually developed a specialty in eye care, and had served a residency in ophthalmology on one of his furloughs in the United States.

Dr. Silver often talked about the first cataract surgery Dr. Gess did in Rotifunk. In those days, the patient was kept immobilized after surgery and the eyes were bandaged for ten days. In that particular case, the bandages were removed on Christmas morning. Dr. Silver said, "It followed the Biblical account, the blind were made to see." It seemed like a miracle. There were few, if any, eye surgeons in Sierra Leone, and Dr. Gess attracted large numbers of patients who needed eye care.

After several years, he moved the eye facilities to Tiama (after I had left) which was nearly as inaccessible as Rotifunk. Then he established an eye clinic in Bo. Eventually, he set up headquarters in a suburb at the edge of Freetown. In addition to the eye clinic, a general hospital was established on the grounds as well as a hotel for itinerant workers and a small church.

Since then, Dr. and Mrs. Gess have returned to Sierra Leone every January, spending several months treating eye diseases and doing eye surgery. In addition, they have done work in several other countries and have been able to encourage qualified eye surgeons to donate a month's time in Africa to treat patients with eye difficulties.

Dr. Gess was one of the first doctors in Sierra Leone to recognize onchocerciasis. This disease exists in South America, and in Africa from Senegal and Angola on the west coast, to Ethiopia and Tanzania on the Indian Ocean. It belongs to the class of filaria which are thread-like parasite worms that live in the bloodstream. The disease is transmitted by black flies.

Two major symptoms characterize the disease: large skin nodules which contain the worms and river blindness when the organism infects the eye. Diagnosis is made by snipping the skin nodules and exposing the worms.

The medical community in Sierra Leone was of the opinion that onchocerciasis was not present in the country. Dr. Gess had wide experience with the disease during his stay in Nigeria and quickly recognized it in Sierra Leone. He was able to both diagnose and treat patients who were infected.

Dr. Gess was a man of many abilities. He was an ordained minister and brought a depth of theological insight to the local church and the church as a whole. He also had considerable administrative skills, at one point carrying the responsibilities of mission superintendent.

The next doctor was Bob. Physically, he was a big, cheerful man. Young, he had adequate skills but wandering attention. His mind was busy with schemes to solve all the health problems of West Africa. At one point, he decided to initiate clinics outside the hospital, but he developed no regular schedule, visiting a different village on every visit.

Then he proposed the church should establish a medical school. He started developing plans for faculty, buildings, and a curriculum. I was aghast! The financial implications were mountainous. The church was barely able to meet the costs of the hospital and the three small dispensaries that it sponsored. The medical school was an item on the agenda for the medical committee which was to meet in a few weeks. Alone at Tiama, I fretted and fretted about the matter. I was sure the discussion would be heated and probably disagreeable.

The day for the meeting came. I was the secretary for the committee. The item for the medical school was not on the agenda. I waited anxiously for the matter to come up, but it never did. After the meeting, I cornered Don Theuer.

"What happened to the plans for the medical school?" I asked. "I've been worrying about the discussion for weeks."

Don laughed. "Bob decided a month ago that the idea was impractical."

I still had not learned my lesson that worrying was useless. I couldn't solve any problem by worrying. If the problem happened, I couldn't do much about that either, but had to deal with it as it came.

Bob's visits to Tiama were often stressful. He sometimes made demands on the staff that was beyond their ability to accomplish or that couldn't be done because we had neither the equipment or personnel.

At one point, the cistern at my house ran dry because there was a leak in the cement. The house had a double cistern, one for each side of the duplex. Since no one was living on the other side, we tried to switch the pump to the other side, that cistern also had a leak and there was no water there either. When Bob arrived, we discussed the matter.

"We really are in trouble without water," I said. "The rains won't come for another two months."

"That's easy," was his reply. "I'll get someone to teach you how to mix cement and you can repair the cistern."

I had learned a lot in ten years, but I didn't intend to learn how to mix cement. "I came here to deliver babies not learn how to mix cement. There are two maintenance men on the mission staff. Surely, one of them can come and fix it for me," I protested.

And one of them did come and fix it. In the meantime, we were able to use water from the larger cistern at the maternity unit.

Dr. Bob was reluctant to accept local customs. One day we had taken a woman in labor to Rotifunk for delivery. A young Muslim man, Fofana, had driven the vehicle. The women who came along with us carried the laboring woman to the veranda of the hospital. Dr. Bob came to examine her and commanded Fofana to pick up the patient and carry her into the ward.

There was an animated discussion in Mende between Fofana and the women. It was strictly taboo for a man to touch a pregnant woman, and neither Fofana nor the women were willing to disobey the taboo.

Dr. Bob became very angry, picked up the woman himself, and carried her inside. I felt sorry for Fofana who was not being rude, but was obeying local customs.

Probably my favorite doctor was George Harris. Everybody looked forward to George's visit. Soft-spoken, patient, hardworking, George seemed to be able to solve any problem. With an African disregard to time, he was always willing to stay until the last patient was seen. But best of all, he had a delightful sense of humor and his sly puns enlivened the day.

We had a standing joke between us. I was always on the alert for a patient with tuberculosis. George was concerned about hernias. We would keep score as to which person had seen more of their specialty that day.

One of George's stories was about a case of incarcerated hernia in which a loop of bowel twists on itself inside the pouch of skin that is the hernia. If left unattended, the patient will die due to bowel obstruction. Usually, surgery is performed to correct the situation.

In this instance, the patient had arrived at the hospital at Rotifunk shortly after George had arrived in Sierra Leone. He was the only doctor at the hospital at the time and felt he wasn't capable of doing the surgery. He decided to take the patient to Connaught Hospital in Freetown; an arduous trip, part of the way over a dirt road. There was also a ferry to cross. Eventually, he got the patient admitted to the hospital. He stayed in Freetown overnight, and in the morning went back to the hospital to see the patient. To his amazement, the man had been discharged without being treated. With a great deal of effort, George searched the city, found the man, and brought him back to the hospital. This time he waited until the man was seen by a doctor and was sure that the patient would have the necessary surgery. After that, George was no longer hesitant to attempt surgery in Rotifunk.

On one interesting occasion, George and Lowell Gess came to Tiama to do a cesarean section. Early in the labor, I had decided that this was an obstructed labor and the woman would not be able to deliver vaginally. Tator Bagrey, one of the midwives, caught a lorry to Mano and was able to phone Rotifunk on the railway line (the phone only functioned between 8:00 a.m. and 5:00 p.m.). Both George and Lowell were at Rotifunk. They packed up their equipment, including a portable operating table, and did the surgery successfully.

On another occasion, a ten-year-old boy came who had stuffed a bean in his ear. The boy was sedated and George tried to extract the bean with a forceps, but the boy was restless and would not lie still. Additional sedation was given; George kept trying. An hour passed and the bean was still in the ear. I suggested that we take the boy to Bo where he could be given a general anesthetic. George was not willing to admit defeat. A third sedative dose was given. Now I began to worry that the boy would be so heavily sedated that we would not be able to wake him. A second hour passed and George continued to try and grasp the bean. After three hours, he achieved success. With unsteady legs, the boy walked away, ear empty and intact.

On a few occasions, the missionary maintenance man from Moyamba came with George to do some necessary repairs (like fixing the cistern!). Don Appleman was rather like George, easygoing, comfortable, relaxed, and unbothered by schedules. One day we had done a morning's work and were having lunch. We had a pleasant meal and good conversation. At one o'clock I was ready to go back to work, but the two men kept chatting. I fidgeted and fidgeted which went unnoticed by the two of them. Finally, I sat back and relaxed. If they were in no hurry, why should I be? When they were ready, they went back to their tasks and the work was done.

George was very skillful mechanically. He spent much of his time at Rotifunk repairing and maintaining equipment. I was always grateful he was able to do small repairs for me on this trips to Tiama.

CHAPTER 46

ᴔfrican Trek

In 1962, I took two long and exciting trips: the first down the West African coast to Nigeria and the Camerouns, and the second by road to Monrovia, Liberia.

I have mentioned my growing interest in tuberculosis. The World Health Organization (WHO) estimated that 10 percent of the African population had active tuberculosis. I also knew that a positive tuberculin skin test in a child under the age of three years was diagnostic of active tuberculosis. BCG was used as a preventative immunization against tuberculosis and was utilized in many European countries including Great Britain. The American medical establishment did not accept this practice and still doesn't.

I had heard about an international conference on tuberculosis which was going to be held in Ibadan, Nigeria. I made a request to attend, and the mission board gave me the funds to make the journey.

The night before I left Tiama, I knocked my glasses off the bedside table and shattered them. I am extremely nearsighted and have worn glasses since I was nine. Of course, there was no chance of replacing the glasses before I left Freetown, but I had an old pair of uncorrected glasses. The sights of Nigeria and the Camerouns were all seen through a slight blur.

The flight from Freetown was scheduled to leave on Saturday afternoon. But, of course, it didn't; instead, we left early Sunday morning. Ted Stapleford took me to the airport. The plane was full and again I was the only woman passenger. (Why don't African women travel?) Ted thought this was an uproarious situation.

The delay in taking off meant, of course, that the whole flight was off-schedule. We should have arrived in Lagos, Nigeria, in the morning where we could have conveniently gotten transportation to Ibadan; about a three-hour trip north of Lagos. Instead, the plane omitted the scheduled stop in Accra, Ghana, and flew nonstop to Lagos, arriving about four o'clock in the afternoon. Now there was no scheduled transportation to Ibadan. The choices were to find a hotel near the airport or take a taxi. Three of us, a young Englishman, an older Lebanese man, and I decided to risk the taxi. It was a good choice, and we arrived safely in Ibadan.

The conference was held on the spacious grounds of the University of Ibadan, a large Nigerian government institution that was a fairly new university. The grounds were beautifully landscaped with an abundance of trees and flowers.

People attending the conference came from all over West Africa and included both Europeans and Africans, most of whom were employed in the area. About 100 of us listened to lectures on current diagnostic methods and treatment. A number of hospitals in Nigeria were giving BCG immunizations. Now in 1996, it is given universally in underdeveloped countries as well as some developed countries, to prevent the spread of the disease. Drug therapy such as streptomycin and INH were relatively new in treatment and were proving very effective in curing the disease.

The guests at the conference were treated to a number of spectacular entertainments. The first evening there was traditional dancing led by a dignified chief in his royal robes and accompanied by a large group of women dancers. Traditional Nigerian clothing is characterized by bright colors: red, blue, yellow, and purple. A woman's traditional dress includes a blouse and a length of cloth wrapped around as a skirt and tied on top of the blouse. The most distinguishing feature is the large, ornately tied headdress. I often wonder how they tie and put on the head tie in the first place and how the material stays in place especially through the vigorous dance. The materials are often very rich with silver and gold threads woven into the cloth. (See Colorplate 8).

On another evening, there was an exhibition of "talking" drums. An infinite variety of drums can be found throughout Africa, all made of many sizes, shapes, and materials. Some of them have the ability to vary the pitch of sound. They are usually used to accompany singing and dancing, but years ago they were also used to convey messages from one town to another. On this occasion, there was communication between two groups present in a large auditorium. Someone in the audience with a drum would beat out a message to the person on stage who would interpret and repeat the message with great accuracy.

A third performance was a presentation of *The Taming of the Shrew* by members of the dramatic department of the university. The acting was excellent. The stage was almost bare of props, but such was the skill of the cast that the hilarious story came alive.

At the end of the conference we went to Lagos, the capitol city of Nigeria. Here we toured the University of Lagos Hospital. This large hospital was organized along British lines with patients cared for in large, open wards. Tuberculosis patients were not isolated. The theory was that with careful nursing and medical care, the disease would not be transmitted to other patients.

For our final meal, we were treated to lunch at one of the large, luxurious hotels on the beach at Lagos. It was delicious; Jollof rice and fried plantain with a dessert of cooked mangoes in a sweet sauce. I ate heartily.

I had made plans to extend my journey as part of my vacation and was to go on to the Camerouns to see my friend, Joy Thede, now married to Gayle Beanland. The conference in Nigeria ended on Saturday, and my plane didn't leave until Monday morning. I was able to find a place to stay at the guest house of the Sudan Interior Mission. Soon I was paying for my sumptuous noon meal, finding myself with severe diarrhea. I felt I just had to catch that plane on Monday, my funds were limited, and the plane only made two scheduled flights a week. Plus I wasn't sure I could get a flight back to Sierra Leone on such short notice.

Like many travelers, I carried medication for such an emergency. I took some sulfaguanidine tablets which were a specific treatment for diarrhea, but that brought further complications. I was allergic to the sulfa and found myself with a rash, severe itching, and large ugly welts on my skin. One of the doctors who had been a participant at the Ibadan conference was also staying at the guest house. I asked him if he had something that would counteract the allergic reaction and he gave me an antihistamine. However, instead of calming me down, I became highly stimulated. I felt as though I had taken ten cups of coffee. I had some tremors in my hands, couldn't sit still, and walked around the room in frenzied activity. It was now Sunday evening, and all of the guests were gathered outside in the garden for an evening worship service. To the accompaniment of the harmonious hymns, I stood under a cold shower until I was relieved of my discomforts. By the next morning, I was well enough to travel.

I had a great time with Joy and Gayle who were working with the Presbyterian church. She gave me a guided tour through a large area of the country, and I was very much impressed with the medical work. At the main hospital, there was a large operating room with a number of operating tables. Two American surgeons had trained the local people to assist with surgery; a number of cases would be conducted at one time. While the assistants opened and closed the cases, the surgeons did the major surgery or supervised the assistants. One of the Camerouneon assistants had become extremely skillful in doing ureteral transplants. The ureters are removed from the bladder and brought out to the surface of the skin where urine drains into a bag, similar to bowel surgery when a colostomy brings the feces from the bowel to a bag on the skin's surface. Ureteral transplants are done when there has been severe damage to the lower urinary tract either from trauma or disease.

Another stop was at a large leper colony. Prior to Camerounean independence, leprosy patients were forced by law to live at the colony. About 2,000 patients lived in the compound. The buildings included a church, school, hospital, and houses for the patients. After independence, the law was repealed and many patients had gone back to their homes and families. When we visited, the compound looked deserted with only a few people wandering around.

With the development of medication that cures leprosy, leper colonies no longer exist. Patients are encouraged to stay in their villages and with their families. Treatment and medications are administered by teams that visit the patients in their own homes.

After several days good visit, I started home. I was to fly to Abidjan in the Ivory Coast, wait for two days for the next plane, and then fly to Freetown. When I had picked up my visa for the Ivory Coast in Freetown, I explained to the French consul that I didn't speak French. He assured me I wouldn't have a problem, that a lot of people spoke English in the Ivory Coast. I should have known better than to believe him.

I had not made a reservation for a hotel, but had the names of two mission guest houses. Both were full. I couldn't afford an Ivorian tourist hotel, but the taxi driver found me an Ivorian hotel that had a more reasonable price. I stayed there for two days, but there were several problems. As I walked through the lobby, the residents didn't look very hospitable. Although I wasn't carrying much that was valuable, I didn't want to lose what little I had. The first evening I went to my room at 6:00 p.m. I locked the door and put a chair with my suitcase in front of it to block the entry. The next night I was a little braver and didn't lock myself in until 7:00 p.m. Of course, nobody tried to enter and I was a little ashamed of myself for being so paranoid.

While I made little contact with the other hotel guests, my room was another matter. I had plenty of company, cockroaches and other bugs of various kinds.

The next problem was finding something to eat. Breakfast was no problem since it was included in the price of the room. For other meals I had to look at a menu, in French, of course. I was able to recognize the words for beef, eggs, and bread and simply pointed to them on the menu.

During one of these meals, a young boy walked through the restaurant carrying two large ivory tusks. I wondered how much they cost. Even if I could have afforded them, there would have been the problem of carrying them home on the plane.

Trade in ivory is now discouraged in much of Africa due to the declining elephant population and stress on preservation of endangered species. It is now illegal to import ivory in the United States. In 1991, the Kenya government publicly burned tons of ivory in an effort to reduce poaching and smuggling. Where had those tusks in Abidjan come from? Even in 1962, elephants were almost non-existent in West Africa. It was just as well that I couldn't ask the price.

I did some walking around Abidjan. On subsequent visits, I have seen a great modern city with many magnificent skyscrapers and elegant buildings. Like Conakry, there are some lovely, graceful boulevards. Even in 1962, there were some graceful buildings including the large, austere palace of the President set in the midst of a green park graced with palm and mango trees. The whole compound was enclosed in a seven-foot-high fence.

After spending two days walking in the area around the hotel, I returned to the airport and flew back to Freetown.

CHAPTER 47

Overland to Monrovia

For some time, Esther Megill, the missionary laboratory technician at Rotifunk, and I had talked about driving overland to Liberia. After the three women died in childbirth, I was severely depressed and even more anxious to get away from Tiama for a short time. However, after the car's engine caught fire, I was hesitant to start on a long drive. One day Clyde Galow, now the mission superintendent, stopped at Tiama.

"When are you going to take that vacation?" he demanded.

"Esther and I have talked about driving to Monrovia, but I have had trouble with the Kombi," I said. "Twice the battery cover jiggled loose and shorted the battery. I am reluctant to start out on a long trip."

"I think you need to get away," he advised. "If your car won't take you, we will lend you our car."

So we made plans. We decided to risk it with the Kombi, which was large enough to easily accommodate four people and our supplies. In addition to Esther and myself, two British women from Njala went with us. One of the women was three months pregnant. I discussed this with Dr. Bob.

"Do you think she should go with us?" I asked. "Those roads are rough. What if she would start to miscarry?"

He reassured me. "She is past three months so her chances of a miscarriage are pretty slight. Besides, if traveling on rough roads would cause a miscarriage, there would probably be a lot of women taking trips!" She withstood the bumpy roads with no problems, completed her pregnancy, and had a healthy baby.

We drove east to Bo and Kenema, then continued southeast to the easternmost end of Sierra Leone at Kambia. The first night we stopped at a government rest house where we camped out. These rest houses had a few beds, and a minimal amount of furniture. We carried our own bedding, food, and a small stove. The next day we stopped at the market at Kambia, a town at the corner where Liberia, Guinea, and Sierra Leone have common borders. The market has a great reputation for both variety and quality of goods. Among other things for sale was the herb used to create the blue dye used universally in West Africa. It is what Americans call indigo, but in Sierra Leone it is called "garra".

At the Liberian border, we had our first encounter with Liberian officialdom. The border post was manned by one officious soldier carrying a menacing-looking gun. He was demanding and rude. He was also slightly drunk. Eventually, we reassured him that our papers were in order, and he allowed us to pass into Liberia.

Once inside Liberia, the road was a delight. Although it was not paved, it was very new, wide and without potholes or ruts; unlike the rough road we had just driven on in Sierra Leone. The eastern end of Liberia was still very sparsely settled and also uncultivated. As I enjoyed the easy driving, I thought of Graham Greene and his cousin, Barbara, who both described the arduous trek across this same territory as he related in his book titled *Journey Without Maps*. We drove through a path of towering trees, bush with thick undergrowth, and a wealth of flowering trees and bushes.

The next night we stopped at a small mission station where we stayed with some acquaintances of Esther's. The missionaries belonged to an organization where each person raised funds for their support. Usually, they cannot go to the mission field until sufficient money has been raised for their support throughout a full term, including necessary travel. In some groups, there seems to be no limit to the amount of money that can be spent on house, appliances, and furnishings. We were a bit overwhelmed by the seeming luxury of some of the houses. Even more amazing was the presence of four electric generators on the compound, all of them working.

House of Representatives, Monrovia, Liberia.

The next day we went on to Monrovia. On the way, we had the first problem with the Kombi. It had a reserve tank that held one gallon of gas. I have mentioned that there was no gas gauge in the car so that you were not always sure when the large tank was empty. When that happened, it should have been possible to pull a small valve on the reserve tank and the gas from the reserve could be used to drive a few miles. But I had never been able to work the valve. I started to walk to find gas. About 15 minutes later, Esther drove up behind me having figured out how to release the valve.

In Monrovia, we were able to stay at the Lutheran guest house, the same place I had stayed in 1957 while waiting for the ship to go home. The next day we expected to explore Monrovia. To our dismay, it was a public holiday and everything was closed; but there was going to be a big parade.

Numerous books have been written about Liberia. Settled in 1822 by freed American slaves, the government was based on the American system with an elected president, supreme court, and two-house legislature. In 1962, the executive mansion was a rather modest, two-story building in the center of town. The parade came down main street past the executive mansion. I think it was Armed Forces Day as the parade was a show of military strength, accompanied by the lusty music of a military band.

That afternoon we explored Monrovia. We visited the government buildings, some of which were open, including the legislature and supreme court; all miniatures of offices in Washington, D.C.

We also drove to visit the port. Although the port did not have the natural advantages of the Freetown port, it was still a bustling, thriving enterprise. It was a "free port" and attracted a great deal of international trade. Liberia, like Panama, provided facilities for the registration of marine vessels so that many international shipping companies registered their ships in Monrovia in order to avoid the stringent safety regulations of the more restrictive countries.

It was at the port that the second problem arose with the car. The battery cover jiggled loose again and shorted the battery. This time there was no fire, but the battery was dead. We got out and looked at it with dismay.

Of course, we attracted a crowd of curious spectators. After a few minutes, a lively American drove up and offered to help. It was evident that he was amused to see these four white women stranded on a dock.

"Whatever possessed four women to go exploring alone?" he asked.

I explained who we were, where we had come from, and why we were traveling.

With a mocking voice, he said, "I'm surprised that the good Lord doesn't take better care of his missionaries."

I replied, "I think the good Lord never wanted us to start out on this trip. He put too many obstacles in our way."

He laughed, soon removed the offending battery, and was able to recharge it for us so that we could go on.

The next day we completed the necessary official duties by registering our passports with the police. We then headed back to Sierra Leone, making three stops along the way.

On the way to Monrovia, we had passed acres of spindly rubber trees. Since rubber trees weren't cultivated in Sierra Leone, we were curious about their presence in Liberia.

The largest income-producing industry in Liberia was rubber cultivation. In 1926, the Liberian government signed an agreement with the Firestone Plantation Company; it granted Firestone a 99-year lease on a million acres of forest as well as other production rights.

In addition to the Firestone plantation, several other foreign firms cultivated rubber trees as did a number of Liberian landowners.

The major road in the country ran through acres of rubber trees. These spindly trees are planted in rows, all leaning away from the wind. To collect the raw rubber, a diagonal slash is made in the bark of the tree about four feet above the ground. A small cup, which will hold about eight ounces, is placed at the end of the slash. The liquid latex collects in the cup. On alternate days a laborer walks through the trees, empties the cups into a bucket, and makes another slash below the previous one. The bucket of latex is emptied into a large tanker and is taken to a central processing plant.

The liquid latex is added to an equal amount of water, then formic acid is added to the mixture which causes the latex to coagulate and form a curd-like mass of crude rubber. This rubber is shredded, dried, and compressed into 75-pound bales which are shipped to the United States for further processing.

We stopped at one of the main processing plants and were given a tour to see the latex turned into a solid.

We also traveled to Ganta, the site of the Methodist Hospital. Apparently, I was not impressed by the hospital since I have no recollection of making the visit. Years later, after the EUB Church and the Methodist Church united to become the United Methodist Church, I became a United Methodist member and in 1980, I returned to Ganta and spent six months teaching at the School of Nursing.

Finally, we stopped at the Lutheran Hospital at Zorzor also run by American missionaries. The hospital was founded in 1924.

There was very little road construction in Liberia. In both Zorzor and Ganta, the early missionaries walked or were carried in hammocks from Monrovia to their stations. For about five years, the major means of transportation to the Lutheran outstations was by airplane. In June of 1958, the road was opened as far as Zorzor. The road had some notoriety after it was a prominent part of the book *The Zinzin Road* by Fletcher Knebel.

If I didn't remember Ganta, I did remember Zorzor. While the small hospital had only about 25 beds, it sometimes had a daily census of 100. I was impressed by their small mud huts that had been built to house the patients with tuberculosis. A school of nursing and midwifery was functioning. There was also a small compound for leprosy patients. The compound had electricity and a good water supply. An x-ray machine was functioning as well as an efficient laboratory.

Esther and I looked at all of this with some envy and with a vision of what could be accomplished at Rotifunk.

The trip back to Tiama and Njala went without incident and again, it was good to be home.

Epilogue

During my stay overseas, I wrote home almost every week, and my family saved many of the letters. The letters, written from 1960 to 1963, are almost complete. In rereading them, several final thoughts come to mind.

During those three years, there seemed to be a steady stream of visitors through Tiama. Because the church in Tiama was so outstanding in its growth and interaction with the local people, visitors often came to observe and participate in the activities of the congregation.

The constant flow of strangers was a far cry from the months in 1952 and 1953 when I felt so isolated. It was good that I had been bound to the town so completely those first years as it enabled me to make myself a part of the community and be accepted by them.

A second advantage was the opportunity to travel that a vehicle gave me. I transported patients and visitors and explored parts of the country both by myself and with friends.

The third impression my letters gave me is the degree of frustration I encountered. There were constant problems with equipment. In particular, the generator frequently stopped functioning. Even though we only used it for a few hours every evening, it was a nuisance to be without it. It had been placed on an insecure foundation that had to be replaced. Once I forgot to add oil and created damage. It would often be weeks before the generator could be repaired.

Early in 1960 during a storm, a tree fell on the east end of the house roof damaging it. This went unrepaired for months. During the height of the rains, water poured into the building, threatening severe damage to the ceiling.

We had moved into the house in 1957, but plumbing in the duplex and dispensary was not completed until January 1961. While I had plumbing on the side of the duplex that I lived in, the unfinished work presented problems when there were so many guests staying overnight in the other side.

Although problems with staff were minimal, they were still

troubling. Twice I caught staff members stealing money. Each time we "talked the palaver" with pastor and were able to resolve the problem without firing the staff person.

Undoubtedly, the greatest frustration was dealing with complicated deliveries and babies that died. Many times I realized that if we had surgical facilities, we could have saved the life of the baby and sometimes even the mother. If we had been able to immunize children, fewer babies would have died. If the community had had a sewage system and safe water, fewer babies would have gotten sick and died.

Looking back, I can see that I constantly talked about safe water and good nutrition. Abraham Lavaly accused me of preaching the gospel of orange juice and dug latrines.

At one point, my frustrations reached their limit and I sent in my resignation. I was later talked into recalling it, but Pastor Carew and the mission superintendent realized how badly I needed a vacation and made arrangements for me to have some time off.

These frustrations, however, were compensated for by all the blessings that came my way in Tiama. If some mothers had difficult labors and some babies died, there were also many wonderful deliveries and beautiful, healthy babies. Often after a safe delivery, the women in the delivery room, friends and relatives of the mother, would sing and dance around the room. While I didn't join in the dancing, in my heart I was echoing their joy. I was grateful when the lives of babies who were sick with malaria or diarrhea were saved with the medicine we provided.

A protein deficiency condition among children called Kwashiorkor is common in West Africa. The children affected have very thin arms while the abdomen is distended. Their hair turns red and becomes straight and thin. The children are listless and whiny. The treatment is a generous diet of non-fat dried milk. The first sign of recovery is when the child smiles, and the day that first smile appears is a day for rejoicing.

I loved being a midwife. In one of my letters home, I talked about the large number of visitors and a few deliveries. I wished it had been reversed with few visitors and a lot of deliveries.

I am glad I could live in Sierra Leone during the time of change from Colony and Protectorate to independent nation. I learned all the words of the new national anthem and appreciated the wise leadership of Sir Milton Margai.

Another blessing was the people who became friends and family. I still keep in touch with many of them. Amos Lavaly and his family have visited me here in the United States, and I visited them several times both in the United Kingdom and in Sierra Leone. Donald and Tuzylene Wonnie lived in Milwaukee for a year while Donald was in school and we have exchanged a number of visits. Sierra Leone students studying in the United States have often been guests in my home.

But the most significant blessing was the church life in Tiama. It was exciting to be a part of the lively, enthusiastic congregation. The growth and depth of spiritual life was due to the leadership of Pastor B. A. Carew.

"Indeed, contentment is great gain."

I left Sierra Leone in June 1963. Since then I have been back six or eight times. During the months I lived in Liberia in 1980, I visited three times including several weeks over Christmas. My last visit was in 1989 as I was returning from a visit to Kenya.

It seemed to me there was a gradual deterioration throughout the country. I have written about the closure of the railroad. Road construction and repair have not kept up with the transportation needs of the country. Potholes were frequent and made driving hazardous. The electricity supply, even in Freetown, was intermittent.

One indication of economic problems was the drastic devaluation of the leone, the official currency. Immediately after independence, the leone was worth $2.50. In 1980, one leone equaled one dollar. By 1989, the rate had fallen to about 600 leones to a dollar and in 1996, the official rate is about 900 leones to a dollar.

In 1991, a rebel force arose in the eastern end of the country. Although the rebels were a poorly defined group, they have managed to create havoc throughout the whole country; burning and looting entire towns and killing and raping indiscriminately. Schools and hospitals have been destroyed. Thousands of people have fled their homes, trying to find safety in refugee camps, some of them traveling across the border to Guinea and the Ivory Coast.

In 1992, young army officers successfully staged a military coup and sent the president into exile in Guinea.

In April 1996, elections were held and the military officers turned the government back to the civilians. However, the rebels have continued to sack and destroy.

I am grateful for the good years in Sierra Leone. My prayers are that peace and harmony may be restored. To quote the words of the national anthem:

"Blessing and peace be ever thine own
Land that we love, our Sierra Leone."